On Retirements

Kaslo B.C,
October 30, 2015

For Sandra, with many
thanks for your volunteer
services to retirees.

Barney Gilmore

On Retirements

Playing Seriously
with the Work
of Growing Older

Jon Barnard Gilmore

BPS
books

Published in 2010 by
BPS Books
bpsbooks.com
Toronto and New York
A division of Bastian Publishing Services Ltd.

ISBN 978-1-926645-26-1

Cataloguing in Publication Data available from Library and Archives Canada.

Excerpts from FIFTH BUSINESS by Robertson Davies, copyright © 1970 by Robertson Davies. Used by permission of The Estate of Robertson Davies and Curtis Brown Canada Ltd., by Viking Penguin, a division of Penguin Group (USA) Inc., and by Penguin Books Ltd. (UK).

Cover design: Gnibel
Text design and typesetting: Casey Hooper Design

Printed by Lightning Source, Tennessee. Lightning Source paper, as used in this book, does not come from endangered old growth forests or forests of exceptional conservation value. It is acid free, lignin free, and meets all ANSI standards for archival-quality paper. The print-on-demand process used to produce this book protects the environment by printing only the number of copies that are purchased.

To
Our muses:

The ones I've loved who know it
The ones I've loved who doubt it
The ones I've loved who have yet to suspect it
And all those others I may never know.

May many of them come visit with you.
Too.

Contents

Part Three ◆ Arabesque

An eight-year-old, dubious about going to school, was encouraged with the words: "But these are the best years of your life."

"I don't know," he replied. "Retirement looks pretty good to me."

Prologue, or Perhaps
Epilogue, and Perhaps Both

To browse in proper bookstores (such few as remain today) is to be met with a growing number of books about retirement, the majority of which are primarily devoted to "powerful strategies" for assuring that one's "wealth" is up to the task of supporting a "lifestyle" that may be more appropriate for people and societies that do not age.

Retirement, however, is much more than a financial challenge and much more than simply a new "lifestyle." Retirement involves the personal and psychological work of moving beyond work: It includes all the work of aging, and sooner or later it includes the work of dying. Books necessarily have significant limitations in helping one to achieve this new variety of personal work, particularly books that simply equate retirement with income management. "Wealth" plays only a peripheral part in facilitating the work of the retiree, "work" that often may best be undertaken playfully and without cost. Because such work is so individual, and because it changes so much from month to month, no book touching on the psychology of retirement can do much more than encourage you along your own path and offer you certain hints about where your next good idea might be found.

As this book reveals, I have found many such encouragements in encounters with my friends, in various works of fiction and non-fiction, and in some of the landscapes through which I have passed and on which I have settled. I suspect that many other retirees, particularly those who happen to notice their own eyes scanning this particular sentence, are likely to find some of the same encouragements in many of these same places. I hope so. I hope, too, that some of those places may come to include a few to be found between the covers of this book.

Retirement Anticipated

For the twenty-eight years prior to my early retirement I served as a professor of psychology—an academic. During most of those years I was affiliated with the University of Toronto. There I enjoyed a wonderful tower office in University College in the centre of the main campus located in the heart of the city. My home was close by, at the edge of Chinatown, a three-minute walk away. I loved Toronto, the university campus, learning from my colleagues, and my work itself. Early retirement and a move to a place far from any city were not things I expected I would ever choose. And yet, in the end, both were exactly what I did choose. Or, to be more accurate about it, early retirement and a move to remote mountains each chose me.

I began considering retirement casually, in fits and starts, beginning in my early forties, often while daydreaming during periods of sabbatical research carried out in pleasant foreign lands, e.g., in New Zealand, Switzerland, rural England, and northern California (the land of my birth, a land that in some ways was becoming the most foreign of all). Although I had been born and educated in the United States, my first academic job in 1964 happened to be in Canada at Ontario's new University of Waterloo, chosen by me for the simple reason that it offered the best salary and best teaching conditions available at the time. I soon discovered that it offered as well a splendid student body, splendid colleagues, and comfortable farm and small town environments in which to live. Within a few years, however, I had been lured to Toronto, had become a Canadian citizen, and was specializing in teaching Introductory Psychology to very large classes.

In the fall of 1979 I paid a visit to California to see both my mother, who was still living at Lake Tahoe (where my younger brother and I had spent our high school years), and my father, who was living in Walnut Creek, about fifteen miles east of Berkeley. My parents had met at the University of California Berkeley, where she was majoring in economics and he was preparing for law school. My father was playful, intelligent, and handsome, and he was a pretty good dancer, which, my mother later told me, was part of his allure for her. My mother loved to dance, play the piano, and play competitive card games. My father was not particularly competitive, which may explain why as a lawyer he specialized in drawing wills and trusts. He appeared before the bar in court something fewer than twenty times during a legal career that lasted nearly fifty years.

My parents had separated in 1952, divorcing two years later. My mother made Crystal Bay, Nevada (at Lake Tahoe), her home. It wasn't until I attended Stanford University (Berkeley's great rival) that I saw my father again with any regularity. He would come down to walk the hills behind campus with me of a Saturday, or I would drive northeast to spend the afternoon and night with him and my new stepmother, Helga. I was very fond of Helga from the beginning. She shared many of my enthusiasms. Many years later, long after she and my father divorced and after she retired from her profession of creating radiation treatment plans for cancer patients, Helga also moved to Canada. Initially she lived in the small village near my own retirement home in British Columbia, but presently she moved to a kinder winter climate and to the greater cultural riches of Victoria.

In 1979, on that fall visit to California, I found my mother in high spirits, preparing to go down to Puerto Vallarta in Mexico, where she had recently created a winter home for herself, one that assured her plenty of beloved sunshine, warm sea air, and comfortable friends. On this same trip, I found my father happily reminiscing about the vacation through Greece that we had shared early the previous summer. My father had done practically no foreign traveling before that time, and there was much in Greece that I had wanted to show him. We even obtained permission to enter the Orthodox peninsula of Mt. Athos, where for five days we walked from monastery to monastery, the Aegean Sea always in view. In Greece I had found him to be the picture of intelligent interest and contentment throughout our wonder-filled wanderings. Back in California the next fall, we sat in the new garden that he was landscaping, beside the ornamental olive trees screening his neighbour's fence, and we made plans for another walk, this time in Point Reyes National Seashore north of San Francisco.

I also paid a visit to Helga while in California. She celebrated our little reunion by creating an elegant lunch for two at her small apartment overlooking San Francisco Bay, a rather special meal that featured fresh cracked Dungeness crab, a hearts-of-palm salad, and a California fumé blanc. (What was not to love?)

And then finally, because I happened to be close by at just the right time, I also elected to attend the twentieth reunion of my Stanford University graduating class, held on the main campus west of Palo Alto. There, by chance, I renewed an old acquaintance with a former classmate, Elizabeth Hodder, an encounter that led to a courtship, to her emigration to Toronto with her two teen-age children, and to our marriage at the close of 1980.

In the summer of 1981, while both of Elizabeth's children were visiting their father in California, the two of us drove from Toronto to Vancouver and then down to California, where I was to initiate a sabbatical year of work. We had no set itinerary during our leisurely drive across Canada. On the first night following our circuitous route across the Canadian Prairies, we happened to find ourselves camped at Radium Hot Springs just inside British Columbia. The hot springs pool there was so pleasant that we got out our maps to see whether there might be other hot springs, farther west, where we might also enjoy the waters each evening. The result was that the next day we detoured south, then back north along Kootenay Lake, there to explore the beauties of a place on the map called Ainsworth Hot Springs. We spent a wonderful night there. The following morning, we continued north to the village of Kaslo, and then turned west toward our next temporary destination: the Nakusp Hot Springs.

Ainsworth and Kaslo each made a very strong impression on us. As we left Kaslo both of us agreed that the people living there might just be the luckiest people in the world. Looking back on it, I think that for me Kootenay Lake and its surrounding mountains had evoked echoes of my childhood home at Lake Tahoe in the 1950s, a time when Tahoe itself had still been a place of few residents and unspoiled beauty.

At the end of that sabbatical, late in the summer of 1982, Elizabeth and I returned to Ainsworth for a three-night stay, interrupting our long drive back to Toronto. It rained quite a bit during our stay, but we thought it was magical nonetheless. We vowed to return for a much longer stay at some future opportunity.

Six years later, in the summer of 1988, we had that opportunity. We found and rented a lakefront cottage located fifteen minutes south of Ainsworth Hot Springs and we spent nine enjoyable weeks in residence there. After five weeks, mildly amused by the florid real estate flyers being delivered daily to the mailbox in front of this cottage, we decided, on a lark, to look at a few homes for sale in the area. Eventually, and to our surprise, with time running out on our late summer rental, we impulsively made an offer to purchase a lovely parcel of undeveloped, forested lakefront land. This land was conveniently located just six minutes north of Ainsworth and fifteen minutes south of Kaslo. After five nail-biting days of difficult negotiations, the owner of this property agreed to sell it to us on mutually satisfactory terms.

Our impulsive purchase suddenly put us very consciously on a path to a potential early retirement, the possibilities for which we only then began to explore in earnest. Elizabeth had for some years been working part-time as a technical writer and trainer, teaching the use of certain electronic equipment and software applications. Because her work was largely done on a contract basis, she anticipated being able to continue this work, if she so desired, wherever we might live. (By this time, both of her children were living independently back in the United States.)

During each of the three summers that followed the purchase of this land, we rented various homes nearby and slowly oversaw the building of our Gatehouse at the front edge of our property, a property that we began to call Junipers after the deep green bushy groundcover that thrives there. The Gatehouse was meant to provide a small apartment for us each summer until we retired and sold our Toronto home. With the money from that Toronto sale we could then afford to build our retirement home. That home was planned for a location around the hillside on the property, out of sight from both the Gatehouse and the street. Our Gatehouse was then supposed to offer us rental income to supplement my pension cheques, and perhaps it might someday serve as a private home for caretakers in our old age.

Meanwhile, during the winters that we spent in Toronto, I had begun searching out what little information I could about retirement life and also about the University's requirements for arranging an early retirement. In 1991, I formally applied for that retirement and in due course it was approved, effective as of the end of June 1993. What little I first knew about retirement was about to expand considerably as that date approached and then was left far behind. The chapters that follow in this book constitute a personal report about certain things that I've learned since 1991, and about some of the themes that are likely to be encountered during the course of many other retirements.

Part One
Reports from Kaslo

1 | *Kaslo May Days*

*T*oday, Victoria Day Monday, the Village of Kaslo, British Columbia, observed its one-hundredth anniversary May Days celebration. The celebration was held after the traditional May Days Parade down Front Street to the park where the Kaslo River meets Kootenay Lake, the park where the Maypole is erected each year.

I have now watched four of these parades and can report that this was quite the longest (and the windiest) I've yet seen. Moreover, the crowds were larger today than in the recent past. Still, the local Historical Society has pictures of some of these celebrations dating from the first decade of the existence of the town when Kaslo could be reached only by steamer up the lake from Bonner's Ferry, Idaho, or from Nelson, B.C.

In those days Kaslo was four or five times larger than it is today, flush with prosperity from the surrounding mines, now all closed. Special excursion steamers arrived with many hundreds of passengers

for the day of festivities. It seems unlikely that the number of specta-
tors and participants, in the parade and its attendant events, has ever
exceeded the numbers achieved in those early years, just prior to the
turn of the century.

The large crowds today must have come close, however. Today's
numbers were helped by the centenary effort this year, and may be
helped again next year when the centenary of Kaslo itself is celebrated.
Still, I can't quite believe that the parade is going to continue to be this
big. Or, to be more accurate about it, I don't want to believe this.

In a year's time Kaslo is also going to become the village nearest to
my retirement home, so I take a proprietary interest in the changes that
the town may undergo. You should understand that Kaslo is located in
what is currently one of the loveliest mountain settings imaginable. It
has the charm that only a small friendly village can have, a village where
somehow there is just one fine exemplar of everything you may need: a
bakery, drugstore, gas station, grocery store, fine restaurant, health food
store, hotel and bar, building supply outlet, credit union, loggers supply,
nine-hole golf course, hospital, library, gift shop, cultural centre, school,
ice rink, etc. A village where it is easily possible to know by sight half
the people you'll ever see at the post office or at the town dump, except
in July and August, when the tourists join us.

Things were neither so charming nor so lovely long ago, however,
when the Maypole children first danced in a raw and muddy townsite
denuded of trees, surrounded by a range of mountains fast losing their
own blankets of mature forest. And if too many people should discover
this village and move here (as I plan to do), it will not stay as lovely as
now. The size of today's parade, and the size of the crowds watching it,
could threaten just such a fate for Kaslo: the dangers of "discovery" and
unseemly growth.

I arrived to spend another summer here just a week ago, and on
my first trip into the post office I was met with a very disturbing

petition being circulated by Alderman Mackle. You should know that I quite admire Alderman Mackle, and would have helped elect him had I been present and properly informed at the time of his election. But this friendly village is not quite unanimous in sharing my current political views in such matters. There are some, for instance, who feel that an alderman ought to cut and wash his hair more often, and that an alderman's dog should not come to council meetings or sit in one of the councilmen's chairs, etc. And, I learned just recently, some also feel that an alderman should certainly accept the political process and should refrain, then, from standing in front of the post office circulating a petition urging the repeal of, in this case, council's decision that the May Days Parade this year should go down Front Street only once.

Now, to me, one of the most attractive features of the May Days Parade in Kaslo is that it "always" goes around twice. This allows one to scoot across the street, or jump up on a better fencepost in time for the grand second coming. Good things as complex as the village parade cannot be properly assimilated in one brief passing, especially if you happen to run out of film just as the Kootenay Kiltie Pipe Band swings into view. And if the boys on the passing logging truck should happen to catch you with a water-filled balloon on their first pass, well, there is always the second pass to have your revenge.

Going around twice is a local tradition, the undebated curtailing of which seemed to me unthinkable. I was glad indeed for Alderman Mackle's petition confirming this tradition, and for the chance to sign it.

Of course it later dawned on me that there had to be reasons for ordaining a one-pass parade, but when I asked around for them I got ones that seemed hardly worthy of the name. It was rumoured that the horses that are often the penultimate group in the parade (with the children's "bicycle brigade" following) left messes in the road that the Legionnaires, marching behind our two Mounties and the Pipe Band, found unacceptable the second time around. I even heard it said that our village pride had been hurt by the shaming of nameless outsiders who had grander parades that didn't need to go around twice. (So much the worse for them, I would have thought.)

Actually, the first year I saw the May Days Parade in Kaslo, for some reason it went around just once, maybe because the new Mounties in town hadn't led the parade before, or because the drum major for the band took a wrong turn. Nobody was ever quite sure. Anyway, somehow it all went terribly wrong. And everyone seemed to agree that year that it *was* both terrible and wrong. The next year everyone seemed very pleased that all was again right when that parade came around again.

Today, however, as decreed, the parade went by just once, and I think we all saw the reason for it, however sad some of us may have felt about the deliberate change of a unique local tradition. The parade was simply too long to fit once around the block, and two passes would have meant routing it around two or more blocks, as indeed was required for the *staging* of today's parade. Last year, you see, there was a bit of a traffic jam when the head of that parade got back to the Post Office before the tail had started out of the intersection. Thus there ensued a wait for certain gaps to close up, providing a seemly spacing for the awaited second coming. One can see that it would be asking a lot of future paraders, some of them on foot, to go two long blocks (instead of one) back up A Avenue for a second circuit. The parade route is already a full kilometer long.

I must also report that one other tradition died this centennial year. Normally the May Queen and her Princesses (from the high school) ride on the first grand float. Traditionally, that float has been a fine and funky replica of the old Kootenay Lake sternwheeler *Moyie*, which now is beached at Kaslo and has been restored beautifully as a local museum, just in time for the two centennial year celebrations of 1992 and 1993. The parade route this year passed the *Moyie* on her starboard side, then finished the Front Street portion of its route and turned south toward the river. But the traditional *Moyie* float was not in the parade this year and instead a sporty little modern runabout boat, devoid of Victorian charm or pedigree, and riding on a flatbed, carried the Queen and her court to the Maypole. Many of the towns-people, dressed for the occasion in wonderful Victorian garb, waved as usual from the sidelines while the begowned Princesses dispensed favours and waves in return. Nonetheless, *Nostalgia* took another sharp jab to the ribs on this, her day, as that little speedboat slowly brazened by, bearing its regal treasure.

The park where the parade ended, and where the Maypole was set up in front of the stage for the visiting dignitaries, was green and lush. We had only peek-a-boo sunshine, but sufficient to warm the crowd. The north winds that had so chilled us on Front Street finally began to die, and in any event they were partly screened by the trees surrounding the park.

People were seated three deep on the grass, in a large irregular el-lipse with the Maypole at one focus. Behind them, many more specta-tors stood, in some places five deep. Six youthful citizens, one with a large video camera resting on his shoulder, sat along the metal roof-peak of a well-placed concession stand nearby. And the limbs of a large tree shading the dignitaries' platform held half a dozen small boys. Just below them, in rows of chairs, were two dozen former May Queens, including two from the 1930s and last year's Queen.

Some time was taken arranging the Maypole ribbons spoke-like out on the grass, ready for the children who were to perform the dance. The children (all first graders), dressed and garlanded for the occasion, were shepherded off their Maypole parade float and seated on the grass beside the dignitary platform. Meanwhile, the crowds following the end of the parade came on foot down to the park. Considerable time was devoted to taking the centennial pictures of the children arrayed around the Maypole with their teacher, each holding an extended ribbon. Everyone waited for all the little hands to leave all the little faces, all eyes to come to the cameras, and all sight lines to reestablish. Presently, the Kiltie Band gave a brief concert and then piped the Mounties, the Queen and her court, and the many dignitaries around the Maypole and onto the platform of honour. And after we all shyly sang "O Canada" in a difficult key, and after the public address system was compensated for the crowd noise, the Maypole dance began.

Each year the same traditional song is used for the dance, usually performed live on guitar, flute, and tambourine. The children do essentially the same set of brief figures with their ribbons. (There are actually two sets of children, each of which does the same figures, sequentially.) The winding and unwinding of the pole is never carried very far, and the song starts and stops rather unpredictably when the children reach their assigned places for each figure.

Because the children are so young, and because there is never a lot of practice time available to their teachers, there are always dependable missteps and tangles. Now we have had one hundred years of loving indulgence and inevitable interventions to get things sorted out. One hundred years of held breath and village anxiety. One hundred years of Victorian ingathering.[*]

If truth be told, there are some in town who cannot understand why the dances cannot be performed by children in grade two, children who could learn and remember the simple designs in much less time and with far greater reliability. These are not generally welcome views, however, and speaking for this reporter, I would miss the precious moments of simple chaos each year, moments that bring us so briefly together around the children and each other and the Maypole.

---

[*]   When this was written I was under the misapprehension that the Maypole dance had been held consecutively for all one hundred years of the local May Days celebrations. In fact the dance has been held annually but only since its first performance, approximately seventy years ago.

Late in the afternoon there was a fine magic show for the crowd. But a threatening thunderstorm soon arrived with a crash, ending the festivities in mid-trick. (The trick involved an endlessly replenishing water jug!) Then, just before sunset, the storm cleared and another of Kaslo's frequent double rainbows appeared over the Maypole and over the empty park. The rainbows here are particularly vivid, and the primary rainbow today had two vivid inner bands of purple. One for Victoria. And, I have no doubt, one for Kaslo.

2 | *Eastbound*

*T*oday I have been driving east through vast empty wheat fields, taking our car and many of our belongings back for one final winter in the big city, my last year of employment at the university. Such long hours of solitary driving can invoke a low-grade anxiety, if one is so inclined, and despite the beauty of the empty country through which I have been passing, I *have* been so inclined.

My current moments of disquiet were sparked by what I have heard today on the car radio. It was a talk about forest fires, or, more particularly, a discussion of a new book about a team of firefighters most of whom perished a few years ago when the small Montana fire they had been assigned to fight exploded and jumped the river that was to have protected them. Just three of a dozen men survived: These included the crew boss, who at the last minute lit an "escape fire" and then stepped into its embers when the oncoming flames arrived, and two novices who did exactly as they were told and followed the crew boss.

The drama of the story is that no one knows why the crew boss decided to light the escape fire, himself included. It is not something he was trained to do or expected to try. Still, enough fuel was consumed by that smaller fire, and consumed fast enough, so that those who took refuge behind its expanding perimeter escaped death. The others died trying to outrun the oncoming fire.[*]

The unpredictability of fire, of the road, of retirement, and indeed of all life in the mountains travels with me today, away from Kaslo. Despite the urban pleasures that lie ahead in Toronto, leaving my summer home outside the sleeping village this morning has been for me a sad business. As I left, the dawn air was especially clear, and the snow, recently returned to our mountains, sharply defined every horizon. I found that before departing I filled my lungs repeatedly, as if to store up a year's supply of clarity. (Or was it perhaps resolve?)

The story on the car radio made me recognize that although Kaslo village had its normal small quota of troubling deaths this summer, happily our predictable local forest fires had spared all those who were fighting them and living nearby. Near the end of this particularly warm sunny summer, the village had been visited by a series of severe thunderstorms, the first of which produced rather more noise than actual rain. Because the forests always become so dry and flammable by August, any lightning without heavy rain is a routine recipe for late summer danger in our mountains.

And sure enough, with the arrival of that first bad storm, the short paved airport runway above the village, on the road to the dump, became a hive of forest service activity. Helicopters and supply trucks were

---

[*]   Sixteen years after writing this I heard on *Ideas* (a long-running CBC Radio program) a history of fires that included another account of this same event. According to this account, only the crew boss stepped into the escape fire and survived. Two others also survived, but they used a different strategy. Apparently, a century or more before this fire, natives and settlers commonly used this technique to escape from prairie fires.

visible coming and going for many days, and the drone of the water bombers flying in from Nelson had heads craning to follow their routes up and down the lake.

The first planes I followed were attacking a fire that turned out to be uncomfortably close to my home, just behind a very high hill to the northwest. A wind was blowing the smoke from this fire north, toward the village. Were it not for the noise of the arriving planes, I would not soon have discovered that the fire was there.

Once I realized the meaning of the heavy engines overhead, I took off in my battered pickup truck and found a parking space off the highway where I could watch the bombers readying to fight what was still a small, if intense, fire. As is typical, the planes made a number of practice or reconnoitering passes. The rising and falling pitch of their labouring engines, as they repeatedly approached, dived, and then retreated, seemed at the time more ominous than any of the city sirens I hear so often during the fall and winters in Toronto.

Typically the small bombers will circle a fire a number of times, then suddenly they will come in rather lower than before and discharge a cascade of burnt-orange mist that billows out from under each plane in turn and falls into the smoke of the fire. There follows a momentary pause, then the smoke becomes thick, dark, and angry. Slowly one becomes aware of a great quiet, as the planes climb out far away, returning home in a hurry to refill before flying back. Before they arrive again, however, the fire and smoke flare anew. It can be frightening business when the fire is so close. Despite strong wind that day, this first fire that I saw was controlled within a few hours, and so, happily, my anxieties were short-lived.

Then, a few days later, a very severe storm passed through with a great deal of lightning, starting dozens of fires in just half an hour. On a trip into the village soon afterward, I could see two of these fires in the forests to the west, at high altitudes, threatening large tracts of timber including some of the watershed on which the village drinking supply depends.

The bigger of these visible fires, pouring tremendous amounts of smoke into the western sky, was receiving the bulk of the aerial attention by the time I arrived in town. I watched the now familiar circuits of the bombers and the pyrotechnical display of their payloads cascading down like great umbrellas descending over the smoky heart of the fire. Flames were clearly visible from my vantage spot four miles away, flaring, then fading, while the fire stepped uphill from tree to tree. It did not seem possible that this fire could be stopped before nightfall, when the planes would be grounded.

And yet, by the next day when I returned to the village for our mail, both western fires appeared to be under control. By this next day, however, I had first noticed the fire on Mt. Kaslo.

Most mornings, if the lake is flat and calm, I go down to the waterfront to record the day's water temperature and lake level. Both the temperature and lake level can change noticeably in twenty-four hours, although usually in August they remain rather stable.

The walk down to the water has become one of my greatest joys because the pathway and staircase we have built passes through a veritable Japanese garden of mosses and wildflowers, grand stone, lichens, firs, and pines. There is a steep cliff above our shore, and the steps twist and turn echoing its various ledges. There are seven runs, seven platforms, and seventy stairs over the steepest part of the descent.

Below that, I have created another dozen steps out of stone, turning the jumbled rocks at the base of the cliff into a further staircase. The overall descent to the lake is about seventy-five feet, and underwater the same cliff continues to plunge another one hundred feet, and then soon an additional two hundred feet again. Above the water's edge we have built a small, simple deck, which gives us access to the lake and rocky shore. From this deck, and only from there, is it possible to see beyond the eastern tip of our peninsula, up past Mt. Kaslo, eight miles to the north of us.

Mt. Kaslo is three miles from the village, directly across the lake to the east, rising six thousand feet higher than the town. Contrasted with the dramatic mountains behind it, the mountain, when seen from the village, looks more like a nearby hill. It has a gentle, some-what conical appearance, and just barely visible at its rocky summit is a kind of obelisk that, when seen through binoculars, looks like a Saturn rocket aimed for takeoff. This strange device is in fact one of a series placed on various mountaintops in the Purcell and Selkirk ranges. Geologists use them to measure the creep of the mountains as they lift and migrate. Or so I have been told. This is the only ru-mour about their function that I have found credible, and I have yet to reach one of these mountaintops to see what might be written or explained there.[*]

In any event, on this morning I noticed, from our waterfront deck, "clouds" surrounding the top of Kaslo Mountain. Immediately, however, these clouds resolved into smoke, and in the steep bowl below the tree line, on the southeast face of the mountain (invisible from the village), I saw a small and intense new fire pouring smoke up to the summit.

The fire was on the steeper, back side of Mt. Kaslo, which holds alpine bowls and ridges that are heavily forested to within five hundred feet of the peak. The fire must have remained very small, smouldering for almost two days before breaking out, because it was not there the

---

[*]   A year after writing this report I was told by two independent and authoritative friends in Kaslo that these various cones are, in fact, covers protecting radio relays for communications by the RCMP. (I do not like this explanation, but I have been unable to doubt it ever since it was told to me.) Then, one year after learning this, I finally did climb to investigate one of these structures first-hand. They are made of fiberglass, dusty gray in colour, and have a clear plastic window high up on one face in the direction of a nearby town. Nothing written on them suggests their function. Unless that function is simply to preserve alpine graffiti.

day before, I am sure, and the lightning strikes that had peppered that area had occurred the day before that.

But when I first noticed it, this fire was very active, pouring a pencil-thin column of thick smoke up the canyon and on into the sky. With my binoculars I could plainly see the place where the fire was burning, though I could not discern any flames. There was no sign that the fire was being fought. Indeed, getting ground forces to the spot would have been very difficult under the circumstances. I knew there were larger fires still requiring attention, and this fire looked as if it would soon burn up to the timberline and then burn out. Moreover, any generous rain would be sufficient to stop it.

The same evening Elizabeth and I went into the village for dinner and did not return home until after dark. The local fires were a topic of discussion at dinner. Our hostess had already heard about the fire on the back of Mt. Kaslo, high up in the Powder Creek watershed, but no one else had seen the fire or heard of any steps being taken to fight it. In the village one could see only a little smoke rising behind the mountain shortly before dark, and soon nothing more was visible.

However, on the drive home we came to the place on the highway that has much the same view as we get from our waterfront deck, and Elizabeth, looking over her shoulder, told me to look, too. There, very clear in the night air, were two bright orange fires burning vividly, like two matches that had just been struck at the far end of a long dark corridor. These fires were perhaps three hundred yards apart, so the fire on Mt. Kaslo was now two fires, each much larger than the apparent solitary fire seen that morning. One fire seemed to be moving laterally, eastward, toward a dense patch of forest above Powder Creek, a forest on gentler and more vulnerable slopes. It seemed clear that this fire was not going to die and would have to be fought at next daylight.

Each of the next three days and nights, I returned to our waterfront deck to see if the fire had been controlled, but each time it seemed to have grown in extent. At night, flames were always clearly visible, yet by day only great quantities of smoke could be seen. I saw signs that another fire (it seemed much smaller), a few miles south of the one on Mt. Kaslo, was being fought from the air, but the larger fire was apparently being ignored and left to burn out. By the third day, the fire had long since reached the tree line, but it still smouldered, and, more significantly, it had also been burning slowly down and across, contacting great masses of new fuel. The villagers I asked about the fire were either unaware of it or assumed it was not significant or dangerous. No one was aware of any attempt to fight it.

In fact, crews were trying to contain this fire, occasionally using aircraft and subsequently working on the ground. But I didn't learn this until nearly ten days later, so I was left on my own to monitor the fire daily, trying to convince myself that the fire was harming neither forest nor watershed, neither the natural beauty of Powder Creek nor the proper unfolding of the universe.

Every day, despite the constantly enlarging perimeter of smoke, it was still possible to imagine that with any luck and action, this fire could surely be put out in just another day. And yet, one full week after the fire started it was still as prominent as ever. True, it had not left huge ashen scars on the mountain, as far as I could see, but of course the smoke prevented a clear view. The perimeter of the fire grew each day, but not as swiftly as each night it seemed it must.

We had windy days that brought the smoke down over our heads, but in the steep bowl to the lee of the mountain peak the fire did not seem to increase in the wind. Only during the nights, when brilliant orange beacons shimmered in the fire zone, did it sometimes seem that everything was completely out of control.

I lost track of the days. The fire burned on. It seemed like two weeks had passed when, shortly before we had to leave at the end of summer, our friend Holley decided to rent a small boat and invited us to join her for one last picnic across the lake at the mouth of Powder Creek. It was all decided at the last minute early on a Thursday morning. Elizabeth and I soon found ourselves with Holley crossing the flat lake, the earnest purr of a small outboard in our ears and the delicious lake air streaming into our lungs.

On this sunny morning, poking along close by the eastern shore of the lake, with the Mt. Kaslo fire invisible behind the looming mountain in front of us, the calm was suddenly broken by the heavy chatter of a helicopter passing low over our heads then disappearing around a little point in front of us. Underneath the helicopter was a long sling, and at the end of the sling was a heavy but empty cargo net. The sling could mean only one thing: that this helicopter had been, or was, fighting a fire somewhere. We rounded the little point to discover what was going on and saw through binoculars that the helicopter, hovering over the lake shore, was lowering its cargo net to a man standing beside a portable pump.

A heavy fire hose led from the pump into the lake, and another led to some barely visible collapsible water bags. The man on the ground was supposed to fill the water bags and put them in the cargo net. But the pump refused to start. As we watched, the helicopter landed carefully, cut its engines, and the two men inside went down to the water's edge to help with the pump. Eventually the pump was repaired, the helicopter was restarted, and we turned around to begin our picnic half a mile away at the mouth of Powder Creek. No sooner had we beached our boat than the helicopter came around the small point again and roared over our heads at low altitude climbing up the canyon. Swinging underneath it was the cargo net filled with four or five bulging water bags destined for ground crews fighting a fire. The flight path led straight toward the Mt. Kaslo fire in the watershed east and north of us.

In no time at all the helicopter roared back down, an empty net drifting far out behind it as it flew out of the twisting canyon, following

Powder Creek to the lake. These trips up to the fire continued for half an hour and then ceased. By the time we returned home that afternoon, almost no smoke could be seen from Mt. Kaslo, and by the next morning the fire apparently was out.

It turned cold the few nights prior to my departure, and the weather was very unsettled, with intermittent showers. By Saturday morning there was snow on the summit of Mt. Kaslo, while on many of the higher mountains light snow covered all of the ground above tree line. The precipitation cleansed the smoky air and made every tree stand out on the ridges around us. Ainsworth Hot Springs began doing a thriving business as the Labour Day weekend arrived and a hot soak at last seemed welcome after the heat of August. The fires in these Ainsworth waters flare on a brisk fall day, but this time it is to heal us.

I left home this morning in the dark to catch the first ferry east, before the Labour Day crowds could gather with their inevitable queues two hours long. (Elizabeth will fly over me on Wednesday, and will greet me in Toronto on my arrival Thursday night.)

The passage across the lake, as dawn broke through pink-layered clouds, was beautiful to the point of causing immediate homesickness. My route took me far south to the end of the lake, then continued straight on through the Kootenay River Valley and south into Idaho. In northern Idaho, hops were being harvested in the morning sun, and one bounced off a passing truck to join me in the car, becoming a malty companion on the dashboard. I turned east on Highway 2, the straightest and perhaps the most dramatic route east, and climbed gently against the Kootenay River as it passed from Canada south, looped west through Montana, and then flowed back north into Canada and Kootenay Lake through the pointing finger of Idaho.

Six hours after leaving home, half a lifetime away, I crested a small rise and left the southeast corner of the huge Kootenay River watershed to enter the Flathead River watershed. No sign announces the change, but none is needed. There is the raw scar from a huge old forest fire here, and the exhaustion of the land is suddenly palpable. People and time so often do this to the land. And it seems so needless. Is this what lies ahead for Kaslo? For me?

This last drive to Toronto will be a journey through watersheds. Today it has been the Kootenay, Flathead, Cut Bank, and part of the Milk River watersheds—twelve hours on the road. Tomorrow, another twelve hours should take me through the Milk River, the Missouri River, and into the Red River watersheds. The third day, bearing straight east, I will cross the Mississippi twice (each time on nondescript little bridges a few car lengths long) and will arrive in the St. Lawrence watershed. The fourth twelve-hour day will see me through to Toronto, across what is much less than half of the full St. Lawrence drainage.

Already Kaslo seems far away, and the question I will soon face from my many city friends — "But what will you *do* all day in Kaslo after you retire?" — looms large. Whenever they ask this question I feel I don't know how to begin to answer, even though the answer has long been perfectly well known to me.

The truth is I will be watching fires, and bears, and people, and boats. I will see our house built and my book on the common cold finished. I will study the snowline and wash my pickup truck. I will memorize maps. I will give unasked advice on the subject of "retirement," and I will seek advice concerning galaxies perhaps, or muons, or immunoglobins. I will read, of course. I will sit long hours beside the lake, beside my wife, and (I hope) beside my aging parents. I will write down certain of my thoughts. I will send letters. I will drink B.C. cider, slowly. And from time to time I will go to bed. (But always, first, I'll make sure that the screen is safely in front of the fireplace.)

3 | *Moving the Cat*

While the official date of my retirement is still some thirty-six days into the future, I am already learning more than I expected about retirement, early or otherwise. Well planned though this retirement has been, and well schooled though Elizabeth and I have now become concerning our change of status and lifestyle, it certainly remains true in our case that, just as the old proverb reminds us, "The best laid plans o' mice an' men, gang aft agley."

This proverbial conjunction of mouse with man I have always taken to be a flourish of poetic licence, emphasizing, I suppose, that we humans are no less vulnerable than those unfortunate wee beasties so preyed on by all the rest of the animal kingdom. But now I have reason to infer that the author of this proverb must have been owned by one or more cats and that it was no poetic whim that made him choose the mouse to link with the man as being at the mercy of the fates. I have met the fates and they look to me to be mostly cats.*

The move to Kaslo has not been going according to plan because the house in Toronto has not sold according to plan (suggesting anew the recklessness of "planning" the sale of a house). This in turn has meant that the move of our possessions to Kaslo has not yet taken place.

Originally, the plan was that our cat Sophie would be couriered by Elizabeth, flown with her to Kaslo, while I played the savvy teamster in a rented moving van, efficiently cruising from truck stop to truck stop westward along U.S. Highway 2 to B.C.

Instead, Sophie and I led a slow micro-caravan of two packed cars: we in our plucky little Honda Civic, and Elizabeth and our friend Janis following in Janis' car, hers being the big comfortable one with the cruise control and air-conditioning, both of which ceased to function within minutes of our setting out on our five-day westward odyssey.

Sophie is a thirteen-year-old polydactyl tabby cat (you could look it up, but in this case it means six-toed) given by me as a kitten to Elizabeth on our wedding day that many years ago.

Sophie is generally known to be one mean tabby. This because it can take a half-liter of one's own blood to transport her to the vet, and because the vet invariably elects to put her under complete anesthesia before taking her temperature, or looking in her ears, or doing other routine $200 jobs on her. But in fact, especially lately, Sophie has suddenly become, well frankly, a pussycat around the house.

Sophie's recent change of personality took place about two months ago when the last one of three other cats that periodically had been imposed on her domestic life left Sophie (and us) for life in a calmer

---

*   Years later I encountered further confirmation of such truths on a sign in our veterinarian's office. The sign read: *"Dogs have masters. Cats have staff."*

home. This last cat was the one Elizabeth's son Dan had left in our care "for just a few weeks" until he could find a place for her in a dorm at New York University, a place where he could surely, quietly, keep her (unnoticed). Nearly two years later, long after Sophie made that little cat's life miserable, Dan decided it might be some time before he could claim his cat and so, yes, we could give her to a good home.

Elizabeth could not at first bring herself to part with this guest, her baby cat, but while she was working out of town one week, and with her neutral acquiescence, I advertised to my large Introductory Psychology class the existence of this poor suffering harlequined beauty. After class the perfect home came up to claim her.

It took Sophie about three days to believe she really finally had the whole house all to herself. Suddenly, after many years of self-imposed Coventry, Sophie began jumping up on laps again, and sleeping at the foot of the bed. Notwithstanding this remarkable transformation in personality, Janis still regularly refers to Sophie not by name, but as "that rottentabby."

Now Janis is a little more complicated to introduce. Janis is gentle, beautiful, and small of stature. She is a dear friend of Elizabeth, divorced a few years ago, a charming woman eleven years our junior who gave up a successful career in Germany as an operatic soprano to return to her hometown of Toronto, there to work for a time as an arts administrator for a major cultural institution and later for a major dance company.

Elizabeth first met Janis at the home of a mutual friend who had been Janis' landlady until 1972. Recently, both of Janis' parents died, leaving her their automobile and just enough money to go touring, starting with our corner of B.C. Janis has only just learned to drive, however. Prior to our trip out to Kaslo, she had never driven on the open highway. She was nervous about that and asked if we would let her come along with us. Janis is the sort of person people are delighted to help in such situations so of course we said yes. One other thing (full disclosure): Janis was long ago and briefly a student of mine, and is the woman with whom I lived in Toronto between 1969 and 1972.

Rottentabby Sophie does not like to travel, especially in cars. That is why our original plan was to fly her to B.C. When it became clear that it made much more sense, financially and practically, for us all to drive west with Sophie, quite a bit of thought went into how to make this tolerable. It was decided that Elizabeth and Janis might ride in another car, Janis' car, so that Sophie could be insulated from them by a number of car lengths, two sets of steel car doors, and plenty of road and radio noise. Unexpectedly, the radio in Janis' car also ceased to function, at about the halfway point of the trip, but by then the fascinating and inaudible antics of the cat visible in the Honda up ahead made Elizabeth and Janis all but indifferent to this less serious entertainment loss.

At the moment of our scheduled departure from Toronto, Sophie was not home, although she had been very much under foot until shortly before. I went around the neighbourhood calling her, falsely suggesting that I had food to offer. She appeared a few doors down our back lane, doubtful, but she did not quite evade my grasp when I got close to her.

I put us both into the Honda, shut the doors, and then released her, expecting loud and instant complaint. Instead I got active curiosity and only a bit of sarcastic conversation from her. We had long ago learned that travelling in her transport crate particularly annoyed Sophie. She did better when she could roam the car. For a time, then, I was permitted to imagine that I might be spared complaints in this interesting new environment, this basement on wheels.

We were well north of the city when Sophie started strong audible complaining. I tried, successfully, to ignore her because I knew I had five days of driving ahead of me. Nothing I could do was going to make her any more comfortable than would the freedom of the car she had already been given, with the two nests I had built for her among the luggage. To my surprise, however, Sophie soon stopped all but a constant meek little cry, the sort that tells you that she has realized in these last few moments of her sad little life that she is powerless to make you reconsider your desperate cruelty.

Later Sophie gave up vocalizing altogether and began to try to sleep, but the jiggle of the car always awakened her as her head sank onto her paws. Naturally neither of the specially cushioned nests that I created to avoid this problem held any attraction for her. Finally, as was to happen periodically during each day of the trip, Sophie walked across my lap to look out the driver's side window, then settled down to rest her chin on my lower forearm, the one that was trying to steer the car.

We stopped for lunch and I slipped quickly out of the driver's side door to keep Sophie from escaping. We offered Sophie water and she drank nothing. We put out a box of kitty litter. Despite her big breakfast, she did not use it. While the car was motionless, Sophie stayed in constant motion (we could see her from our table in the restaurant). She searched out every window for signs of us. Whenever she saw us, she appeared to be mewing loudly. Elizabeth and Janis found this amusing. I suggested that perhaps Liz would like to drive the Honda for a while, and after lunch she did so.

From Janis' car we could see Sophie's ears in profile as she wandered around the Honda in search of comfort. Sophie frequently came to the back window to stare fixedly at the front tires on Janis' car, her mouth moving six times a minute in what was obviously a loud if rote complaint.

The day got hotter. It was time to rotate drivers and so I got back behind the wheel of the Honda and Elizabeth returned to relieve Janis. As we started up, Sophie started panting in what I took to be heat exhaustion. I stopped and offered her cool water. She would not drink. She would not use the kitty litter, which I kept having to fetch from the rear of the car where it rode covered by plastic. And on we went.

From time to time I would pull over and stop.

"Why are we stopping?" the women asked me.

"The cat is desperate again," was the reply.

It did not help matters that they found this obvious answer somehow amusing.

Late in the afternoon, Sophie became more vocal and more mobile. She successfully convinced me that she desperately had to leave the car to answer the call of nature and to cool down. So with Elizabeth and Janis following blindly, I swung off the road at a wide siding, pulled far over to the edge of the dirt, and prepared to let Sophie touch the earth. These preparations were not easy, however, because we had brought no proper halter or leash.

Actually, we did spend a lot of money for a halter just before we left Toronto. We had put it on Sophie the evening before we left so she could become accustomed to it. While we were putting it on her, she reverted to her true tabby self and she drew a few lines of blood from me. But I got the halter securely in place, and, despite several heroic attempts, she was unable to wriggle out of it. She calmed down soon enough, and by our bedtime, when she asked to go outside, she seemed to have forgotten all about the contraption.

The next morning, Sophie greeted us and her breakfast wearing no halter. We searched all her outdoor haunts but failed to turn up this expensive red toy. All I had in the Honda when it came time to let Sophie escape from the car was a long piece of nylon cord.

I tied the cord securely around Sophie's midriff, held the other end tightly in my hand, and flung wide the car door. Sophie didn't move. Elizabeth and Janis, parked some distance behind, watched in fascination.

Their version of what happened next goes as follows: Out of the car steps a grim man with gray hair. He is holding onto a long white line, or a fuse, or something that leads back into the car. He is backing away slowly from the car, staring intently at something inside it. The long line goes taut. He pulls on it. Nothing happens. He pulls again. There is a gray blur and something springs out of the car and dives for cover deep underneath it.

The man, muttering, gets on his knees to look under the car and pulls again on the taut line. The line suddenly moves away from him and wraps around one of the front tires. The man races around the car to embrace the tire and untangle the line. He bends down again and stares under the car at the other end of the line. And stares. Minutes pass. The muttering continues.

Then a cat bolts out from under the car and jumps up through the wide open door back into the car. The line now runs from the man's hands, completely under the car, and back into the car on the other side.

At this point Elizabeth and Janis are laughing too hard to see what happens next.

What happens next is that the Honda door is slammed shut and quite suddenly we are under way again.

By the time we stop at a motel that evening, Sophie has neither drunk any water nor has she used her litter box all day. On arrival in our room for the night we immediately offer her both. She takes a quick drink, ignores her box, and instead approvingly examines the entire motel room. She purrs. She stretches out on the carpet. We offer her food. She purrs louder. She eats. She drinks again. Next morning again, she drinks, she eats. But when it is time for us to leave, it is clear that she still hasn't used her box.

We cannot outwait Sophie. We must be on our way. The litter box is covered and put in the back of the Honda. The cat is caged for the move to the car. When she is released inside the car, there are no complaints. Perhaps we will yet have a quiet day. But no, not yet we won't. Sophie soon is complaining more loudly than ever. And not sleeping. She is shedding, and she does a lot of grooming.

At a morning rest stop Elizabeth and I decide that Sophie's intestines might be blocked by hairballs. We decide that if we see a large pet store or veterinarian's office, we will stop and buy some hairball paste. Elizabeth is now quite concerned about Sophie's urinary health and favours the vet idea. It will give us a chance to ask if Sophie is in any danger. Visions of long delays and extravagant expenses dance in my mind's eye.

"Yes, dear," I say.

We have both noticed that I only call her "dear" when I am annoyed.

Miles later, coming out from the Michigan woods into the small towns of northern Wisconsin, I spot a veterinarian's office on the other side of the highway. Janis and Elizabeth do not see it and so cannot imagine why I suddenly do a U turn, and disappear back up a hill. I pull into the parking area in front of the office, and, leaving Sophie in the car, I go inside. The young woman sitting at the reception desk, wearing faded jeans, is busy on the telephone, giving someone sage advice about dog foods. She gives no indication that she will be with me soon.

Then an older man in a brown lab coat comes out from the back and asks if he can help me.

"Do you have any hairball gel for cats?" I ask.

He asks me why I want it, and hardly hearing my answer, immediately convinces himself that only the doctor, who is busy at the moment, can determine if it is safe to sell me this powerful substance.

I am a bit confused because I believe I have asked for a simple Vaseline derivative of no possible danger to anything having nine lives. Apparently I am wrong, however. I have the right product in mind, but only the doctor can let strangers leave with this strong (and probably expensive) medicine.

Elizabeth comes in the door, all smiles at my astute find: a vet who is open and in. I explain that actually the vet is busy somewhere and we are not to be allowed to buy the hairball medicine until we talk to him.

At this moment, the scruffy young woman in front of us finishes her phone call and introduces herself. She is the doctor.

"Can you please tell me why you need this preparation?" she asks.

Now that she has taken over, the male assistant finally feels it is appropriate to get out the product and lay it on the counter between us, where, who knows, I might grab it and run.

I happily let Elizabeth take over the answers, but almost at once she is describing Sophie's state of near death. It looks to me as if, in another blink of the eye, we will be authorizing immediate surgery and boarding the cat for a week.

Now if Sophie were a male cat, thirty-six hours unrelieved, she would indeed have been pronounced near death. But given that she is female, and given that she is unused to travel, and given that she had eaten well and been drinking last night, we were to be allowed to move cautiously westward, under the strict advice that should Sophie not have urinated by this very evening, she must immediately be placed in the care of a vet. The hairball medicine was soon given over with no fuss, but at great cost, and we were sent on our way.

Before we resumed our journey, and against my better judgment, Janis thought it best to tell Sophie she had better use her box soon, or else. And I thought it best to repack a few things so the cat box could be open on the passenger side floor at all times. Sophie was offered more water. She declined it, declined to use the box, and was driven back onto the highway, her chauffeur's nose now distinctly out of joint.

Sophie became more and more agitated late in the afternoon. For the first time, her wandering took her into and out of the cat box. Hope rose again for the umpteenth time that maybe, finally, biology would triumph over psychology. For the sixth time that day, I looked for a place to pull over and stop so that road motion would not deter Her Highness from enjoying a performance in the Royal Box. But it was not necessary to stop. Sophie simply decided to relieve herself. Relieving me. I flashed a big thumbs up sign to the women in the car behind me. But they were not relieved, assuming that my gesture was a comment on some flash of scenery that they had both missed.

That evening, while we were at dinner, Sophie finished off our worries, much too soon for the hairball medicine to get any of the credit.

Janis suggested that the credit was perhaps hers, because she had threatened Sophie with a stay at the vet's.

I suggested that the credit belonged to cat biology.

Elizabeth suggested instead that Sophie was now becoming an experienced traveler.

The experience Sophie had gained was the experience of complaining, not the more useful experience of how to travel. By the time we arrived at our destination, at the end of the fifth day, she was the mistress of every nuance in the feline lexicon of complaint.

We have been back in Kaslo over a week now, united with our mountains and with my stepmother, Helga, who has at long last moved into her house in Kaslo, our favourite village house, the one we chose with her two summers ago, before a nasty broken ankle delayed her immigration here from San Francisco. Janis has just found a small perfect cottage to housesit while the owners are away in June. Sophie has been bringing to our doorstep copious mice and shrews, and recently, one large bat. (Happily, this last was only playing dead; it flew away later when our backs were turned.)

It looks as if Elizabeth will soon be away for six weeks, doing a contract job in California, where I may go to join her briefly. Helga once loved a cat of her own named Minnie, so this evening I asked her if she would like to board Sophie for a time.

Helga paused and then replied quietly, "You know, I never really had an affinity for Sophie."

I understood. Completely.

4 | *The Stag Under the Stairs*

Today was to have been a very special day, and it has indeed been quite memorable, though not in the way I expected or intended.

This is the day we expected to begin the site preparation for building our new home, the retirement home that we are hoping will be ours for the rest of our lives. Since last July, when finally we sold our Toronto home, we and our belongings have been shoehorned into our wee one-room Gatehouse here, located at the boundary between the eastern end of Woodbury Village Road and our lakeside lot. The main house, our future home, will be built out on the steep hillside, above the rocky cliffs that plunge down to the lake at the eastern tip of Woodbury Point. The views to the east and the south will be spectacular there.

The house itself is not supposed to be spectacular, however. It is supposed to be very comfortable, easily livable, and economically reasonable. Also, it is supposed to be ready for us by, oh, September or October.

"No problem," estimates Chris, our builder. "We can definitely start on March first."

But today it has been raining, and somehow our builder hasn't been able to reach the excavator quite yet. Moreover, our building plans still need approval from an engineer . . . perhaps next week. Chris tells us not to worry. He urges us to have patience. It *will* still be in March that we get under way.

"Isn't that what was promised?" he asks. [*]

Retirement is proving to have many unexpected lessons to teach, patience being but one of them. Even before retirement we had been given considerable opportunity to learn patience here in the Kootenay region of B.C. Our remarkable cliffside staircase leading down to Kootenay Lake, built in the summer of 1989, took twice the time and thrice the money that we had been told to expect. The stairs take one from the cliff-top end of a woodland path, down seventy winding steps, past seven unique landings, to a sculpted platform at the lake's edge that is set among large tumbling rocks. The substantial cedar posts and beams of the staircase blend with the cliffside firs and pines, augmenting the reflected sunlight that bounces off the rock and the surface of the lake below. Speaking only for myself, this work of outdoor art was worth every extra dollar and day that it took to build. Moreover, our special Gatehouse/garage, built during most of the two summers of 1991 and 1992, also took twice the time and thrice the money that we had been told to expect. It, too, proved to be well worth the wait and the wages.

But now, with retirement, has come a small pension in place of an ample wage. So while it may be argued (naively) that we have plenty of time to spend in building a home, we no longer have forgiving incomes. It is commonplace that the financial lessons of retirement can be the

***

[*] It was. And eight months later we would move in to a wonderful realization of what we had planned.

least enjoyable to learn and also perhaps the most frequent and difficult to master. All the more reason that these lessons need to be learned quickly. Here in the Kootenays, however, things rarely happen quickly.

Another lesson that retirement invariably teaches is the unreliable nature of one's familiar self-images. Unlike in the big city, no one here calls me professor, for instance. This is something I expected and encouraged by moving here. But I was quite used to being the professor in the outside world, and I realize now that I drew a certain comfort from all I could contribute while in that role. Since taking early retirement, however, it has sometimes become much less clear what I may be contributing, and to whom. Every so often this ambiguity creates a concern that is surprising to me, a concern over who I now may be and where I now may fit in this ever-changing world.

All this might have been predictable, I suppose. Yet I really did think that somehow, magically, I might be spared any new identity trials. Certainly so during the years prior to turning sixty-five. However, five days ago, with the stag slowly dying under the stairs, this identity problem arose again in a surprising new guise.

Some weeks earlier there had been a kind of precursor to the events below the stairs. I was alone at that earlier time, living in the village, caretaking Helga's house, her new cat, and our cat Sophie. Helga was away visiting old friends in California and Elizabeth was visiting her children in New England. I had decided to take a walk, a fine two-mile circuit around Kaslo that leaves Helga's house and drops down to circle the alluvial fan on which the lower village is built. This walk proceeds counterclockwise, first via the riverbank, then along the lakeshore, then back beside Kaslo bay. In the bay a number of ducks and Canada geese are wintering over, and on the day in question I decided for the first time to take all the old bread left in Helga's kitchen and feed the fowl.

I was quite unprepared when I arrived at the little beach on the bay to discover that another gentleman, definitely a senior citizen, had already attracted many of the birds around him. Not that his presence or offerings created a problem at the feeding station. There were appetites and space enough for all the treats we both had brought. The problem (if that is even the correct word) was somewhere back behind my eyes. Suddenly I saw myself, white-haired with walking stick, solemnly throwing feed to the fowl. It was an *old* man that I saw. Just like that other old man, standing off to my left and talking baby talk to the geese, offering them grain and seed. For the first time, I felt "retired" in that somewhat pejorative sense of "used up," "simple," and "out of the loop." Standing there in that unrecognized paradise, not yet aware of all that may be right about feeding the birds again after so many years, and forgetting what even that same morning I had in fact been putting *into* the loop, my thoughts came full stop. The gap between the roughly forty-year-old me that I normally imagine and feel myself to be, and the roughly seventy-year-old me that I imagined I saw feeding the ducks, was too great. I shuffled off toward home followed by a dark and gloomy cloud.

I soon got over it. For one thing, I managed to adjust the forty years up a bit closer to the true chronological mark. And besides, I was distracted by a surprising phone call that came to Helga's house soon after I got home. Candace, a friend who teaches second grade at the Kaslo school, located just above and adjacent to Helga's home, told me a note was about to be sent home with every student, from kindergarten right up through grade twelve. The note was advising parents that cougars had been spotted recently on the edge of the village, and that cougar tracks had that day been found "behind the school" (i.e., on the bench of land right beside Helga's house). Parents were asked to accompany their children to and from the school bus or the school during the next few weeks.

I thanked Candace for her call and rushed from the house in the waning winter daylight to scour a thinning layer of snow for cougar tracks. To my surprise I soon found fresh, large prints, prints that were much too big to be from the paws of any domestic cat or even a bobcat. I was puzzled, however, because the animal had a stride shorter than I would have expected in a cougar.

For a quarter of an hour I followed these prints back and forth near Helga's house until, as I rested and pondered, the large black dog making these prints trotted past me on his way home.

When I called Candace back, she could not tell me precisely where the cougar tracks had been seen behind the school, nor just who it was that had confirmed their origin. Whatever the case, it seemed prudent to keep our two cats in at night for a while, and to keep a good lookout each time I left the house.

No further sign of cougars was reported, and soon after Elizabeth's return from the East, we set off together to visit our families and some friends in California. To conserve holiday time and avoid winter driving, we elected to fly south. I arranged to fly home early, alone, in time to prepare for the excavators that we had expected for today. Thus, five days ago, after an absence of two weeks, I had occasion to break a fresh trail through the new snow to our stairs down to the lake.

All winter long our property has been visited by multiple small groups of mule deer, and each morning there have been circuitous doodles in the snow tracing out the wanderings of the previous night's visitors. One of the first things that struck me this day, as I set off on the path to the stairs, was that there were no animal prints at all in the new snow, nor in the remains of the snow from two days before. But then, when I reached the point on this path where it bends sharply back to start its descent to the top of the stairs, at the point closest to where our home is to be built, I was startled by the rattle of hooves on rock and looked up to see five does trotting smartly straight uphill, right out of our invisible master bedroom.

I reached the stairs and carefully began the descent, my eyes fixed on each snowy step and on the vibrant mosses cascading down the steep cliffside to my left. As I neared the bottom of the stairs I was suddenly startled by a loud snort and a quick triplet of hoof-beats. There, directly in front of me at the foot of the steps, was a magnificent stag with full antlers, standing erect, head raised, large brown eyes intently focused on mine. We were very close, and the event was so uncanny that for a long moment I wasn't in the least surprised. In a dream this animal would have spoken to me, and, dreamlike, I waited for just that to happen.

But nothing happened. There was no sign of whatever fear or pain the stag may have been feeling. There was only his level gaze and rapt attention. One of us moved. And then the stag turned and hobbled a few more steps away from the stairs, turning away from me and suddenly freeing my thoughts. How did he get to this rocky amphitheater at the edge of our lake? If the stairs were not used (and the snow on the stairs was completely undisturbed), then only a mountain goat would have had any chance of climbing down into this place without injury. A deer might conceivably swim in, but it would soon swim out, too. I could only assume that the stag slipped over the edge and down our cliffs, although a later search did not uncover any evidence of where this might have occurred. A fall over the cliffs seemed much more likely when I finally realized that the stag was hobbling on just three legs. His right rear leg, held off the ground at all times, hung limply in the air.

How long had he been here? I could see evidence that he had bedded down for some time in two different bushy locations at the base of the cliffs, beside the stairs. And numerous droppings on the ground suggested that at least one night had already been spent in this location. What was the matter with his leg? The stag turned and hobbled just a bit further from where I still stood on the stairs. I could see no sign of exterior injury on him anywhere. Perhaps he fractured his hip in a fall over the cliffs.

A wave of sorrow and a feeling of responsibility for this animal swept over me. Again I felt a crisis of existence. Just a week before, on city corners in California, I had passed the homeless and unemployed who were asking for work or spare change, and had watched the others who were walking by without seeing, as I tried to do. I heard, too, about two friends of friends, one who was facing a choice between paying for badly needed medical treatment or paying for what seemed to her to be all the necessities of her life, while another had just enjoyed heroic medical care paid for by expensive health insurance.

I had pushed these stories out of my mind. But faced with the stag at the foot of the stairs, immediate, alone, and so clearly in need of help, there could be no similar denial or escape. What was I going to do? What should I do? What in fact could I do? The retired professor had no answers. He felt useless. Stupid. With nothing to contribute.

Something soon permitted me to suppose what I most wanted to suppose: that this stag was not really in pain, nor in any danger. That the animal might well be doomed to starvation in this small and rocky prison was, at least for the time being, unthinkable. However, to salvage a sense of competence and to bolster my optimistic form of denial, I hunted the empty Gatehouse for food to offer the animal, to help him on his way. I found a pathetic cup of rolled oats, which I took down and placed on the stone step at the base of the stairs. It was nearly sunset. The stag was now farther on, standing among sharp large stones, looking back at me. Gone was the majestic look, and there was no apparent interest in what I was placing on the step.

I phoned Elizabeth in California for advice and condolence. I did not want anyone to shoot this animal on the pretext of doing it a kindness. Elizabeth suggested that I telephone our friend Jill in Kaslo. She reminded me that Jill has lived here longer than we, has constant animal visitors to her local orchard home, and has made many more connections in the local community having to do with wildlife.

When I called Jill she gently explained to me how, if a large animal could put no weight on its leg, it almost certainly had to be very painfully injured, and eventually, one way or another, that injury would prove fatal. The stag was probably dehydrating and starving, confined as it was to such a small contour of land. Jill suggested two people to call who might help me "put down" the stag. But I was not even close to being ready to make any such call.

The next morning I awoke from a troubled sleep and immediately went down to see if the stag was perhaps better. I soon saw that the small pile of oats I had put out remained untouched on the stone step. But I did not see the stag, and for a moment I took heart that perhaps he had swum to safety. Then, as I continued down the stairs, underneath the tallest landing near the bottom, the stag struggled to his feet and hobbled a few steps out into the open to a place from which he could see me. I thought I might reassure him if I pretended to ignore him, as if going about other business. So I walked right on by and away from him, on down to the deck beside the lake.

The lake level had dropped considerably in the two weeks I had been gone. I made my regular measurements of the new lake level and water temperature, then returned up the stairs. The stag stood nervous and alert as I first passed within twelve feet of him and then passed over his head. He lay back down under cover of the landing after I reached the top of the stairs.

It was no longer really possible to imagine that the stag would recover, but that did not stop me from trying anyway. All day long I worried over what I had seen and what I had been told earlier by Jill. By sunset I could no longer deny that something would have to be done, but whatever that something might be, it would have to wait until morning. All evening I considered whom to call. Somehow I could not bring myself to call a hunter. I decided that when the time came, I would call the RCMP.

In the morning I checked one more time on the stag. He looked weaker, and he did not move when I approached him. Reluctantly I went back and called the village RCMP. Because it was a Sunday morning, my call was automatically relayed to Nelson where a very calm woman answered. I explained about the injured stag, that I did not own a gun, and that if the animal must be killed I had hoped to see any resulting venison given to someone who needed it. I said I understood that the RCMP might be able to help me.

The woman replied that our village officers were not on active duty this morning and that in any event it might be best if a Conservation Officer handled this matter. She took my name and phone number and said that someone would be calling me very soon.

She was as good as her word. Within minutes I received a call from Officer Christie in Nelson. He said he would come right over (it is a forty-five-minute drive here from Nelson) and would do whatever was necessary. I thanked him and gave him directions to our house.

Officer Christie proved to be a quiet young man, fit looking, and serious. I was at once grateful that it was he who had come. We spoke briefly and then he went to his truck and collected his gun (a shotgun, not a rifle), a pair of ear protectors, and a few shells. I led the way to the stairs and down to the landing above the stag. We were talking as we descended, quietly, briefly, but this time the stag did not stand up until we were very close. Officer Christie loaded his gun and I urged him to be careful of any ricochet off the rock cliffs. I was now behind him on the stairs and so was potentially in a line of fire if he went abreast of the stag to fire back under the stairs. I was allowed to retreat back up the stairs while he put on his ear protectors and readied to shoot. I went a considerable distance back until I could no longer see the stag or Officer Christie.

Sooner than I expected I heard an explosive roar. I flinched involuntarily. I waited, expecting another shot, but there was absolute silence. Then, from far across the lake, came the soft rattle of a dozen echoes.

"Will there be another shot?" I called down.

"No," Officer Christie said.

I heard him open the shotgun to remove a shell. I went back down to where he stood on the stairs, not eight feet from the fallen stag. There was a small hole beside the open eye of the animal, and blood was flowing out from under his head. We watched without saying a word. There was a twitch. Another. Officer Christie got down and gently touched the eye of the stag, but there was no response. Then the two rear legs started sleepwalking and I winced. Officer Christie explained that this was normal, and to myself I thought that, of course, if inhibitory neurons release first, then the excitatory neurons . . . etc. And while my mind raced on, my throat tightened and choked off any further conversation.

Officer Christie lay his gun aside and stripped off his good jacket, preparing to butcher the carcass. I left him and went back to the Gatehouse, but I could not continue my work. I sat looking at the mountains. Waiting. Looking at the big 4 x 4 truck parked at the end of the road. Watching the trail up from the stairs. After a long while I decided to go back down to see how things stood. On the stairs I found the hindquarters of the stag, and a few steps below, the forequarters. Officer Christie had just finished his work. One hundred pounds of venison was now destined for the Salvation Army in Nelson. A handsome pair of antlers was saved for me.[*] The remainder of the stag's head was now at the bottom of the lake, and his entrails, on the ground, were already attracting curious ravens, circling overhead.

We made three trips up the stairs to the truck. On the first two trips, we each grasped a leg of the stag and hoisted the meat over the snow and up the hill. It was very hard work and I was frequently out

---

[*] They had come off the stag's head with the shock of hitting the ground. This is the season when antlers are normally shed.

of breath. On the third trip, the gun, jacket, and antlers came up the stairs. Afterwards, Officer Christie came indoors to wash his hands and to drink a large glass of water. We speculated about what may have happened to cause the stag's injury. There was a four-inch gash on the inner thigh of the injured hind leg, but this surface wound was healing and did not seem infected. There was no external sign of a broken bone or fractured hip. And no other marks on the animal. It was all somewhat puzzling.

Then, a few hours after Officer Christie left, I got the news about the cougar. According to a neighbour, a cougar had been seen sweeping through our neighbourhood during the previous few days, scattering deer in all directions. One deer was spotted swimming across the lake. A deer kill had been found on the ridge above us. And quite recently, a most unwelcome hunter, using dogs, had come through our properties, hot on a cougar's trail. That a stag had gone over our cliff was suddenly no longer surprising.

It has now been two days since the stag died. Already the ravens and a pair of bald eagles have consumed everything that remained on the ground. Rain has since washed away most of the blood at the site, but it has hardly touched the new guano that is scattered everywhere around. This afternoon I have been speaking again with Officer Christie on the phone. I have just learned that, yes, it is still legal (with a permit) to hunt cougar here. Officer Christie says that as a matter of fact this very morning a small female was brought to the Nelson office to be legally registered. It had been killed yesterday in our neighbourhood by a hunter using dogs. Local children and pets should now be safer. The deer, too. So some are saying.

5 | *Troubles of the Heart*

SATURDAY MAY 14, 1994
KASLO, B.C.

*E*very Garden of Eden has its serpent, and Kaslo is no exception. Actually, there seem to be two serpents here. One of them has been fostering considerable friction between those in our garden who would pick the tree entire and some who would only look on it in awe. The second seems to be a constrictor, one that has been throwing coils around my own chest. I feel that both these serpents have emerged together out of some deep den, but why here, and why now?

Two evenings ago a town meeting was finally held to consider the potential effects of recently revised plans for major local logging. A number of concerns were expressed at this meeting, concerns that have eclipsed all others in Kaslo. The tensions created whenever large-scale logging is proposed are not unique to Kaslo, of course. In most of the forested regions of Canada, logging periodically becomes the focus of considerable conflict among the members of three general interest groups, in all three of which the members themselves are often fractious and mistrustful of each other.

The first group consists of people in the logging industry and those depending on it for employment or trickle-down business. The second is that group of citizens who, for environmental, economic, moral, and/or aesthetic reasons, fear the damages that logging is so often permitted to do to our watersheds, our viewsheds, and to our greatly diminishing natural habitats. (As perhaps you have already guessed, I count myself most closely aligned to this second interest group—except occasionally when I empathize too much with members of either of the other two groups.) The third group comprises the membership of the relevant governmental forestry agencies: those who set the industry codes, manage Crown lands, regulate cutting and road building in the forests, set stumpage fees, oversee reforestation and fire control, and etc.

Thus it happened that last Thursday evening, community representatives from all three of these estates met at the Kaslo Legion Hall to question, and to trade information about, an application from the Wynndel Box and Lumber Co.* Wynndel is applying to Forestry for permission to carry out large-scale logging directly across the lake, both inside Powder Creek Canyon and on those flanks of Mt. Kaslo that face the village.

The meeting was well advertised and it attracted an audience of perhaps eighty people in addition to the dozen and more experts and presenters who sat at the table in the front of the hall. Two men drove the one hundred kilometers up from the Wynndel mill at the south end of the lake, crossing over on the ferry, to defend their logging plan. A third forester, who works at Meadow Creek for a different mill, located thirty kilometers away at the north end of the lake, sat at the head table and supported these two.

---

*   Pronounced either *win-dell* or *wine-dell* with roughly equal frequency, although I persist in pronouncing it *wy-en-dell*.

Two government men also made the long drive over from Forestry headquarters in Nelson. One of them has responsibility for assessing the "sensitivity" of proposed logging sites to environmental and visual damage, and his evaluations affect the intensity and degree of logging that is permitted in any given area. The other Forestry official turned out to be the first man's boss. He was a younger man of poise and obvious intelligence who at first I thought was just one of the many Forestry staff charged with evaluating logging proposals before issuing permits to cut. His title seemed to include something that sounded more like "recreation" than "silviculture." But it was the "silviculture" planned for Powder Creek that was the main topic of our meeting, and in the end this man proved to be the Forestry expert on it. (The jargon of our forestry bureaucracy can be quite thick and impenetrable at times. It created plenty of its own kind of haze at the meeting. And it led me to wonder if there might not be some linguistic equivalent of "clearcuts" and "slash burning," which, however ugly it may also be, could at least thin out the jargon and make the "harvesting" of ideas about logging a more straightforward business.)

One of the spectators sitting at the back of the meeting hall with the rest of us turned out to be our local member of the provincial parliament, Corky Evans, a member of the political party that was recently returned to power after some years spent in the wilderness, the same party that is now under considerable fire for caving in on many of the environmental promises that it made prior to the recent election. Corky happens to embody a particularly effective blend of eloquence, good looks, and deep concern for preserving "mountain values" (read: living in harmony with nature and with neighbours while respecting the beauty of what we have). Significantly, Corky is also a former logger, one who is committed to a visible, honoured, and enduring logging industry here. It is Corky's government that sets the rules under which logging becomes either possible or impossible and profitable or unprofitable.

Only the two Forestry men among those three government people who were present did any considerable speaking, until late in the evening when Corky finally rose to close the meeting with his own impassioned observations and commentary. (I will describe what he said presently.) In contrast to these two "neutral" Forestry people, and in contrast to the three logging company people (who naturally favoured the proposed plans for logging on the east shore), almost all of the speakers from the audience were opposed both to building the logging road that is even now being punched into Powder Creek and to the planned initial "harvest" of four significant cut blocks scheduled to begin later this summer.

Last summer we had been told by Wynndel Lumber that only one of the first set of cut blocks would be clear-cut, but quite recently, at a time when we are finally facing an imminent deadline for filing any of our concerns with Forestry, the company suddenly amended its application so as to be able to clear-cut all of the first four blocks. Some of these initial clear-cuts will be visible from many different places along the lake. More significantly, over the next few years a large number of further cuts are planned in the same area (to justify both the great cost of the road going in and to satisfy certain inflexible rules that require logging companies to achieve given minimum harvest levels each year in order to retain their exclusive timber license for cutting on a given portion of Crown land).

Thus, most of the people at the meeting, including those who depend on local tourism for their livelihoods, those who understand the probable consequences of the disappearance of any more of Earth's scarce natural areas, and those who simply live here counting on the daily tonic provided by our mountain air, our unpolluted lakes and streams, and those majestic views full of forest that are still available to us, seemed frightened by the direction that these proposals were taking, a direction that seemed to many to be so transparently misguided.

As might be expected, some of the worried folk who spoke from the meeting floor were periodically discourteous, or incoherent, or they were blatantly and simply egotistic. By contrast, the government and industry presenters and the local organizers who had arranged this meeting (they were all actually rather nervous I think) invariably spoke respectfully, often speaking directly to the point as well. Most of those from the audience tended to speak at length when they finally reached the public microphone, as if they had just this one chance at having an impact and did not want to lose that important opportunity. But what struck me most was how deeply many of the speakers felt about the impacts the logging could have on their lives. They were speaking from troubled hearts. And because my heart was troubled, too, I found to my surprise that I could not speak at all.

My heart troubles all started about two months ago with a moderate chest pain that sometimes appeared and sometimes did not whenever I engaged in hard physical work. I had experienced this angina earlier when I helped Officer Christie carry the mass of venison up our snowy stairs, but at the time I had not recognized the pain for what it was. After a time, however, I knew I must not ignore these episodes any longer.

And then, from the moment when I first consulted our Kaslo doctor until the time that Elizabeth and I arrived by car in front of St. Paul's Hospital in Vancouver for specialized treatment of a serious coronary condition, only nine short days had passed.

During the first three of these days I just had time to adapt to the new headache pain caused by the nitroglycerine patches suddenly prescribed for me and to imagine all the reasons that my earlier pains hadn't really been angina after all. (For one thing, my EKG at the little Kaslo hospital, done just after I left the doctor's office, had been pronounced "normal.")

Then I took a stress test at the Nelson hospital. To my surprise (and that of the doctor in charge), I had hardly begun exerting myself when I started to feel angina at the same time that danger signs appeared on the EKG tracings being taken. The treadmill was immediately stopped and I was made to lie down, but for a moment the tracings apparently got rather worse. I was given nitroglycerine, then oxygen (I didn't feel I needed either), and I was made to rest completely for fifteen minutes until well after the angina had passed and the tracings had become normal again.

Despite sympathetic and helpful interpretations of my situation from the cardiologist in Nelson, both Elizabeth and I left the hospital in a state of shock, hardly believing what we were being told. Nothing explained why I might now have coronary disease. I am nowhere near sixty-five yet. (I will be fifty-seven in a few weeks.) I have never smoked. I am not diabetic. I have never been overweight. My diet has long been mainly vegetarian and, I had assumed, low on fats. Both my parents are over eighty years old and still healthy, and I have no family history of heart disease.* Much later I would even have it confirmed that my blood cholesterol level has been normal as well. My desperate need to know why me, and why now, was not helped when one doctor in Vancouver, exasperated by my questions, said to me, "You are over fifty, you are male, AND THAT'S ENOUGH!"

Within an hour of taking the stress test, an appointment was arranged for me to have the necessary angiogram performed six days later in Vancouver, to confirm the diagnosis of coronary insufficiency, and to locate exactly where the problems lay.

In those next days of waiting it continued to matter as much to me that I find something (hopefully something reversible) that could ex-

---

* In saying this I have denied one significant exception, however: My maternal grandfather, a portly Italian whom I was never to know, died of a heart attack when my mother was a girl.

plain the existence of this coronary problem as that the problem be soon treated. And when at last I considered "stress" as a causal candidate, I simply could not believe that any recent stress (of which there has indeed been a modest amount, not noted in these pages) could compare with the considerably greater stresses of one year earlier, created while trying to sell our city house and to get ourselves moved to British Columbia. In retrospect, even that previous stress appeared to me to be both brief in duration and long since finished.

The sudden new stress of this surprising diagnosis, however, and the risk of a potentially fatal heart attack implied by it, might well explain any subsequent worsening of my condition, not to mention the stresses associated with the prospect of being hospitalized for the first time since I was a child.

I arrived at the hospital in Vancouver with my fears only partially under control. I have never believed that personal acts of will have any power to control the genesis of thoughts and emotions, and in my clinical practice as a psychologist I repeatedly found that, by themselves, acts of willpower rarely modified thoughts or emotions after they had arisen. Like it or not, fear was something of a regular visitor to me on arrival in Vancouver, and only my brother's advice as to how to study and learn from that fear really helped me to get past it. Fortunately, I was also blessed with loving care and some effective distraction from many of the uncertainties that lay ahead, primarily from Elizabeth, but also from a visit we paid to our old friend Dorrit Klarke, who is an M.D. in general practice living in the suburban town of New Westminster just upriver from Vancouver.

Before I left Kaslo I had already heard from two neighbours who had themselves undergone angiograms that the procedure was almost painless, and even "interesting" as well. Dorrit had told me that the procedure was common and safe, and also that the man who would be my Vancouver doctor, Dr. Dodeck, was apparently a cardiologist's cardiologist, among the most respected in Canada. If I still was fearful on arrival at the hospital it was mostly a fear of hospital pain, a fear of possible bypass surgery, and a fear of the unforeseen complications that any stay in hospital may create.

Of course there are very many who have good experiences in hospital, and in the end I was fortunate enough to be one of these. For the most part I was blessed with painless IVs, fine nursing care, a doctor whom I immediately liked, a very professional and reassuring technical staff, and, best of all, the news that I had a single coronary blockage for which angioplasty was an appropriate treatment, a treatment that could take place as soon as the following day.

Angioplasty is a procedure in which a thin tube is threaded from the groin up through the main artery that serves the legs and thence into the heart to the site of the blockage. A small balloon-like device on the end of this tube is then inflated with fluid, pressing aside the plaque that blocks the artery, and thereby opening up the obstruction to let normal quantities of blood again flow to the heart muscle downstream.

One is fully awake during the procedure and, except for some unremarkable angina while the balloon is briefly inflated, and some pushing and pressing around the groin area (which is under the influence of a local anesthetic), one feels nothing special. There is a lot of high technology around during the procedure, including television monitors displaying views of the heart in action.

Somehow I found it all very reassuring, though I am sure there are some who would be more frightened than reassured by the heroic seriousness of all that equipment. In the end, angioplasty worked well for me, reducing the degree of blockage from almost ninety-five percent to a safe thirty-five percent.

That was the good news. The bad news was that the blockage is located near the beginning of the main coronary artery that serves most of the left side of the heart, a location around which no subsidiary and compensatory arterial growth is naturally possible. There is no alternative then to keeping that particular channel open, for my life will certainly depend on it. Still, I should be able to work outdoors soon as fully as ever I did, except that I must be especially careful to avoid sudden extreme exertion such as comes with pushing a car stuck in the snow, or straining to lift very heavy objects, or for that matter climbing rapidly uphill across a clear-cut strewn with destruction and debris.

I have not been told so yet, but I suspect that avoiding strong anger or outrage is just as important as avoiding those other sudden tensions. Sitting in Thursday's meeting at the Legion Hall, I was tempted to feel outrage, as for instance when hearing believable accusations of government and logging industry collusion to push through still more clear-cuts, more burning, and more monoculture replacement "forests" on grossly disturbed soils. However, my attention having so recently been so wonderfully concentrated by the recognition of my existing mortality, other priorities easily prevailed.

High on my list of new priorities is to do whatever may be required to avoid further coronary difficulties. And in my case, what seems to be required is quite happily done. A brisk thirty-five-minute walk every day, whatever the weather, is number one. Then there is a simple aspirin to take each day. For another month or more there is also a calcium channel blocker to take. Then there is the task of finishing up that last little bit of French vanilla ice cream and getting used to 1% milk.

There are some other priorities, too, all of which follow whenever I now succeed in relinquishing my habitual and unconscious assumption that I may count on many more years of health to accomplish the goals I have set for my retirement years, including what were supposed to have been the young and healthy years.

There is still a book about the common cold that I would see finished. There are still very important friendships to be nurtured. There is a home to be built. And there is what may be a fleeting time of natural beauty remaining to be enjoyed here in the Kootenay Lake basin. Perhaps the timber really will disappear again, just as it did one hundred years ago when the miners deliberately burned much of it off, the faster to read the rock outcrops for any signs of ore and the sooner to take away all the ore that could be found.* Both the heart and the lungs of this area — its waters, soils and forests — do appear to be in trouble. (And at such an early age, too.)

At the end of the logging meeting on Thursday, two things happened. One, I was troubled anew by a case of "indigestion," which in the past had never been very common with me. Two, Corky Evans accepted an invitation to comment on the things he had heard during the evening, and to tell us how things looked from the government benches in parliament. He rose and began to wax optimistic about the potential for assuring sustainable and sensitive logging practices in British Columbia. But then he shared a telling story with us. He mentioned that his own next-door neighbour, a sensitive soul, was recently persuaded to sell his land at a good price to an individual who at once logged it for an immediate return on his investment. The consequences were a sudden eyesore and an unexpected heartbreak. Every day now, from the windows of his home, Corky sees another of the unhappy results of clear-cutting.**

That clear-cut represents one of the consequences of recently higher prices for lumber and the correspondingly increased prices paid for logs

---

* I have been told since writing this that the local miners never deliberately cleared forests by burning them. That is probably true in general. But for whatever reason, most of the regional forest was cut or burned within the first twenty years of the arrival of the white man in the basin.

** In the years that immediately followed, Evans went on to run for the party leadership and he was for a time minister of fisheries in the province. Many of his actions and inactions seemed to favour logging practices that were unsustainable and unsightly and risky for some of his constituents. His moving story, alas, later seemed to me to be more campaign strategy than a concern for forest stewardship.

from private land. Yet unless timber prices (and the stumpage fees charged by the government for taking timber from Crown land) do rise, it seems that there can be no economically persuasive alternative to clear-cutting in many forest areas, such as those we now look at across the lake. It is Catch-22 all over again. Higher lumber prices (with lower rates of permitted cutting) would help enable economic alternatives to clear-cutting. These alternatives might then make it possible to save the heart of our remaining carpets of forest. But those same high prices would induce more and more individuals to devastate their own private woodlots instead.

Corky's heartfelt comments at the close of Thursday's meeting passed over this conundrum, however, and in the end he chided some of those who had earlier appeared to advocate further trashing of the already injured forests in our back yards, thereby to save the views in our front yards. Trash is trash, he reminded us, and we must find a way to stop trashing nature everywhere, not just outside our front windows.

The next morning, as the builders arrived to continue work on the foundation walls of our home, Elizabeth left for a one-week business trip and I left to take my prescribed daily walk. My "indigestion" seemed somewhat more pronounced as I began my walk, but previously walking had tended to settle it nicely. Yesterday, however, nothing made it any better, and by noon I was face to face with the frightful possibility that my chest pain represented renewed angina and not indigestion. Three spaced doses of nitroglycerine under my tongue produced no improvement. Reluctantly, I phoned Phil Olsen, our local doctor, and drove myself to the small Kaslo hospital for the necessary diagnostic EKG.

My symptoms soon were proved to result from a true indigestion and not, after all, from an expression of angina. When one is a beginner at it, it is not always easy to tell the two similar symptoms apart. Dr. Olsen and the nurse on duty were very supportive and helpful with their naive patient. Further medication was prescribed to control my indigestion until it goes away on its own.

For the time being, then, the two serpents that I spoke of seem to be back in their den. The deadline for comments on the Wynndel logging plan is still more than a week away. The mail continues to bring me delayed expressions of sympathy and concern from friends far away. On Front Street in Kaslo, people I know only slightly cross the street to welcome me back home. Alpine flowers have now appeared beside our cliffside stairs, where these wind down to the lake. And today, across the water, the spring green of new forest growth shimmers in the sun.

All of these are heart medicines as effective as any I now take with my meals. In my new-found sensitivity to sensations around the heart I am aware of another kind of lump now sitting there, and it feels like gratitude. But tell me, what does one do with overflowing gratitude?

6 | *A BC Tel Tale*

*R*etired persons use the telephone a lot. Retired persons living in rural settings and building their homes particularly count on an easy and dependable phone service. Until recently, dialing just four digits in Kaslo could put you in touch with anyone in town: with Dr. Olsen, with the Building Supply, with the volunteer fire department, with the production office of the visiting movie crew, even with the RCMP. Always assuming, of course, that an electrical storm hadn't knocked something out and that the local phone exchange was in normal working order.

Earlier this summer, on Friday, July 15, to be exact, Kaslo leapt forward into the 1950s when the miracle of modern telephone technology brought us our own seven-digit local dialing. Those who had gone very late the day before to the post office found in their mailboxes a last-minute notice of this changeover, an afterthought from dear old BC Tel. But most of us had no idea why on that Friday morning we kept being told by a disembodied voice that "your call cannot be completed as dialed." Four-digit dialing had become a Kaslo habit that everyone here had long taken for granted.

I dialed Helga's 7-5-2-0 a second time that fateful Friday morning, carefully this time, but got the same new message. I am used to hearing a message saying, "The number you have dialed is no longer in service." This happens frequently here. When that happens, I'll just dial 7520 a second time, or sometimes a third time, occasionally a fourth, and Helga answers. That is par for Kaslo. But not this. Five times I got the same new message – five times, that is, when I didn't first get a busy signal because the error message itself was swamped with diverted calls.

The phone exchange in Kaslo is housed in a windowless tan box of a building beside which there is a rather ugly microwave tower. On all sides of this building are attractive Victorian homes and gardens, generous trees, and the occasional church steeple. That stark tower and this one building are perhaps the only things that don't fit nicely in the town, if you don't count all the ugly utility poles and wires in the village—more about which another time.[*]

Inside this BC Tel building, I am told, there is a veritable museum of ancient phone equipment, the marvel of all who have seen it. The building dates from the 1920s and is rumored to have the oldest equipment of its kind still working in Canada. I have talked to a few phone employees from outside the area who have seen it. They all had a faraway look in their eyes while telling me about it. And a pitying smile on their face.

It was with some great Holmesian (or perhaps Watsonian) pleasure that I was soon able to deduce what the problem must be on the day of changeover. While no one had told us that we must now actually dial the 353 prefix in front of all local telephone numbers, we *had* been told that

---

[*]   Sadly, some years later it became necessary to add to this short list the less-than-charming light industry yards along the highway at the southern edge of Kaslo's incipient sprawl.

beginning July 15 we would finally be able to dial Nelson as a local call, without the customary long distance prefix of "1" and without the previously attached expensive charges. This change had been "voted" on by all Kaslo telephone subscribers many months ago. We knew that electing this extra service would boost our monthly line charge by a few dollars. What we didn't know, and were not told, is that by electing this service we would give up our rare privilege of four-digit local dialing. But since Nelson has different prefixes than Kaslo, naturally the switching equipment would need to know which prefix was intended, so all seven local digits would now have to be dialed. I punched in 3-5-3-7-5-2-0, and sure enough, Helga answered. Later that same day I found BC Tel's belated notice of this new seven-digit situation in our mailbox.

In case you may not guess, let me say that BC Tel is not my favourite provincial monopoly. With some marvelous exceptions, the majority of whom happen to live in Kaslo or in Nelson, the people who meet the public at BC Tel seem to have been trained at Lily Tomlin's Ernestine School of Telephone Torture. Graduates with Master's degrees in either Advanced Officiousness or Blind Stupidity appear to receive preference for promotion within the company. Had my coronary problem occurred a couple of years earlier, I would not have needed to wonder why. BC Tel-induced stress would have been the obvious and sufficient reason. It was back then that I was dealing at length with the company, asking to get off our ancient four-person party line and get connected to a private line.

"But sir," I was told, "all our lines are private. Do you wish individual line service?"

"Oh yes, yes! With the emphasis on the service. Please."

The contrast with the local medical service is particularly strong. It has been just over four months now since my angioplasty in Vancouver and my return home. At this writing there have been no signs of any reoccurrence of the coronary blockage. I had been under the impression that the first three months were the main risk period for any renewed troubles, with their likelihood of occurrence being as high as one in four. Then a friend in Toronto sent me a clipping from the *New York Times* dealing with a newly discovered viral trigger for certain cell growths blocking coronary arteries, similar to mine. This article quoted a far higher likelihood of early relapse, and a risk period extending for six months instead of three. This is news fit to print? This is a friend? With friends like this, who needs BC Tel?

Our most recent dealings with my corporate nemesis concerned the pre-wiring of our new house. In a manner most uncharacteristic in the Kootenays, work on our house has moved along rapidly and efficiently. There have been a few financial surprises and scares, but by dint of continuous care and yeoman's worry on both our parts, Elizabeth and I find that some of our retirement savings still exist, and our house is ever closer to being a beautiful reality. I will defer to another time a more complete description of the saga of building a retirement home. Suffice it to say that recently the house reached the stage where the drywall was to be installed, but this could not occur before insulation and vapour barrier were in place, and these could not be put in place until the wiring was finished.

Well, our electrician finished all his electrical wiring in excellent time. But BC Tel wanted rather more than the three-week reminder they were given to come pre-wire four phone jacks.

"I can schedule you for August 29," said the nice service representative whom I reached after the third transfer of my call, each transfer with its associated long period spent sitting on hold and subject to punishing Musak.

August 29 was much too late, I informed her, explaining why this pre-wire would be brief, not major.

She explained why the charge would be large, not reasonable.

I explained that the insulation crew and the drywall crew were booked for the only times available two weeks off.

She then failed to explain why all that must wait.

Finally, when I asked who had the power to grant my request for earlier service, and asked for their phone number ("I am not allowed to release that information, sir"), she said I might soon expect a call from the service-scheduling foreman in Nelson.

Duped, I hung up, satisfied.

No such call ever came.

In the end, and at the last minute, after two more useless calls to some remote "service" representative, our electrician persuaded the very helpful Kaslo phone serviceman to give us the necessary phone wire, and I spent all of a Saturday using the electrician's tools, stringing the phone wires from boxes in each room through the open walls to the main phone cable coming in underground and waiting at the main service box. Two days later, insulation and continuous vapour barrier sealed off the walls I had worked in. I had by this time persuaded the phone company to finish connecting our phone service boxes in the week following, a week earlier than originally scheduled. The Kaslo phone serviceman was finally able to swing by, one day before this new date, and he quickly made the connections that gave us working phone jacks. All in all it took him much less than an hour. I am now looking forward to the large bill that we will soon get from Vancouver for this lengthy "pre-wire service."

Two years ago the charge for *changing* our service from a party line to a private line, one that would enable us to use a phone answering machine, a fax machine, or a modem, was supposed to be modest by comparison. However, a private line, known to the phone company as an "ILS" (Individual Line Service) might not be easy to arrange. Only a few ILS lines were available out of Kaslo to our neighbourhood and apparently all of them had long since been subscribed.

We began what threatened to become a very long wait in the ILS queue.

Moreover, I soon learned that the charge for my ILS, when at last I received it, was going to be $335 per year, plus long distance charges and taxes, while in Kaslo itself the cost of ILS is $75 per year. Distressed, I wrote to BC Tel with three pressing questions.

My first question asked the company to explain the punishing monthly charges for our own ILS. My second question asked for the name and address of the person who had the power to allocate more ILS lines to properties outside Kaslo. My third question asked for the name and address of the person who had the power to initiate a lower out-of-Kaslo phone rate for ILS lines. I sent a copy of this letter to the CRTC, the federal regulatory body that supposedly oversees provincial telephone monopolies, their rates, and the quality of their phone service.

The CRTC immediately acknowledged receipt of my letter and asked BC Tel to report to them on the matter of costs. Dear old BC Tel, busy doing good perhaps, never responded to my questions, even after a second request was sent to them ten weeks later, with a copy of my original letter. In due course they responded to the CRTC, but concerning the rate information only, and from the CRTC I eventually learned about the math, if not the policy, that determined the high charges for ILS out in our quiet boondocks.

I learned that our village of Kaslo is "urban." And around the edges of this urban town runs an invisible telephone boundary. Inside that boundary is the Kaslo "Base Rate Area" (the BRA), where the ILS rates are uniform and the ILS service is almost plentiful. Outside the BRA one is charged a set price each month for every quarter mile of distance from the nearest point on that boundary. This distance is supposed to be measured as the crow flies. At first, however, I was told (untruthfully) that the pricing distance was to be measured from the switchboard building in the center of town, and/or that it was to be measured along the actual phone lines as they wandered their way out to our property. According to the rate books, our house was fourteen quarters (i.e., fourteen quarter-miles) away from our Kaslo BRA. A \$335 yearly charge was to be the result.

During another year of waiting, with further letters (plus phone calls) to remote BC Tel personnel, I was repeatedly told that an ILS line would become available for us "very soon." Finally, however, I got the name and phone number of the Nelson Field Service Manager. It was he, I had learned, who controls new service runs in this area.

I called his office and got a nice honest assistant who gave me the bad news and the good news. The bad news was that all along, in fact, no further ILS lines had been planned in our area for at least another two years. There never had been any reason to suppose that we might be receiving ILS service "very soon". (We were not even first in the ILS queue.) The good news was that anticipated surplus funds might just make it possible to have a few more ILS lines outside Kaslo, after one more year.

Since I had recently learned that the CRTC frowns on service backlogs that run on for more than a few months, I thought perhaps they, too, might be interested in my potential three-year wait. I wrote a letter of surprise and dismay over this new news to BC Tel's Nelson office, with a copy to the CRTC. I received a prompt call back from the Nelson Service Manager himself this time. He was suddenly able to promise me an ILS connection sometime before our arrival back in the Kootenays eight months hence.

Alas, however, between this promise made in good faith, and delivery on this promise, there stood some graduates of the aforementioned Ernestine School who would have to schedule our new service and to handle all of the paperwork. This would be done far to the west of Kaslo and Nelson in some large city room as I imagine it, where over in a corner black kettles still steam and boil, the lights are always low, and red, rich choruses of phones ring quietly in the background, unanswered for hours on end, and concentric circles of women warm to their work, sharing happy news with each other of each new triumph of one-upmanship.

Since we were to be absent in Toronto, concluding our employed lives at the time that our ILS service was finally to be connected, it was arranged that Helga would be the local contact person in this matter. The paperwork was duly begun, but then everything was put on hold by a remote employee of the phone company who assumed (correctly) that we didn't know that the basic cost of this new service was going to be $967 per year, and that we might in consequence want to reconsider. I was invited to phone this employee at the witches' den, but of course she was away from her desk each and every time I called long distance from Toronto.

Because this new prospect of a yearly charge that amounted to nearly three times the one I had already been complaining of so energized me and so monopolized my attention, I finally spoke to the first witch who would listen. I explained that some mistake must have been made, and that I had multiple written confirmations of the earlier $335 figure.

Oh no, it was explained, you are not fourteen quarters away from the Kaslo BRA as you may have been told, you actually live forty-eight quarters away, hence the high cost of your service.

When I asked who told her that distance, and who could correct her mistake, I was merely referred to my good friend the Nelson Field Service Manager.

No one had been able to tell me where the Kaslo BRA approached closest to my house. I had hoped I might find out from Nelson. On a topographic map, the forty-eight quarter-miles airline distance that this nearest boundary was now said to be would clearly put it well beyond Kaslo itself.

I finally reached the Nelson Field Manager's assistant (the manager again being away, of course), who could not (or at least would not) tell me where the Kaslo BRA boundary lay, but he did confirm that the mileage to the nearest point of the BRA is to be direct air mileage, not road mileage. He advised me to get some sleep and said that he would call me back in Toronto the very next day.

His return call came just before dinner eastern time, and yes, at the time I was sitting down.

"Good," he said, "because I have some surprising news."

The rules, he told me, call for rates to be calculated based on the quarter-miles from the *nearest* BRA.

"You live on Woodbury Point," he said. "Your nearest BRA is the Riondel exchange, a little over a mile across the lake." (Riondel is that small cluster of houses we see over the water, but it has its own unique exchange and prefix numbers. For us it has always been a long distance phone call away.) "Consequently," he continued, "you will be charged for five quarters of distance, not the fourteen you were originally quoted, and certainly not the forty-eight quarters recently claimed."

After just a few more guerilla skirmishes, BC Tel surrendered. Those skirmishes involved appointment calls placed only to our vacant Gatehouse, ignoring the agreement to call Helga to arrange access. Later there were two broken appointments made with Helga, who waited patiently and in vain out at our Gatehouse for the promised connection to take place. Finally, however, BC Tel gave us our ILS service and have charged us the low five-quarter rate for it each month since.

I do not usually talk much about this splendid victory, because should this account ever become a public embarrassment to the Ernestines at BC Tel, I am sure they could find a simple way to retaliate against me as easily as our local employees were eventually able to find a way to satisfy me. So please, keep this tale confidential, and if you must tell someone else then tell him or her not to tell. Of course it also goes without saying that you must never *ever* tell *anyone* while using a BC Tel party line.

7 | *Orky Comes Up for Air*

Sunday September 4, 1994
Kaslo, B.C.

*I*n addition to my regular pension cheque from Montreal Trust, I received another paycheque a few days ago, and it was welcome indeed.

This additional cheque came to me from Glenorky Productions, the folks who have been putting Kaslo on the map this summer by shooting part of a full-length feature film here. Their cheque increased my August income by a handsome $39. Others here have been getting many hundreds of dollars every week, typically for renting their homes to members of the sizable film crew that has encamped in Kaslo for the six-week period of filming.

I'm sure that come next spring Revenue Canada will be expecting a generous donation from me in consequence of this deduction-free payment for acting services rendered, but for the time being I expect to enjoy the full use of all of my hard-earned movie dollars. Actually, I was thinking about saving them to buy a video copy of the movie *Glenorky* when it becomes available sometime late next year. I figured that if I don't have my own copy of the film handy, people who only hear my description of it may never believe what they hear.[*]

A video may not be necessary, however, because this morning on the CBC national radio show *Sunday Magazine* there was a special long piece about the filming of *Glenorky* in Kaslo. It confirmed much of what I have been telling people. You see, Kaslo plays the title role in the movie. Glenorky is a town located somewhere in the great northwest (below the greater northwest called Canada) on a lake that some say is the home of a large monster named Orky. Many people in Glenorky, like many people in Kaslo, would be pleased if generous quantities of tourist dollars were attracted from seekers after Orky, and they are quite happy to skate on the thin ice of absurdity in pursuit of those dollars. Ironically, this movie could be seen in part as a spoof of tourists and in part as a spoof of those who woo them. No one here seems likely to see it either way, however. As the long piece on *Sunday Magazine* made clear this morning, we in Kaslo have fallen in love this summer. We have looked into the fun-house mirror and briefly seen ourselves as we might wish to be. (God help us.)

The plot of this film is both hard to pin down and hard to describe, although not for the same reasons.

It is hard to pin down because during the filming here, throughout July and into the first week of August, the script kept changing daily. Obsolete copies of the script became a kind of second currency in town, and a recent script casually placed on a coffee table could instantly catapult the owner into the highest of social circles. There were infinite possible gradations of this kind of status because each script had a date and time on it, along with a printed warning meant to suggest that all earlier scripts were now as worthless as the fallen needles of a winter larch.

---

[*] As a later report reveals, this movie was eventually released under a different title, *Magic in the Water*.

The plot of the film is hard to pin down because even today no one can say exactly what that final plot will be. As a consequence, the local rumour mill has been quite active this summer, and for Kaslo that is really saying something.

The plot of *Glenorky* is hard to describe because no one likes to sound foolish. Still, you will need a rough idea of the plot to make any sense at all of the following report on some of the filming that I saw while acting as an extra. (Yes, I can almost see the headlines back at my university now: "Retired Professor of Psychology Trades One Distinguished Acting Career for Another.")

In brief, the plot of this film runs roughly as follows: Sweet loveable living breathing lake monster (Orky) is disbelieved and dishonoured by most residents of the little town (Glenorky) that lives off his fame. Orky is now seriously ill from man's pollution of his watery home, and he is desperately trying to send out an environmental SOS through various locals, each of whom he has saved from drowning and shown around the cavernous underwater beaver lodge that he calls home. Unfortunately, Orky's intended message loses quite a lot in translation, so that his confused and grateful survivors, who subsequently spend most of their time babbling and building huge sand castles, are simply treated as insane by the overly sane, disbelieving, resident therapist in town (Wanda). A sweet loveable misunderstood little girl (Ashley) believes, however, and she seeks both comfort and Orky while visiting the mountains (played by our Purcells) with her divorced Type-A dad (Jack), another disbeliever, and her brother (Josh), who doesn't need an Orky to make *his* life interesting. This poor fractured family is renting a cabin on the lake that belongs to a sweet, irascible, wise old Indian (Uncle Kipper), one who knows that truly there *are* more things 'tween heaven and earth than are dreamed of in any philosophy our side of Hollywood's.

Meanwhile, the Japanese have just brought to town a state-of-the-art submersible scientific research vessel that should be able to sniff out any living lake monster, at any depth. A young Japanese boy (Hiro), who is the son of the vessel's inventor, falls hard for dear sweet misunderstood Ashley and soon endeavours to spend every moment he can with her. Late in the film, one of those moments takes place in the cockpit of a fake, mechanical lake monster, secretly built by certain sour persons in town for the purpose of finessing any negative publicity that might otherwise result from possible Japanese press releases implying the Orkylessness of their lake.

In the scene in question, the children have furtively commandeered this mechanical monster. It is careening wildly out of control, at dusk, as Ashley, Josh, and Hiro try to steer it to safety and slow it down. Fire belches from this monster's mouth. The monster bears down on a small boat moored peacefully near shore and it is supposed to hit the boat, set it ablaze, then careen off toward shore as the flaming boat explodes. On shore, oblivious to the unfolding drama leading up to the explosion, elegant tourists dine and dance aboard the *Moyie*, Kaslo's beached sternwheeler museum, here transformed by plaid bunting and Hollywood magic into the "Orky Emporium, Laundromat, and Micro-Brewery." (I swear, I am not making this up.)

Naturally, the casting of the dining and dancing extras for this dramatic climactic scene was a very sensitive business. The slightest false note could bring ridicule on the movie, thus negating all the hard work of so many in Kaslo, not to mention the work of the one hundred and twenty film crew members who had been filling every available tourist bed in town for well over a month. Thus it came as a pleasant surprise when, in late July, Elizabeth and I were asked to take an afternoon away from building our home to fill the roles of persons of a certain age celebrating their wedding anniversary with other happy revellers in the restaurant aboard the Orky Emporium, in the scene where the mechanical Orky runs amok. We could not refuse.

As directed, we reported to the Senior Citizens Hall for makeup and wardrobe at 3 p.m. one very hot afternoon. The next three hours were spent waiting, while trying to coax a failing air conditioner into sporadic service. Finally, at 6 p.m. a pretty blond in shorts, wearing a headset and constantly conferring with the walkie-talkie in her left hand, called us to our places aboard the *Moyie*. This was Laurie, the extras' rehearsal coach, who assigned us our places and began directing our rehearsals.

While an outdoor camera tracked along the curved windows of the forward lounge on the *Moyie's* upper deck, shooting through the "restaurant" and out to the lake beyond, we revellers inside were to move to our carefully orchestrated positions.

Elizabeth and I, each holding a wine glass (filled with red cranapple juice), moved forward with the camera, as if to partake of the buffet laid out temptingly at the forward end of the lounge. We were to fill our plates and exclaim silently to each other how delicious the food looked. But we were under strict instructions not to eat the food because each item had to be returned to exactly the same place, time and time again, for each rehearsal change and retake. We were also instructed to look only at each other and at the buffet, not at the fire-belching mechanical Orky misbehaving just offshore out our windows, nor at the moving camera passing by.

My normal dinner hour is about 6 p.m. By 7:30, with no dinner yet, and with all the fine food passing endlessly back and forth through my hands, though never near my lips, I began to get peckish. Soon I was positively peevish. For one brief moment I wondered if this might really be an elaborate psychology experiment, filmed for later analysis back at the labs, with me as the naive subject.

It was 9:30 when the daylight finally failed and the filming was halted for the day. The scene beyond the *Moyie*, out on the water, had not been finished. But hungry as we all now were (no, we were not invited to eat the buffet, though mostly we did anyway), none of the extras had any regrets or complaints. The entertainment outside our windows had been worth every minute of the heat and deprivation.

In the first rehearsal of the day, the mechanical Orky did not zig and zag correctly, nor did it come close enough to the moored boat that it was supposed to graze. In the first take of the day, the pilot light went out on the mechanical Orky so that it breathed no flames at all. Also, one of the three camera crews could see, and had filmed, another of the camera crews. Camouflage netting was adjusted accordingly. The pilot boat went out to light the pilot light in the fake Orky's mouth and the second take occurred.

This time the moored boat burst into flames many seconds too soon, before the Orky got anywhere near it. The flames were turned off (they could be turned on and off at will for they came from a hidden propane tank inside the boat) and all prepared for the next try.

On the next try, the Orky pilot light failed again and no flames came from the mouth. On the next try, things worked pretty well, but the flames on the moored boat were thin and unconvincing. On the next try, some of the cameras didn't have the right settings for the rapidly fading daylight. And on the next try it got too dark before filming could start one last time.

The people of Kaslo watching from behind the various cameras on shore, and those of us aboard the *Moyie* found it all magical and funny and touching. They would get it right. Sooner or later. That much was clear. A few days later they did, too. And afterward, when finally, once and for all, they blew up the moored boat, the people of Kaslo spent many hours in that special state of grace that makes even strangers your friends for a time because you have shared a great anxiety and come through it famously.

While we were aboard the *Moyie* as extras, there were others on board as well, from CBC Radio, interviewing members of the extended film crew (in their time of anxiety) and some of our townspeople as well. Mayor Mackle (for such the alderman has now become) was interviewed, as was our poet laureate, David Herreshoff.

On the broadcast today all of Canada heard them, with the others, the multiple directors and various members of the film crew. The mayor was delighted that everyone was having such a profitable time, and that for one magical month the good citizens of Kaslo had been diverted from fighting over the proposed downtown sewer system and the economic development which that system may or may not encourage.

Perhaps the most telling observation about Kaslo's summer experience was made off the air, however, by Gerald Garnett, a local science teacher. He put it this way: It has been as if a balloon drifted over Kaslo dropping one hundred dollar bills at random. Everyone has been scrambling hither and yon trying to pick them up. By chance, some people have come up with a fistful of bills, and some people have come up empty-handed. It hasn't been fair, but there seem to be few if any hard feelings.

Still, it will be good to say goodbye this week to all the extra summer crowds. The valleys will all soon empty and Indian summer will arrive, providing us with our own turns to vacation here. Of course, along with the mild fall days will come the burning. The smoke from the residue of summer logging, forest fire fuel no longer, will be lazing in the air. The mountain ridges will disappear behind a blue haze. And Orky will certainly cough if he ever again comes up for air.

8 | *Wild Ate*

Sunday March 19, 1995
Kaslo, B.C.

*I*n the opening chapter of Homer's *Iliad* there is a tragic scene in which Agamemnon loses his civility, his reason, and a considerable portion of his respect because of his mad reaction on having to give up a lovely prize of war in the person of the maid Chryseis. Much later Agamemnon can look back on his egregious behaviour in surprise and sadness, and only then can he recognize that he had been at the time under the temporary sway of a god who had set "wild Ate" (madness) on him.* This madness, a mixture of rash pride and pout with a certain impulsive rage at the denial of his dominion, blinded and bruised the great king. But despite his later recognition of his abuse by a god, this sad episode was by no means the last time that Agamemnon or the others among his splendid male compatriots would endure their towering testosteronic trials.

---

* *Ate* is pronounced with two syllables, having two long vowels, to rhyme with *bay tree*. Ate is the name given to the Greek goddess of destructive mischief and rash action.

I like to imagine that with the recognition of his madness
Agamemnon was on the road to wisdom and that he actually arrived
there before he died, sometime after Homer had done with him. There
is no historical suggestion that Agamemnon *did* attain wisdom, however, and even if he did it does not seem to be in the nature of the gods
to be defeated by mere mortals when the gods have determined to set
wild Ate on us. Wisdom, it seems, is easily neutralized; at least at first.
The wild and willful Ate is more than a match for that softer will urging
us toward reason, courtesy, and expressions of brotherly love.

Now, one of the specific attractions of our Kaslo seclusion is the
peace that normally comes with it. And one of the attractions of retirement generally is the chance to escape the wild Ate that our day
so frequently induces, often, it seems, triggered by exhaustion in the
modern rat race. Today, however (and this was not the first day either),
wild Ate managed to find me here in Kaslo and to bring me both shame
and sorrow.

Today's triggering event had to do with the book that I have finally
finished drafting, provisionally entitled *Medical Intelligence and the
Common Cold.** Basically, the book is a non-fiction medical history. But
it is more, too. It is a travelogue; it is a mystery story; it is an adventure
story; and embedded in it will even be found the occasional sermon,
all prompted by my discoveries during fourteen years of reading and
research devoted to the topic of colds. For most of that long period I
have been writing or thinking about the book as well.

Now at last, finally having been able to complete this, my first book,
I naturally dream of seeing it published. And favourably reviewed; and
widely read; and stored safely for posterity on library shelves around
the world. I know this book is not for everyone. And I know that finding

---

*   Published in 1998 under the title *In Cold Pursuit: Medical Intelligence Investigates the
Common Cold.*

a publisher will not be easy. That is why I have been asking a few of my literary acquaintances for advice about a short letter I have drafted describing this book to potential publishers. Today, certain advice I received in connection with this draft letter brought with it a visit from wild Ate. Out of the blue this Ate came, and I cannot quite see why. Thus, I sit down to write.

In a word, the advice that I received (and this is the third time I have received it) is to write to potential publishers using a hard, contrived, glittering sell in the first line and first paragraph of my brief cover letter introducing the one-page description of this book that comes as a separate second page. In effect I have been told to expect that most editors (and, by implication, my eventual readers as well) will be rushed, uninterested, and even rude. If they cannot be seduced in three sentences, they will read no further. No patience or curiosity or dispassionate hearing should be expected or requested of them. Time is money. And manuscripts, it seems, represent a splendid chance to lose both.

Well bah! HUMBUG! Give me the quiet voice and the patient ear. Or so I ranted. My poor wife, who could see some of the good sense in the advice that I had been given (and the recklessness with which I had chosen the people who gave it), could not at first find particular sympathy for my bombast. Which only made my Ate the more powerful.

"But you can always look into publishing the book yourself," she said hopefully, trying half-heartedly to calm me down.

But her comment only brought with it new visions of a mountain of rejection slips, followed by an exhausting vision of our penury after I mortgaged our bleak future to pay for the printing and binding costs of a book that I could not later even give away. In the space of a few seconds I experienced the full clinical catastrophe: Mania to Depression to Paranoid Madness. It was not pretty. But looking back, it was certainly, well . . . interesting.

In psychology, pediatrics, forensic medicine, and psychiatry, there has been an active and continuing debate about tantrums, and about the extent to which they are (or are not) controllable. When tantrums are not dangerous to others, they are often still dangerous to those who suffer them. It is tempting to think that one can be taught to avoid or interrupt these events. On the other hand, there is also some reason to think that these things are genetically predisposed and in some instances nearly unstoppable. Agamemnon did not doubt that wild Ate was imposed from without and was all but unavoidable by any act of will.

Certain brain diseases clearly provoke involuntary rages that, once triggered, can be nearly impossible to stop, short of full anesthesia. Many signs point to a strong physiological predisposition to visits from wild Ate, and some drugs seem to make such visits either more or less probable. The inference has been strong in some quarters that it is biochemistry, not psychology and not culture, that sets wild Ate loose. And the fact that these mad rages are so often seen in males and so infrequently in females only strengthens this inference.

Of course any inference, no matter how strong, can be wrong. As the wise saying has it: "Biology is *not* destiny." Special medical environments often change genetic and physical destinies. Similarly, special social environments often change genetic and physical destinies. With this in mind, I find it bizarre, for instance, to note the continuing debate about the exact proportion of variations in IQ measurements that can be said to be "due to" heredity. As if there could be any intelligence at all in the absence of food for the mind. And as if some "proportion" of one's mental growth could be said to derive only from the mechanical set of one's neurons.

Well, for a long time medical science was quite comfortable with the idea that the disease called phenylketonuria was one hundred percent hereditary. It was known to be caused by a single defective gene. There was no variation in the progression of this disease in young children, leading invariably to severe mental retardation. Today, newborns diagnosed with this disease are given a special diet, free of the simple protein that they cannot tolerate, and now they develop normally. Shall we then say that this disease was after all one hundred percent environmentally caused, by "improper" diet? Far better simply to recognize how inappropriate was our original drive to quantify the answer to this unfortunate and unanswerable question about the relative proportion of responsibilities attributable to interacting genes and environment.

For almost every genetic trait there is an environment that will greatly facilitate its expression and another that will completely inhibit it. Similarly, for almost every environment there is a genetic blueprint that will wonderfully tolerate that environment, and another that will soon die in it. The reason we care so much about whether our various faults lie in our genes or in our environment (which leaves aside the most important variable of all: our behaviour) is that we ambivalently assume that we are not responsible for the products of our genes, and by extension, the products of our glands and organs. Surely we cannot stop cancer, or thieving, or wild Ate, if these be impelled by heredity. They are not our fault. Still, there are always some who, despite being susceptible, do avoid cancer, many who do resist the impulse to steal, and many who do control Ate. By design or good luck, such people find themselves in environments where these evils can be successfully resisted.

I conclude, then, that my wife was mostly right (as she so often is): The wild Ate who visited me was at least partly encouraged by my reckless choice of person and place in seeking out the particular advice that was not likely to be found where I went looking for it. This is not to say that the advice which I did receive was bad as such but merely to say that I should have known that I would be unlikely to tolerate the particular line I would be fed. One trick in achieving wisdom (and in growing up generally) seems to be learning how to create for oneself those special environments that nourish the good. Learning this is not easy, especially when those environments themselves keep changing. It helps considerably to have skillful social assistance in all this. That is why another secret of success seems to be to create for one's neighbours, one's employees, and one's family, the nourishing environments best suited to them as well.

In this connection I still worry about our local forests. It is not easy to preserve that special nourishing environment represented by a blanket of uncut trees. We in Kaslo continue to fight the rapacious clear-cutting of so much of our surrounding mountains. Nothing has been resolved since my previous report on the subject, nor is it likely to be soon. Wild Ate regularly visits loggers and environmentalists alike here each time that the subject of reduced cutting quotas is brought up. Among some an appetite for lumber and pulp remains fierce, while among others it is an appetite for living forests, fish, cougars, and owls. There are no longer enough resources to satisfy both of these appetites.

Agamemnon would understand our dilemma. But I wonder, were his lovely Chryseis again at stake, if this time around he would free her with any greater generosity than he did that first time—with any more wisdom than industrial forestry has so far exercised over the lands that it now holds ransom.

9 | *Orky's Own May Days*

Victoria Day Monday, May 22, 1995
Kaslo, B.C.

Only recently has Kaslo's weather at last become spring-perfect. The Kaslo River is exuberant again, full of white noise and snowmelt. The local trees and gardens appear to have reached the peak of their late spring blossoming. It came as no surprise, then, that the entire village appeared to have turned out for today's May Days Parade, to share again in the opening of the summer season and the first of our summer series of three-day holiday weekends.

The theme for this year's parade has been (what else?) a celebration of Orky.[*] Amid a backdrop of palpable civic tension and local politicking, Kaslo has gone green today. It has declared a village-wide Green party at a time when the political pun therein might normally be anything but approved. Still, the dark mossy colour of Orky's skin parading down Front Street, the vivid green of our park grass, the

---

[*] Orky will be remembered from an earlier chapter as the gooey-eyed green lake monster to be featured in a Hollywood movie that was made in Kaslo last summer. In the film, Orky's green health is threatened by dark, polluting humans.

colour of tourist money and the local forests was very much the colour of the day today.

Yesterday, Kaslo's annual Logger Sports Competition drew record crowds. Visitors came from more than a hundred miles away to watch and to compete in the bright sunshine. The substantial log-and-sawdust seating area for the Logger Sports spectators was recently increased in that natural little amphitheater beyond the park where last summer so many others sat watching the backstage activity of the large film crew working just behind the *Glenorky* beach-house set. Nevertheless, the crowds yesterday (like those of today for that matter) were so much larger even than last year that there were still many people left standing and craning their necks to watch the axe men below send the chips flying. The Logger Sports competition can be much more interesting than one might think. And often quite amusing. But of that, more another time.

There is much to tell since my last report. My common cold book is now being considered by various remote and silent publishers. We are at last comfortably resident in our splendid new house, with plenty of sagas to relate around a winter fireside in consequence. And teaching? No, I *still* don't miss teaching (though I thought I would) and I still *do* miss the informal morning coffee community back at the college, with its wonderful and different experts, and news items, and interests. It was my computer and the Internet that was supposed to offer me continued access to such collegiality from my sunny retirement garret here in our remote electronic cottage. But the big lie of the Information Highway is also a topic for a later winter fireside. Orky is today's May Days topic. Today's big parade. And Kaslo's fix.

Shortly after my last report, Kaslo received two major pieces of news sending tremors throughout the town. First came the news that the movie *Glenorky* was at last finished and was to be released to the world, on or about May 5, 1995, under a new title, *Magic in the Water*. Second, we learned that the world premiere sneak preview of this movie, complete with many of its young stars in glittering attendance, was to be held in our region's only movie house, the funky old Civic Theater over in Nelson. Tickets for this showing were to be made available only to Kaslovians, a few days in advance.

The first of these two announcements understandably caused considerable consternation. Everyone agreed that *Magic in the Water* was about as dumb and forgettable a title as one might ever hope to dream up. It would be like asking Kaslo (a.k.a Glenorky) to change its name to something like Mountainville, as if such a name would play better in the tourist brochures back home. And it hurt, just a little, that Glenorky the town (née Kaslo) was no longer to enjoy the title role in the film.

But the second of the two announcements caused a sensation. The tickets for the world premiere were to be free, by donation to Kaslo's local Ambulance fund. Tickets could be picked up at a card table that would be set up in the vacant lot on Front Street, between the drugstore and the grocery store. There were to be eight hundred tickets given out, and the card table would be there for three days.

Kaslo and its surrounding area currently have a winter population of approximately one thousand people. In the event, *all* of the eight hundred tickets were gone before noon of the first day. (Elizabeth got two of them for us, numbered 588 and 589.) Immediately thereafter, Nelson's fire marshal announced that only four hundred people could be allowed inside the Civic Theater for the special Saturday matinee screening. In order to keep the peace, it was hastily arranged that two screenings would take place, and those with tickets numbered 401-800 would be allowed in only to the second screening, scheduled to take place right after the first.

Thus it was that I found myself almost at the front of a long queue of Kaslovians one Saturday afternoon early in April when the first four hundred happy faces stumbled out of the theater into the bright sunlight of Nelson's Vernon Street, their world premiere fantasies come true.

"It's good," they said, when they were pressed by those awaiting their turn to go in.

"But is it *really* good?"

"Yeah, I liked it," would come the noncommittal answer.

Still, the slow grins spreading around suggested that, despite the awful new title and despite the increasingly undeniable hints that the majority of our proud local faces all ended up on the cutting room floor, we might still be in for quite a treat when it was our turn to go inside.

Just before we entered, I spotted (but at first did not recognize) three of the movie notables. Like the rest of us, they were attending this world premiere in their finest work clothes, only for us that generally meant our discount jeans while for them it meant their designer jeans. There chatting with some of the locals was the very young Sarah Wayne (she plays the lead role of Ashley) looking at once both smaller and older than I had remembered her from last summer—the very picture of ten-year-old amused poise. There, too, was the young Japanese boy Willie Nark-Orn (he plays Hiro), looking as wide-eyed and happy as the rest of us. And presiding over them was the producer/director of the movie, Rick Stevenson, completely at ease in our Kaslo crowd. Stevenson has wonderful boyish good looks that make him totally believable in the role of father to any youngster in his train. There were, at that moment, a lot of youngsters in his train.

Once inside the theater I claimed prime centre seats, only to discover later that we were seated right in front of the reserved area where Sarah and Willie and Rick and their friends were sitting for the second showing of that afternoon. I took the opportunity to get autographs on my ticket from Sarah and Willie. I had to laugh at myself for being stunned when I saw that Sarah's gracious autograph had the awkward legibility of that of any normal ten-year-old, rather than the flourish of some twenty-five-year-old diva that I apparently had been expecting.

There were a few brief speeches, bouquets of roses presented to Sarah and Willie, and a gracious thanks from Director Rick to all the people of Kaslo for their welcome and warmth and help all last summer. And then suddenly, without further fanfare, the movie was under way.

I think I can speak for many in the audience when I say that within minutes we were completely charmed by, and caught up in, the movie. It is in fact full of fine spoofs of familiar clichés. It soon became clear that the new title made much more sense than might have been imagined from the scripts we were reading last summer. The total corniness of those scripts was in the deliberate service of a very relaxed, polished, and funny story line, appropriate for the sophisticated youngster in any viewer.

Not that I can any longer pretend to any kind of cynical objectivity about this film. Forty-nine years later, Sarah Wayne in the role of Ashley has replaced Margaret O'Brien (*Our Vines Have Tender Grapes*) as my favourite child actress. (Retired persons of a certain age may remember Margaret.) Thus, my readers will have to risk their own judgments of this "family film," judgments that may not (to put it mildly) be the same as mine.

I say all my positive things about this film in spite of the fact that the whole scene in the dining salon on the *Moyie* in which Elizabeth and I participated was cut. Still, I do appear in one scene. That is my right shoulder blade you can see behind the bushes, at the picnic table, way down by the lake, near the upper-left corner of the screen, in a very brief opening shot of Josh and Ashley sitting on the swings on the front lawn of the "hospital," immediately after the scene indoors where Dr. Wanda says meaningfully to Dr. Jack (Ashley's injured father), "I'm going to have to keep you here for observation."

In this hospital scene I play the part of a patient, taking the sun by the lake while attached to a fake IV bottle hanging nearby. (Not my best profile, that, but hey, it's a start.)

Well, May 5 has come and gone without this film yet being released to the world. We are now told that *Magic in the Water* is scheduled for general release in many hundreds of North American cinemas early this coming September. Rumour insists that the delay is because audience reaction to various sneak previews has been so very positive that the movie is now scheduled to be entered in certain film festivals late in the summer, just prior to its general release.[*]

Despite this delay, an updated video copy of the film was supposed to be previewed three times each day this long weekend, at Kaslo's Langham Cultural Centre, in the small auditorium that has bleacher type benches seating about sixty people. These special screenings were meant to be another fundraiser, this time for the Langham itself. Unfortunately, Hollywood apparently overruled the generosity of Director Rick, and at the last minute we were limited to one screening per day. The queue for admission to today's screening was very long, and it formed quite early. In the end, many more were turned away than finally got to see the film.

Everybody got to see today's parade, however. I am pleased to report that with Mayor Mackle in control, the parade did indeed go around twice. That is the good news. The bad news is that the exact parade route was not published in advance, so that many of us who waited on down in front of the *Moyie*, a half a block below the point where the parade was first diverted off Front Street, unexpectedly missed the first pass entirely. I ran up to the premature turning point just in time to catch the huge, green "fake" Orky from the film (now raised out of the lake and carried by a large flatbed truck) making that first turn. Sarah and Rick were high up astride Orky's back, tossing candy favours

---

[*]   The rumour was almost certainly false. The film did not do well, and the "spoofs" it may or may not exhibit are in the eyes of only a few beholders such as I. Still, the pictures it provides of Kaslo and the surrounding environment are lovely to see.

down to those watching from the sidelines. If it turns out, I should soon have a fine photograph of the two of them, with the elegant bell tower of our scenic Village Hall behind them and snow-capped True Blue Mountain in the distance.

The peace of this day, and the joy of this parade, have temporarily masked some deep new divisions in the village. Recent Village Council meetings have been the occasion for some fierce local politics that defy a convincing explanation. A few weeks ago the councillors voted unanimously to fire Mayor Mackle for his refusal to carry out council's unanimous will in starting on the Front Street sewer project. For the time being there happens to be provincial money available to help us pay seventy-five percent of the cost of building a sewage treatment facility in the village. Kaslo badly needs this facility if the strained and aged septic fields in the lower village are not going to pollute the bay and the lake itself. Because lower Kaslo is built on a sieve-like alluvial fan of rock and sand, washed in there over the years by the Kaslo River, evidence of some pollution has already been observed in the lake.

It is not clear why our mayor has so delayed the downtown sewer project. The regional health authority has declared that there can be no further restaurants or tourist accommodations built in Kaslo until a proper sewer system is available to relieve the increasing stress that these new businesses would place on our ground water.

Perhaps it is as simple as that: i.e., maybe the mayor (like many of us) does not want Kaslo to be "spoiled" by any growth and change, assisted by a new sewer. (As if we could stop growth and change.)

This isn't what he says, however. What he says (with some justification) is that "due process" was not observed in getting the necessary agreements from the citizens affected by the sewer project, not to mention due process in the events leading up to his being "fired" by council. Anyway, Mayor Mackle soon fired back, with lawyers from Victoria, B.C., behind him, and within two weeks he was in his chair again at the head of Village Council. This illegal firing (and the subsequent unfiring) was a provincial first, and apparently it made headlines all across the province. The resulting publicity, unwelcome as it was, nonetheless occasioned no end of private amusement and gossip here at the same time.

More recently we've been diverted by "the golf course fiasco." Kaslo has a nine-hole golf course of quiet beauty and real challenge, located on high ground that both overlooks and is owned by the Village. This land is leased to our local Golf Club, which in recent years has been hooking rapidly into the red. There are many trees along the golf course, lining many of the fairways. Some would say there are too many trees for the struggling grass and the struggling players below. Thus, this spring, selective logging of some of those trees was proposed by the executive of the club. Village Council originally approved this plan on the verbal understanding that just three truckloads of logs would be removed, and that the Golf Club and the Village would share fifty-fifty in the handsome proceeds thus generated. (The price of raw logs has kept right on increasing all this spring.)

Well, somehow the number of truckloads that were removed turned out to be sixteen, not three, and somehow all of the council (save for the mayor) was later persuaded to allow all of the proceeds of this local cut to go to the Golf Club, with none left over to help us with Village expenses. The mayor used this opportunity quite effectively and publicly to embarrass his opposition on council, but he was something less than courteous in so doing and this has renewed the strident calls for his ouster.

Still, May Days works well as a time of village truce. For myself, that is proving especially welcome today. Many of the people whom I have come to admire in Kaslo feel that the mayor has played rather too fast and too loose recently, both with the facts and with the democratic process. Many agree that, yes, he has a heart of gold, and, yes, he is a diamond in the rough, but they also insist that he keeps a hidden agenda dedicated to keeping things as they were here in the 1970s. Moreover, they say, he seems not to see the pain his behaviour causes to others.

All this is awkward for me because, despite what I can observe with my own eyes, I admire the mayor extravagantly. His well-concealed intelligence, his various strategic surprises, and his environmental commitment all appeal to me. Riding in today's parade, in a borrowed classic car (he is more regularly seen driving through town either on his motorcycle or on his backhoe), the mayor was the picture of friendly ease. Behind his long straw-coloured beard he might even have been Orky in disguise: the quiet green monster who saves lives while slowly being done in by the pollution of our greedy times. The mayor, too, was enjoying this summer day of truce.

This year, however, no May Days rainbow appeared over the town. The May Days truce appears to be but temporary.

10 | *Close Calls*

*J*ust over a week ago, two nights before our cat Sophie was ambushed, I returned from a ten-day absence spent visiting each of my parents and attending the wedding of Elizabeth's daughter Sarah, near San Francisco. Elizabeth, driving our car and visiting friends, had not yet returned from the wedding, so Sophie and I were still alone. The night I flew home, Sophie had been glad to see me but she was not about to reward my absence with immediate affection. The next day she was positively loving, however, and she spent my second night home on the bed, close by my side, outdoors on our open, covered sleeping porch. (This porch is at ground level at its western, uphill end, but it is a full story above the ground at the east end, closest to the lake.)

The third night was very dark, with no moon. When I fell asleep, Sophie was curled up at the foot of the bed and small waves hitting the lakeshore were covering us in soft white noise.

Then, just after midnight, I was awakened by a sudden ferocious snarling from somewhere directly below me. Sophie was not on the bed. I heard the clatter of slipping rocks as something (or some things) rushed up the steep face of the rocky bench on which the house rests. Coming out of deep sleep I assumed without thinking that I was hearing a cougar's voice and that it must be chasing Sophie. There were heavy sounds, a slight gurgling noise, and the loud snarling did not cease during the few seconds that it took me to fully awaken and to decide what to do.

I sprang from the bed to the railing above the scene and shouted down into the darkness. At the same time I stamped hard on the porch and clapped my hands, hoping to startle the intruder and to save Sophie.

The snarling stopped instantly and I thought I could hear heavy footfalls disappearing south along the side of the house to my right. At the same time, I thought I heard a softer sound, a small rock moving and brief gurgling again, to my left.

I ran into the house for the big flashlight we keep by the front door. In seconds I returned and shone the light first left (hoping to see Sophie) and then right. Nothing. I carefully examined every inch of the ground from the safety of the porch above but did not have the courage to leave the porch.

There was no sign of Sophie. I whistled for her (which almost always brings her for the promise of food at any time of day or night), but I heard and saw nothing more.

For two hours I lay in bed, listening closely but heard only the wavelets against the cliffs below. Finally I dozed off and eventually I drifted into a dream. In this dream my mother came to see me, looking sad.

She said, "I have some bad news."

I said, "Yes, Sophie's dead, isn't she?"

"Yes," my mother replied.

Then I awoke. It was getting light. After another look at the rocks below I quickly dressed and climbed down to where I thought the night struggle had taken place. I searched minutely for signs of blood, or fur. But there was nothing. Not a sign.

I followed a deer path north from our property along very steep cliff sides (on Crown land) looking for Sophie or her remains. Then I followed similar paths leading to neighbouring properties to the south. I spent a long time searching. I checked the Gatehouse. I whistled the standard breakfast whistle that always brings Sophie running. Still nothing. As the day wore on I had episodes of hope, expecting Sophie might after all come down from a tree and saunter home. But late that afternoon I heard about recent coyote sightings, and my hope evaporated.

Our neighbour on the ridge above us reported that his dog had been barking with some regularity at one or more visiting coyotes this week. It then occurred to me that the deep snarling I heard might after all have been Sophie's, not a cougar's. The prey (Sophie) would fight back but the predator, with its mouth in action, would be silent, that is if Sophie's own hunting behaviour is any guide to the behaviour of bigger cats. It suddenly seemed much less likely that a cougar was involved in Sophie's death. And because coyotes take their prey a long way off before devouring it, there seemed to be little chance of ever recovering and burying Sophie's body.

That night I slept outside again, nervously, but I did not hear a sound. And then, the next evening, just as I was preparing for bed, I heard a loud noise outside, a falling rock, somewhere behind the sleeping porch. I turned on the porch light and stood looking out through the glass door leading to the porch. But I saw nothing. Leaving the light on, I turned and continued undressing.

A moment later I turned back and glancing outside I suddenly saw a large cougar standing in the light just beyond the porch, looking down and away from me, directly toward the spot where Sophie had been taken two nights before.

The cougar's prominent tail was closest to me, almost touching the edge of the porch. It was the largest cat I have ever seen, looking healthy to a fault and standing not twenty feet away outside the glass door.

I was tempted to freeze and to watch this elegant cat at work, yet at the same time I felt I must seize this rare opportunity to protect myself and others (even the cougar itself) by helping to make it afraid of houses and people.

Not thinking, I rushed immediately to the door, flung it open, and screamed at the cat, which was still looking in the other direction. It sprang away, without looking back. Four long bounds in three seconds and it had disappeared into the dark woods. (After giving the matter a lot of thought, I elected to sleep indoors that night.)

Elizabeth called the next morning just before starting for home. When I told her about actually seeing the cougar she asked me to sleep indoors a second night, at least until she got home, and to call Officer Christie in Nelson to ask his advice about the risks of sleeping on our porch with a cougar in the area. (Officer Christie was the Conservation Officer who had come sixteen months before to help me with the stag under the stairs.) He was away when I called, but the officer on duty gave me sufficient information to allay any concerns.

I learned that cougars are very shy, as a rule. They are wary of people and are rarely glimpsed even when close at hand. They generally wait for moving prey that can be ambushed along a trail. They prey primarily on deer (taking one every ten to fifteen days on average) and usually they attack people only if (a) they are very hungry indeed, and (b) they are above the person, and (c) the person is small or kneeling. The number of human attacks from cougars has been even smaller than that from bears, and the great majority of cougar attacks have been non-fatal.

The basic rule when meeting a cougar is to stand tall and not attempt to flee. The basic rule if attacked by a cougar is to fight hard and hit out. Cougars almost always bolt if hit hard by their prey. Moreover, and more to the point, cougars are not known to seek out sleeping prey. Still, that second night I found it easy to keep my promise to Elizabeth and to sleep indoors again.

All during the time that these events were unfolding, there had also been some close calls on our local highways. The people of Kaslo were mourning one fatal accident on our dangerous mountain roads this week even as they were also able to celebrate a happier close call, one that destroyed the car involved but from which the motorist was able to walk safely away. I think these recent events, too, had me looking over my shoulder.

Yes, I feel that this cougar and I have had our own close calls now. And it appears that rather more close calls probably await each of us in the future. Today I found myself in a new situation where, for one brief moment, I again thought I was about to encounter Sophie. But of course there have been no signs of her anywhere, at any time. So far at least, there also have been no further signs of the cougar, nor of any coyotes. I am back to sleeping outdoors again, almost soundly. And at least when I am present, my nervous neighbours have now muted their recent talk of hunting down the cougar. I appreciate that.

11 | *Survival Tips*

Monday, October 2, 1995

Kaslo, B.C.

mong the libraries of my retired friends I have noticed a number of books on dining free, by which I mean dining out, i.e., dining on certain of those outdoor foods that nature places in our path. "Foods" here does not refer to fish or game, for my retired friends are almost uniformly peaceable and not given to active killing. No, I refer instead to books describing wild vegetables, fruits, and fungi. Until recently I had no particular interest in such books. However, that was before the recent episode with the mushrooms.

Wild vegetables are not commonly sought out here in the Kootenays, although if we wanted to we retirees could eat almost everything that a bear will eat. ("Vice versa" is taken for granted.) The bears, in spring, eat many a vegetable delicacy, everything from emerging dandelions to the corms of the glacier lily. Grizzlies are fine diggers, and they will rake the earth deeply and thoroughly for their underground alpine breakfasts.

(Not so, retirees.) But it is wild fruit and berries, not vegetables, that can bring bears and retirees into competition.

In Kaslo there are some fine wild cherries to be discovered every spring, scattered far from the great orchards of yesteryear. Each May, at the turn of the last century, a highly prized cherry crop used to be shipped out of Kaslo, by steamer, far down the lake into Idaho, then west to waiting city markets. The arrival of a virus, said to have hitch-hiked in on an imported Japanese cherry tree, soon put an end to this sweet and lucrative industry. Still, even today, there are some wonderful wild cherries to be found late each spring by anyone (and any bear) who cares to hunt for them.

Cherry tree branches are often too frail to bear much bear, and in any event bears tend to stay higher up in the mountains during cherry season, digging for those aforementioned breakfast greens. Thus, in cherry season, with a proper ladder, it is easy to forget all about bears while one picks in peace.

Each fall Kaslo is blessed with wonderful apples. Many of the best apple trees have also gone wild and they may be found almost anywhere along old roads or in deserted back yards. Even fine plums and pears can occasionally be found growing on that vast commons that is our surrounding Crown land. However, it is the retired apple trees that of-fer up the sweetest gifts of all. When served for dessert, in a torte or pie, these special gifts from yesterday's orchards yield a whole new form of ambrosia.

Bears prefer their autumn fruit served on the tree. The fall gatherer had best watch where he is stepping when under any of our local fruit trees. Partly digested apples will pour out of the rear end of a bear as fast as whole apples can be poured in the front end. If you happen to own an orchard here, this is *not* amusing.

In high summer, between the cherries and the apples, come all the wild berries. Throughout the summer there are some wild local blackberries to be found, although these are few in number. There are sweet red thimbleberries along almost every roadside and creek side. And scattered throughout the forests are acres and acres of huckleberry bushes laden with big blue berries. (I gloss over the others: the wild strawberries, the elderberries, and the Saskatoon berries, for instance.)

Certain of the popular local hiking trails are closed for part of every August because so many bears convene in the rich huckleberry patches lining these routes. Considerations both of safety and fairness demand that bears be given the right-of-way. There are many other places to find huckleberries, not all of them populated with bears, so that by fall the freezers of Kaslo are invariably stuffed with bulging bags, their blue-black contents stored safely away for winter enjoyment.

Locally, a common way of showing special friendship is to share the secret location of your favourite (or newest) place for finding huckleberries. However, only the closest relative and dearest friend might ever hope to hear from you where you go to find your special local mushrooms. Mushroom hunters are the defining sign that fall has arrived in what Canadian climatologists call our "interior wet zone." First come the rains. Then come the mushrooms. And then come the hunters, young and old alike.

I don't mean just any mushrooms, either. I mean *the* mushrooms, the ones that periodically fetch over $30 per pound. Wholesale. We are talking the elusive pine mushroom. The *armillaria ponderosa*. The *matsutake*. Call it what you will, it is fungal gold, and hunting it is serious business indeed.

Pine mushrooms are not easy to find, although apparently they can be plentiful here whenever conditions turn favourable. Because they can be so valuable as an income supplement, and because local consumers prize them, too, modern hunter-gatherers (their Walkmans softly thumping) harvest pine mushrooms quickly, quietly, and privately. An amateur, an interloper, a rank beginner, will soon find there is nothing to find. Except for all the lesser sorts of mushrooms, such as the shaggy manes, the boletus, and the lobsters.[*]

Still, these "lesser" mushrooms are not to be ignored by the gourmet retiree stalking his or her wild asparagus. Nor have we ignored them. We have harvested them. We have checked them out in our mushroom books and confirmed their food value. We have prepared them lovingly, and have eaten them happily.

And yes, we have gotten quite sick.

It happened like this. In search of a new walk and a novel view of the peninsula on which we live, Elizabeth and I recently drove a few kilometers to the south, then turned west up a rough logging road there to walk behind that first bench of land that lies one hundred meters above the lakeshore highway. We soon left the logging spur on which we were walking to cut back east, through the bush, toward the escarpment and its view of the lake. As we threaded our way over moss and fallen logs, we encountered a number of new mushrooms that we took to be delicious boletus. (Boletus had been served to us only a few days before, at the home of friends who happen to be experts on wild mushrooms.) So we filled our hats and pockets with our happy finds and returned home.

As a prudent check, however, we first consulted our mushroom book, to confirm that our mushrooms were indeed boletus, and then, just to be doubly sure, we went over to visit with our friends again, to reconfirm with them.

As it turned out, we did have a crop of boletus mushrooms. But it also turned out that all but two of those mushrooms should not be eaten, because, on slicing them in half, the thin trails left by countless pin-sized worms could be seen everywhere. This discovery immediately

---

[*]   I must now confess I have not quite told the whole truth above. Chanterelles can be plentiful in certain spots here, too. They can be used as a wonderful second prize, for awarding to close friends who don't quite qualify to learn the location of your pine mushroom grounds.

led our hosts to take us back outside for a quick field tutorial on their own wooded acreage.

Our tutorial resulted in the discovery of a colourful red heap in the ground, looking more like a soil disease than any mushroom, but a heap that our hosts at once hailed as a wonderful lobster mushroom, a great delicacy. We returned to the house with our newest prizes, a few good boletus mushrooms, and the bulky mass of the lobster mushroom. We checked a mushroom field guide and there we learned how delicious the lobster mushroom can be. We divided the batch of mushrooms in half, and took our half home to eat at once.

The approved boletus mushrooms (sans worms) we fried in butter, and they were almost as tasty as they had been in the thick gravy we had enjoyed the week earlier at the home of our friends. The lobster mushroom, similarly cooked but with a little garlic, was surprisingly delicate and sweet. It had a gentle taste all its own. Being a person who normally does not count mushrooms as culinary friends, I particularly appreciated the understated substantiality of the lobster mushroom. Until later.

Later, I had what I would call severe indigestion. Not really full nausea. But a sleepless night of vague dis-ease where something was very clearly not right with the world in general and with my bowel in particular. Each trip to the bathroom, and there were quite a few that night, brought a grateful if all too temporary relief that clearly indicated something was not right with those mushrooms. Elizabeth, too, had her share of discomfort. We wondered if the problem could be with the boletus or the lobster mushroom, or, with the way we prepared them.

First thing next morning we called our friends.

"Did you eat any of those mushrooms last night?" we asked.

"Yes," they answered.

"And?"

Our friends were silent. Then they said: "Ours were very good. Weren't yours?"

We described our symptoms and asked if they had eaten any of the lobster mushroom, too. Well, no, they hadn't. And why not? Well, it seems that after we left they had consulted another mushroom book and that second book said that lobster mushrooms are epiphytic, which is to say they grow on other mushrooms underground. Sometimes it can happen that lobsters will grow on a poisonous mushroom, in which case they, too, become poisonous. One should not eat a lobster mushroom until one has identified the host on which it is growing, so sayeth this greater book. Consequently, our friends had elected not to eat of the fruit of this ground. (And, they neglected to so advise us; although as things turned out it would have been too late anyway.)

The result of this misadventure has been an interesting discovery, one that seems to me to have implications far beyond any nearby field of mushrooms. I had long supposed that every mushroom fell into one of two categories: poisonous, or safe. I have since learned (the hard way) that the various books on mushrooms actually distinguish not two, but four types of mushrooms. These four are: (1) edible, (2) poisonous, (3) very poisonous, and (4) deadly poisonous.

It seemed at first like a great triumph, to have eaten a poisonous mushroom and survived. I now know that (forgive my choice of words here) a child could do it. A case of the runs. A new conditioned response guaranteeing nausea at the sight or smell of mushrooms. And then it is quickly over. Life goes on.

There are a lot of things like that in life, I would guess. Like someone's forced and unexpected retirement for instance. Probably even cancer. You think this will be fatal, but it is not. Very poisonous to joy, perhaps, but not deadly poisonous. For a time you have the runs. Your stomach won't hold any food. You are sleepless and sweaty with worry. But a time comes when it hasn't gotten any worse, and maybe it is even getting better. Your hunger returns. Someone tells a joke that makes you laugh, at last. And it dawns on you that "poisonous" does not mean "lethal."

So it is with life here. It can be poisonous. It can be very poisonous. But rarely is it ever lethal. You find yourself face to face with a cougar, perhaps. Or you discover that the big dog ambling toward you is really a bear. Such events are not deadly after all. They may even prove to be delicious when served with full attention. The bear pauses with the sun behind her, bathed in a superb cinnamon halo. She stares at you for a long moment, and then moves on. The cougar discovers to her surprise that she is not invisible, and gracefully gives ground.

Delicious moments.

Still, with regard to mushrooms, please permit me to decline them for a while. Gracefully.

12 | *The Stanford Shadow*

Somewhere I was told—probably in a course on comparative religions that I enjoyed forty years ago while an undergraduate at Stanford University—that our sunset years are properly filled by seeking religious wisdom and understanding. At that time this dictum made good sense to me, especially inasmuch as it seemed to leave plenty of one's immediate lifetime for the pursuit of more secular interests in Caesar's world. Then, in some far-off day, those sunset years would be there ready to bring one peace and closure (hopefully, in that order).

I still hope they will. But today I must report that, although recently I have found myself drawn to reading much more religious history, and, although there actually is considerable peace to be enjoyed here in the Kootenay mountains, achieving any sort of closure about the meaning of life seems farther off now than ever it did. I suspect that our drives for fine and final answers may well be impossible of satisfaction, however adaptive, inevitable, and human they may be.

It is true that since retiring I have been rather surprised by the amount of time (still rather small) that I have found myself thinking about religious or personal questions, questions regarding the "meaning" of my past and present life. Normally I would say that I feel lucky, blessed, and sheltered from painful worry over questions concerning my life's work and its value. And normally I would suppose that questions about ultimate "meaning" probably are unanswerable in any event.

But not long ago something happened that gave me some second thoughts about one part of my life, namely that early part when I was myself a student. It began with a dream and with a feeling coming out of that dream. I awoke feeling something of a failure in life, feeling sad. It is not often that I remember dreams on waking. Nor do I often feel troubled or negative in this particular way.

In my dream I dropped in to see a mentor of old, someone who today has become a renowned figure in my chosen profession. I met this man when he was a graduate teaching assistant at Stanford and I was a student in his first class. Later in our lives both he and I moved on to the same Ivy League university, he to his first job as an assistant professor and I to graduate studies leading to the Ph.D. But when I took up my own first teaching appointment, here in Canada, I lost contact with this gentle man. In my dream, there he was today, sitting in his office on a Sunday afternoon, working on a technical paper, and smiling warmly as I entered.

On the surface of it, my dream visit was unremarkable. It was good to see my old friend after all these years. We traded a little small talk, and then, because he was both busy and "successful," I felt I ought to leave. As I did so, I awoke.

Curiously, in the reverie of waking I found myself thinking about Stanford. Sadly. Feeling that I had disappointed my *alma mater* (as he had not). I never became a Nobel Prize winner. I never endowed a grand Stanford project. I never was invited to join the Stanford faculty.

Few of my old Stanford classmates do I ever see, save for my wife, who, on waking too, asked how I had slept, setting me to thinking and now to writing.

It would be cheap and rash psychologizing to say that the feelings I was having signalled either (1) some residual neurotic insecurity, or (2) an after-quake of retirement adjustment. As a clinician, I have no faith in either sort of diagnosis (such diagnoses as yet being primarily matters of faith). No, I was particularly interested in this familiar if infrequent feeling of having let my *alma mater* down, because I believe that, secretly, a large proportion of Stanford alumni (and those of many other universities as well) would know first-hand *exactly* what I am talking about. The shadow of our university passes over one's life unpredictably, perhaps in the arrival of an alumni magazine, in a newspaper article we chance to see, in a meeting with a former classmate, and we suddenly feel vaguely unworthy, unsuccessful, a disappointment.

Mine were not new feelings. I remember something somewhat like them in the dormitory halls as a freshman, and during the campus years that followed. My fellow students and I often felt we were a disappointment. We were receiving some C− grades (and worse!) for the first times in our lives. We were disappointing the fraternity selection teams. Why, even our sports teams were sometimes losing to UCLA and Cal-Berkeley. There were high standards being held up all around us, and we were failing to meet them with some regularity.

I also remember how much fun we were having in our studies, and how fine was our education. We used to joke about the indoctrination we were getting, the hagiography surrounding the more eminent alumni before us, starting always with the founders of the university.

Looking back now, however, I don't think we quite understood at the time what was really happening to us. I don't think we understood the potential chilling effect of the shadow of Stanford while we walked in her sunlight. For it was Stanford's great success that she imbued us with, or amplified in us, some worthy "American" aspirations, aspirations often tinged, however, with elitism and something very near to self-centredness. We were not informed about the costs of that elitism, or the costs of aiming at high financial rewards, or the costs of striving after public acclaim.

Over the years, Stanford has been nothing if not proud. And with some justification, to be sure. But pride, alas, was not accidentally placed first on Aquinas' list of capital sins. Pride throws a long and dark shadow. Soon enough, it interrupts love. It inhibits fellowship. It muddles reason. It tempts to avarice. And it breeds envy. Each of these effects, in their turn, creates further costs to be paid. And among these cascading effects I count episodes such as that of the vague shame that framed my recent morning dream.

To her more successful graduates, Stanford has long been particularly generous and appreciative. But like some parents, she has seemed barely dutiful toward her more anonymous brood with their many smaller and varied successes. (I stress the word "seemed.") For some of us, then, Stanford's long shadow dims the wisdom and honour to be found in quiet competence, in the private pursuit of virtue, and in anonymous charity.

Perhaps there is no escaping this shadow. Every virtue has its shadow side, or so I was taught. Still, I find myself questioning both the inevitability and the intensity of shadows like Stanford's. I have now seen five universities up close and while to some degree all of them foster a "spirit-building pride," not all seem to cast quite the same degree of shadow that Stanford does.

To be sure, these are tough times for universities. It is easy (and perhaps even correct) to argue that the very survival of any great private university, or the continued excellence of any great public university, depends on the loyalty of its alumni. In its turn, alumni loyalty may be said to depend on the development of school pride. Such arguments, I hold, are mistaken.

There is something one could call love of university that is quite separate from pride of university. Love is forgiving while pride is not. Love is generous and non-contingent while pride demands to be renewed. Love wants to make things better for those who follow while pride wants to keep things better for ourselves. Love is earned, by example, while pride is fostered by indoctrination.

The university student of today may do well, then, to look at the distinction between love of university and pride in university. He or she may well attend more closely to the shadow that can be cast over one's life while incubating a school-based pride and a related drive for high achievement. Who can say if attention to such matters will lower the costs exacted by that shadow? My hunch is that a certain amount of pride cannot be entirely avoided, and clearly not through simple acts of will or reason.

Similarly, however, love cannot be created by acts of will or reason.

Much depends on attribution—the attribution of meanings. What does it mean to suppose that "great people" are great because of their teachers? Or because of their parents? Or their intelligence? Or their willpower? Doubtless, these factors have their importance. But what about chance and accident? What about the stars?

Shakespeare's famous line "*The fault, dear Brutus, is not in our stars, but in ourselves*" misleads when it is taken for an easy truth. The line belongs to the jealous Cassius, who is urging Brutus first to pride, and thereafter to treachery. Someone needs to answer Cassius, saying, "There may be no fault in the stars, nor good either; yet the influence of chance upon our lives is much greater than most people dare to suppose."

I do not know the best place for religion in our sunset years. (I am sure that the answer is not the same answer for everyone.) In the evening of our lives, longer shadows are bound to fall across our paths.

These shadows cannot help but teach us a new tentativeness about life and about our attributions concerning its meanings.

It is one thing to be taught, however, and quite another to learn. Reading religious history certainly makes that clearer, if our own student days have not already done so.

13 | *My Brown Paper Bag*

THURSDAY JUNE 27, 1996
KASLO, B.C.

A certain few jokes have always travelled with me wherever I go. Not unlike melodies sounding for weeks 'round the rooms of my mind, I hear echoes of these special jokes in the most surprising and varied contexts.

The joke that I have felt to be the most wonderful over recent years (though few have appreciated it nearly as much as I have) is that sublime tale of the famous physicist who kept a horseshoe tacked up over his laboratory door. And perhaps my second favourite joke, dating from the time some five years ago when I seriously began contemplating an early retirement, has been the old joke about the brown paper bag.

You will doubtless be curious about that first joke, so before I get on with this potentially more relevant second one, let me quickly tell you about the physicist, without further comment.

A journalist went to a physics lab to interview a renowned scientist.

"I see you have a horseshoe tacked up over your laboratory door," he said. "What is that for?"

"Oh," answered the physicist, "that is to bring our laboratory good luck."

The journalist was surprised. "But I thought you didn't believe in that sort of superstition," he said.

"Oh I don't; not at all," answered the physicist, "but the farmer who offered me the horseshoe assured me that you don't have to believe in it for it to work."

(Wonderful.)

The joke about the brown paper bag goes as follows. On the occasion of his retirement from public life, a great philanthropist, newspaper publisher, and rich merchant in town was feted by the local mayor and all the town notables. After many speeches of praise to honour their most famous citizen, the great man himself was finally asked to say a few words.

He rose and gave a long speech of thanks, ending with the words: "And finally, to the young people of our fair city, I say remember this: When I arrived in this town at the age of eighteen, all I had in the world were the clothes on my back and a few small possessions in a brown paper bag."

Soon after the speeches were concluded, a young man shyly approached the guest of honour and asked, "Please, sir, what did you carry with you in that brown paper bag?"

"Well son," came the answer, "in that bag I carried a comb, a Bible, and three million dollars in negotiable securities."

In the year leading up to my retirement I gave considerable thought to the appropriate contents of my own brown paper bag on that day when I would make my anticipated arrival outside the village of Kaslo. Rather like the game of "What Would You Take on a Desert Island If You Could Only . . . " I decided that three million dollars in negotiable securities was not as realistic for me as might be some well-chosen furnishings for my retirement libraries, both literary and musical.

Thus, in that last year of full employment I had a delightful time slowly buying long-delayed treasures. If the purchase was going to be for "my brown paper bag," then it became all right to spend a little more on a fine atlas, or on the complete Shakespeare, or on Berlioz's *Requiem* and *Te Deum*.

It was always my assumption that after retirement I would see our new house built, then pull out my brown paper bag and settle down for a good long read, with fine music in the background—my own "happily-ever-after" script. All this, of course, with due regard for the reputed "dangers" of too much vegetating or making radical changes in one's lifestyle. In the event, however, there have been fewer changes of lifestyle than I expected, fewer items brought out from my brown paper bag, and rather less reading done, even during the winter, than I ever anticipated.

However, down near the bottom of my brown paper bag was an exception to this more general rule. I refer to one of only two video-tapes included therein. It contained a short film by Cynthia Scott from Canada's National Film Board, a film entitled *Flamenco at 5:15.** To my surprise, I have watched Ms. Scott's film many times since retiring, although formerly I rarely watched television at all, on tape or off the air. There is something very wonderful about *Flamenco at 5:15*, and, speaking metaphorically, it now sits on top of all the other treasures in my brown paper bag.

Flamenco at 5:15 records events starting at 5:15 p.m., when a select group of students at Toronto's National Ballet School report for a vol-untary class, held after hours. This special class in Flamenco dancing is taught by two remarkable artists steeped in that Spanish tradition, Susana and Antonio Robledo.

---

* The other videotape happened to contain a memorable recording of the San Francisco Opera production of Boito's *Mephistofele*.

Each time I see this film, I see or hear something new, something wonderful. This surprises me in a film that lasts just thirty minutes, a film I now imagine (falsely) that I know by heart. While I acknowledge many reasons to read a fine book more than once, it has taken some time to get used to the correction of an earlier belief that once you have seen a film, once you know how it turns out, then it has little more to teach, little more with which to entertain.

Recently I was showing *Flamenco at 5:15* to a house guest when, for the first time, I truly heard something that Susana says while telling us about the Spanish culture out of which flamenco flowers. She notes that flamenco dancing is an echo of the national preoccupation of Spain, which is seen most starkly in connection with bullfights.

"Always the play with death," says she, with her heavy Spanish accent. Then she adds: "Will it be happen, or no?"

In flamenco this question translates into an exquisite rhythmic tension: Will the beat, or the gesture, come as expected, or not? Will it be happening now? A moment from now?

In retirement, yes, I continue to find that there is sometimes the play with death—if "play" is even the right word here, if "playfulness" is any kind of achievable state in such a dark context. More often, perhaps, there is the exquisite financial tension, i.e., the play with solvency surrounding the arrival of a pension cheque, a tax rebate, or a temporary job offer. "Will it be happen, or no?"

But also, I turn the key in the ignition of my old pickup truck and I hear myself say: "Will it be happen, or no?" I attempt to set the time of day on my inscrutable VCR. Or, lightning begins to hit close to home and I rush indoors to unplug my computer. Always asking, "Will it be happen, or no?"

The answer is slowly becoming quite clear. Yes, it will happen. The question is simply: When? How soon? Sitting in front of our television screen, watching those exquisite dancers float back and forth, so young, and seemingly so far from "the death," the time that it will happen seems an eternity away. And yet, a career in dancing, for instance, or in singing, in athletics, can be so short-lived. Youth passes, and a forced "retirement" occurs. The little deaths slip past. And the greater ones draw closer.

Timing is everything. One great joy in flamenco dance is that so much of its timing can be exactly anticipated. And the greater joy is that its deliberate surprises are chosen for their aesthetic effect. But unlike flamenco dance, life guarantees us neither sort of consolation. How much the sweeter, then, when hazard throws up a moment, completely unexpected (at a funeral perhaps, or maybe at a meal, or just while driving home), that takes one's breath away with its timeliness and beauty. One is overcome with feeling, as when early some morning the aftermath of a dream brings great peace and happiness, having come on a night when one least expected it. At such times there is at last (however short-lived it may be) the elusive sense of the rightness of all things and the blessedness of this life.

I cannot claim much familiarity with these special states of grace. Retirement certainly provides more time to seek them out, yet nothing suggests that their deliberate courting will increase the likelihood of their occurrence. Still, I now have the consolation of my brown paper bag and its delightful contents. At the same time, I still have my share of moments when I feel myself unemployed and out of life's mainstream.

The reality, of course, is that I am neither. It is mostly just a matter of belief. Unlike the special horseshoe in that earlier joke, it seems that you *do* have to believe in retirement for *it* to work. Thus, those who assert the pun that makes retirement "unworkable" mislead us. Retirement does work—but in unfamiliar ways. Retirement does not require three million dollars in negotiable securities. But it clearly helps to bring along the right brown paper bag.

14 | *Peacekeeping*

*R*etarded dawns, accelerated sunsets, cooling tempera-
tures, and once again the fall colour has arrived. This is
definitely the nicest time of year for retiring at night. My
bed is still outdoors on the private open porch at the back of the house.
The porch rests high over the lake, at the south edge of steeper, forested
land just north of us. Beneath the overhanging house roof, with pillows
propping up my head, I can see the eastern stars, the surface of the lake,
the rising moon. The familiar mountain horizon, dark and distant, appears much farther away at night than it does during the day. As I lie
in bed, tiny airliners wink their lights at me starting far far away, high
above the Rockies. Soundlessly they begin lofting overhead, en route to
Vancouver from the distant East.

The bed outdoors is warmed now by an electric underpad, and a
goose-down quilt cocoons me. Lights rather spoil the nocturnal magic
and thus I rarely read in bed. These days I often go to bed "early" and don
the headphones from my little battery-operated FM radio. Here in the

mountains we receive just one FM station. Fortunately, however, that station is the CBC. On a chilly fall night one can listen to some of the most interesting radio extant while breathing in the cool air flowing down slope out of the woods.

Last night I chanced to hear a program in the CBC series called *Ideas*, a program that consisted of some long and thought-provoking excerpts from a recent talk on the topic of peacekeeping. The speaker was a former American psychiatrist, now a journalist, who specializes in analysing the delusions and neuroses of nations and their associated deliberative bodies. In some respects his message was a very pessimistic one, suggesting to me at least that basic human nature and social nature are such that piracy, pillage, and war can be prevented only by force, while the creation of sufficient force to prevent them always risks increased piracy, pillage, and war.

From the distance of my sleeping porch, the divisions between various nations and cultures appear no deeper than the divisions right here in the Kootenays between (for example) logging companies and environmentalists, or now, between Kaslo's Mayor Mackle and his Village Council. If possible, these local divisions may be even deeper. In this context I cannot help but remember some of the furious battles that I witnessed (and joined) as a practicing academic. I am reminded, too, of the famous aphorism about such battles. It is attributed to various sources, but I believe it was first coined by H. L. Menken, to wit: *"Academic disagreements are so bitter, because the stakes are so low."*

The stakes in the battle over our first village sewer project are not exactly high, by world standards, but the local casualty count certainly has been high. Half the town, and all the principal players (that should also read "principle" players) now number among the walking wounded. One sees them daily on Front Street, looking ever more haggard and harried.

The mayor, who is running for a second term of office in next month's municipal elections, is keeping a low electoral profile right now.

Recently he has been crucified in newsprint and in certain local living rooms for his alleged behaviour thwarting the sewer project in the face of a village council that is unanimously in favour of proceeding. His opponent in the mayoral race, Al Beix,[*] currently one of the village councillors, has been crucified in turn for his part in "railroading" an allegedly unwanted sewer project over the objections of a "majority" of the citizens, who, having been misled about the nature and risks and costs of the proposed project, now wish they had never signed any paper signifying their acceptance of the plan. In some quarters, too, it has not helped him that Councillor Beix has previously been an outspoken advocate for facilitating major local logging, including logging in some contentious old growth forest. At the very least, then, one can say that we in Kaslo continue to live in interesting times.

The variety of means that have been successfully used to delay the sewer project are remarkable. In total they have amounted to something more than a year of delay, jeopardizing the matching funds that the provincial government put aside for this project on the condition that all work should be completed by late next year.

At one point this summer the mayor simply refused to send a letter awarding the first phase of the sewer project to the winning bidder selected by the unanimous village councillors. Eventually, the Village Council met again, and, over the loud objection of the mayor, unanimously passed a motion directing that the Village Clerk should type and fax the letter awarding this contract before the conclusion of that evening's council meeting. This she duly did.

Later that same evening, the mayor quietly returned to the Village office, let himself in, typed and signed a letter countermanding the first one, and faxed it to the company in question.

Those who most desire the new sewer do so because the Ministry

---

[*] Pronounced *Bikes*.

of Health insists that a sewage treatment facility must be operational before it will approve any further building permits in downtown Kaslo. Originally the planned site of the small, low, sewage-treatment building was to have been on the edge of town, where it would be relatively invisible. Now the plan is to put it beside the logging sports complex down at the beach at the foot of Front Street.* With this revised location being "in our face," as some are calling it, and quite literally under our worried noses, many in town are having strong second thoughts about the wisdom and need for any such facility, however unobtrusive and sanitary it may possibly prove to be.

Now it happens that, although I live well outside the Village limits, I will have a vote in the upcoming election for the offices of Village mayor and the various councillors. This by virtue of my name being jointly listed on the title of Helga's village home. Until today I had thought I knew exactly who I would be supporting in this election. But on writing the above it has become clear to me that I am not as sure of my choices as I first believed. I would prefer that my vote contribute to keeping Kaslo peaceful, scenic, small, and affordable. But the candidates running for office probably can promote no more than different small pieces of this wish list. It is not easy now to decide which of these criteria should be sacrificed to preserve some hope of which others.

As near as I can tell, keeping the peace in Kaslo cannot be accomplished by force, by reason, or by my vote. It probably cannot be accomplished by anything that excludes major doses of good luck and economic increase. But this latter would seem to require considerable growth in size, and that could well promote less and less affordable living to those who arrived here prior to 1990. I do not share the fatalistic belief of many that undue development is inevitable here, nor that local

---

*   This location happens to be a few meters west of the site of Uncle Kipper's beach houses in the movie *Magic in the Water*.

development will require massive exploitation of those timber, mineral, and water "resources" that lie all around us. Nor do I share the view that defeating the Kaslo sewer will halt unwanted development.

The Lake Tahoe that I knew as a boy, growing up there in the years between 1949 and 1959, was soon changed forever by constant growth, by bedrooms and more bedrooms. Too many people were brought to the commons, which soon enough became wall-to-wall private property. Asphalt and glass and signage and sewage and road salt and newsprint and regulatory paperwork and all the other detritus of mercantile man have turned rural Tahoe into a garish postcard, a destination, a story line, a kind of outdoor mall crowded with placelessness. This is my worst nightmare for pristine Kootenay Lake.

Kaslo is ready *for* a change, yet seems unready *to* change. The current peace is very fragile, and my choice among the various village candidates is still unclear. Wishing for peace, I am reminded of the telling joke recounted by that American speaker near the end of last night's *Ideas* program dealing with peacekeeping. It seems that Henry Kissinger, against all odds, is prevailed on to come live in Jerusalem and to direct the Jerusalem zoo. Almost overnight this wizard of foreign policy is credited with an economic miracle, for soon tourists come streaming into Jerusalem to visit the zoo and to see its star attraction: a new exhibit where a lamb and a lion graze and sleep peacefully together.

One day the President of Harvard University comes to see this wonder, and that evening he hosts Kissinger at a private dinner. During the sorbet, he leans over and asks quietly, "Henry, tell me, how on earth did you ever do it?"

Kissinger hesitates, then answers in confidential tones: "Every day, a new lamb."

15 | *A Little Wiser*

*Y*esterday I had brunch with my business partner Verne. We have been having these business meetings off and on for about a year now. They have been among the most enjoyable meetings I can remember attending, and I continue to look forward to each one. Our meetings are probably so enjoyable because in the year since we decided to hang out a shingle together we have had no clients and no work. In short, there are no financial and professional responsibilities to get in the way of our dreaming, our leisure, our playful retirements.

Verne retired to Kaslo a year after I did. Prior to taking early retirement he was a professor of communications at Syracuse University, chairman of the radio-TV department there and, for a time, associate dean for academic affairs in the School of Public Communications. Our joint venture was really his idea. I had taught statistics for many years, and taught courses in testing and measurement theory. "We would make a perfect team for doing Survey Research," said Verne during our first business lunch.

Thus was born WISR,[*] the partnership we call *Western Interior Survey Research.* Our first meetings were taken up with the creation of advertising and publicity material. We created mailings. Announced our presence to the world. We speculated on the best formulas for bidding on anticipated contracts. We spent most of one meeting deciding not to incorporate until we had a contract that required that. And so it went. Looking back, it was all very playful. Rather unreal. A lottery ticket purchased against later financial need and incipient boredom.

At our meeting yesterday, Verne and I surprised each other just a little with mutual confessions that we were actually rather glad we haven't had any business this year. Nor would we want our first survey work anytime soon. There has been too much else occupying our time and too much satisfaction in just being retired. We both seemed to see, in greater focus, what we had vaguely known all along: that while WISR is serious business, for us it is also (and primarily) a delightful plaything.

Consequently, at some point in yesterday's conversation we began to ask ourselves why we started WISR in the first place. Were we secretly missing our old professional lives? Were we having second thoughts about retirement? Were there financial concerns that made us dream of business success?

Or was it sheer boredom: the devil's work in idle brains?

It was not this last, that much seemed clear. Then Verne offered a comment about retirement that gave me pause. It could be argued, he suggested, that when each of us contemplated retirement, and for somewhat understandable reasons, we treated it, too, as a game—as not real. Retirement itself may have been treated almost as a type of play, back from which it would be possible to step at any time, i.e., back "into reality." More quickly than expected, however, one's former world moves on after retirement, diverging rapidly, getting farther

---

[*]   Pronounced *wiser.*

and farther away. We discover that, yes, you cannot go home again, back to that life you had been treating as more "real" than a retirement life.

So, to those who are planning retirement, or are living through its early years, I offer this hypothesis: *Whatever your preparation for retirement, whatever your dreams about it, whatever your fears, your hopes, and your assumptions, you are probably in for rather more than you expect.* It may be more than meets your eye, yet it may not. It may be less than you have feared. But in certain important ways it will surely be different. Irrevocably different.

As a psychologist, as an academic, I often secretly felt unworthy because, try as I might, deep in my heart I could not ultimately believe most of what was passing for scientific truth in my field. Nor did I have a great deal of faith in the particular *methods* that academic psychology was using to approach the gods of Fact and Truth.

As I read the history of psychology, and the history of each older science, it seems to me that what once passed for fact and truth has *always* been half denied one or two generations later, modified all out of recognition. Thus it has become impossible for me to imagine that for hundreds of years Truth has been standing still while we have been approaching closer to it. We have become more sophisticated, certainly. We know more now. But I think we are not yet better for this new knowledge, and very possibly we are no wiser.

This is not the place to explore my private view of the work that I left on retiring, and the profession that I felt, in some measure, was already leaving me. Suffice it to say that some time ago I came to believe that even if certain psychological theories do not help us to understand people in general, they *can* still help us to understand those individual psychologists who gave us the theories. I believe, for instance, that Freud's theories of the neuroses rarely find objective confirmation in today's real life patients, and probably did not often do so in Freud's own patients.* But I do suspect that his theory has great merit for describing the psychology of Freud himself. His theory *was* surprisingly "true" for his person, in his culture, however incomplete or false it may come to appear to future psycho-biographers who may do unto Freud as he did unto Michelangelo.

Applying, then, my own theory to my own theoretical self, that is, supposing that my views about retirement may not predict at all the individual experiences of other retirees nearly as well as they successfully postdict my own experience, I am led to this ironic further confirmation of my previous hypothesis (italicized above) for my own case. My hypothesis surprises me, exactly as it predicts what retirement will do; but it surprises me by its blatant exceptions, by how much in fact has gone almost exactly as I had planned and hoped, e.g., by the many new friendships I have made here (including that with my partner Verne), friendships that, unthinkingly, I took for granted would somehow occur.

In this respect my hypothesis has been just like the retirement it tried to predict. Rather more than I expected? Certainly. As much fun? Perhaps. Have I become more than a little wiser? Doubtful.

⌒⌒⌒

Postscript, added two years later
Soon after writing the above, about "how much in fact has gone al-

---

* This is what I make of the fact that so many of Freud's students, colleagues, and analysands came to hold views that were somewhat different (and, in the end, quite importantly different) from the master's.

most exactly as I had planned and hoped," something reached down and rattled my cage sharply. If my angioplasty had not been recognized as the source of a major change of direction in my life, what was about to happen to me could not be so effectively ignored or dismissed. Again, and indeed: "The best laid plans . . ."

Part Two
A Beginner Again

16 | *Affecting Eternity*

MONDAY SEPTEMBER 15, 1997
KASLO, B.C.

*Y*ou would need to be of a certain age to remember those old Container Corporation of America advertisements. They were always quite striking, especially in the first year they ran, sometime in the early 1960s. Nothing else was quite like them. Each advertisement occupied a full magazine page, and each featured a different "modern" painting or collage across which was printed a single pithy quotation, a thought for the week, a philosophic gem.

I remember only one of these advertisements, although I do not remember the author of the quotation it contained. Still, I remember the quotation itself quite well because for a time, when I first began teaching, a framed copy of this ad hung in a corner of my office where only I could see it from my desk. The quotation read: "A teacher affects eternity. He can never tell where his influence stops."

That was heady stuff in those days. Affecting eternity held great attraction. In those days, too, it didn't occur to me there was any need to improve on the designated gender of the teacher in question. It wasn't until many years later that I began to think critically about this quotation, about affecting eternity. By then I had been granted more classroom contacts, with greater numbers of students, than most teachers ever would experience. If a teacher really can affect eternity, then I had been given an unusually clear opportunity for doing so. Did that go a bit too much to my head? I suspect it did.

Meanwhile, somewhere near the halfway point in my working life, my life between starting my first job and taking early retirement, I was drawn to the study of Buddhism. I joined a Zen meditation group in Toronto and attended regular meditations with its members. I was never very clear why I chose to follow this path, but then I never felt that discovering my motivation was particularly necessary. It just seemed obvious to me that Buddhist philosophy and practice was a much-needed counterweight to the cerebral emphasis of my daily working life. Moreover, the Buddhist teachings seemed to say that all thought, all naming of motives, etc., is irrelevant to why Buddhism is to be practiced and honoured.

The Buddhist teachings seemed to say more. To me they seemed to say that anyone, that everyone, affects eternity, with ten thousand invisible threads of influence that commingle, joining others, extending outward forever. And, too, the Buddhist teachings seemed to say that fundamentally this "eternity" is empty, illusory, and that the wish to "affect" it can be an impediment to achieving serenity and to truly helping others. That was some time ago now. But the longer I live, the more I think the Buddhists are likely to be right. We affect eternity no matter what we do. And it isn't only what we do that affects eternity. What we don't do can have equally profound effects. For instance, what we haven't said can be as important as what we have said.

Now there is something I've been keeping to myself, something that for me is very significant. It is so significant that I couldn't write of it here for a long time, although clearly it very much wanted to be written.

What I couldn't previously write was this: One afternoon, early last June, my father died. He was at home, in bed, and by chance I happened to be the only one there with him at the time. I was holding his hand and speaking to him during the last twelve minutes while he died. He had been slipping away for ten days, the result of kidney failure caused by a spreading cancer.

I had arrived to be with my father one week before he died, on the day before my sixtieth birthday. He was being sent home from hospital to receive hospice care during the remaining time he had to live. He seemed cheerful about coming home and he was clearly glad to see me. That day he was still gifted with consciousness, language, and wit. The next day, on my birthday, when the hospice nurse came for the first time and introduced herself to my father, she asked him what he wanted her to call him. He thought a moment and then said confidently, "You can call me darling." I think my father affected eternity in that moment more directly than in any other during his last week of life.

The nurse did not elect to grant him his request, probably hoping it was not seriously intended. Knowing my father, he may himself have been unsure about how seriously his answer was intended. But I believe that it would have been a great mercy had the nurse seen fit to call him darling. My brother, who was also there, agrees. My father's request for the medicine of love seemed to all of us at his bedside to be just what the doctor ordered. Later, when speech and consciousness began leaving him, what he didn't say and didn't do anymore affected us, too. "You can call me darling" became a nimbus around the deepening silence of his last few days of life.

I miss my father very much. In fact, ironically, if predictably, I miss him more than ever I did during equivalent separations from him while he was alive. And the memory of him visits me much more often now than it ever used to, affecting how I view myself and the world around me and how I treat other people. I don't go around calling people darling: I haven't been asked to. But now when people ask me a question, occasionally it is my father who answers. When I hear from someone that they have a dying relative, I now assume that I know what they are going through and so I have a new confidence in speaking to them, one that is curiously presumptuous, but at the same time, I believe, is often affecting.

My father was eighty-six years old when he died. My mother is soon to be eighty-eight. She and my father divorced a long time ago. My father's death has now changed my relationship with my mother, in ways that in turn have affected my relationships with other people. I find myself wanting now to spend more time with my mother. And now when I see her, I find myself asking much more about her growing up and about her parents—my links backward into eternity. With other people I sometimes steer the conversation to ask how different were, or are, the personalities of their two parents. Mine seem so different from each other, somehow. My father: delighted to have his sons with him during his terminal illness. My mother: not wanting to "inflict" that on us, she who sees those last days that I spent with my father as a psychological stressor, as an unconsciously inconsiderate imposition on my father's part, one that could be dangerous for me with my heart condition and all. But I think it was my heart that reaped the greatest benefit from my last week with my father, my initiation into my sixties, my first face-to-face experience with an act of dying.

Among the many internal changes I detect in myself since that first week of June is an eagerness again to read, and a revived interest in Buddhist literature. In this connection it happens that this week I am finally reading a wonderful little book that I have long been postponing for no good reason. Its title is *A Journey in Ladakh* and the author, previously quite unknown to me, is Andrew Harvey. I say "previously," as if Mr. Harvey now *is* known to me, but this is my point: I still do not know him. Though his writing has affected me, and revealed many things about its author, there is a mysterious sense in which "Mr. Harvey" alone is not, simply, the author of that book. (Or perhaps "I" alone am not "simply" his reader.) All the events that led to putting his book together, that led Harvey to finding a publisher, and led to the fates arranging for a worn paperback edition of this book to cross my path, all these events have played their own eternal part in putting these subsequent words of "mine" squarely in your path, dear reader. Do you see it? Eternity. Whether planned for or not.

Isn't it strange? Most likely we will never meet. I cannot begin to imagine you as I write for you now, nor do I try. I am just sitting. Writing. For some eternal muse perhaps. For my brief self, certainly. But I recognize that I would not be writing this, for both of us, if a friend had not put Mr. Harvey's book on my reading pile, and if the cats were not asleep and out of my hair, and if the rain had not made my desk so attractive this morning. The ten-thousand proximal effects that others appear to have had on me, effects that have led me to pen these very words and no others, and the ten-thousand-times-ten-thousand effects that those effects received from a generation before, and so outward through time, these are "eternity."

Isn't it ironic, then, and perhaps sad, to be saddled with that old desire to have "more" effect in the world, imagining that we have failed, or could possibly fail, to affect eternity?

Each of us affects eternity.

We can never tell where our influence stops.

17 | *A Sea Change*

Among my colleagues in psychology who have made it their life's work to understand the workings of human memory it is often considered a truism that we sometimes know more than we can tell. That is, we know more than we can formulate in words, even in the privacy of our own minds. I like to extend this idea and say: We often know more than we know that we know. There are certain things we understand but that we don't remember learning, certain things we did not notice that we noticed, that we can't imagine we might remember or intuit.

This is true despite the fact that it seems to be so much more often and painfully true that we are quite mistaken about very much of what we think that we *do* remember and *do* know.

An example of knowing more than we are aware of knowing is illustrated in that story, told earlier in this book, of the Montana fire boss who saved his life by lighting an escape fire in front of an onrushing forest fire that soon caught up to him. So far as he remembered, nobody had ever mentioned to him the possibility of such an escape strategy, and at the time he himself had no idea why or how he knew to light the fire that saved his life. Yet somehow he did know what he was doing, and the strategy worked exactly as his intuition promised that it could.

I have now had a similar experience, albeit one that was drawn out over a far longer time period. It happened in the silent year since last I wrote here, during the accumulating months since my father died. I did not anticipate most of what was coming, although in retrospect I should have anticipated much more of it than I did. And like the fire boss before me, I did not really know quite what I was doing while taking actions that surprised even me. In consequence, my "retirement" has altered markedly. In one sense it has now ended for a time. (So much then for my retirement plans. As the old quip has it: "If you want to make God laugh, tell her your plans.") The question I now face is, how much do I really know, and how much can I tell my reader, of what it was that actually happened this past year? I am surprised, both by how much I do know now, and, by how much I still don't.

Of course some people hold that autobiography and biography are always and equally fictions. Always partial and flawed understandings. David and Jessie, two of my close Kaslo friends, appear to hold this view. Both are retired professors of English.

David, you may recall, is Kaslo's poet laureate. He often offers us poems to mark and preserve passing local events: a sixtieth birthday, for instance, a dramatic downtown dogfight, the felling of a noble tree, or the inauguration of an artistic set of new stairs down to the lake.

David's wife, Jessie, currently sits on the board of governors of a nearby college, and very occasionally she sits as well beside David in the path of bulldozers set on placing timber profit over prudence in sensitive local watersheds.

Both these friends have given considerable professional consideration to the assertion that memoirs of any sort are *sui generis* fictions.

If I understand them correctly, Jessie and David believe that there is no *fundamental* truth possible in personal accounts of events, but rather there are only various points of view, all of them relative, each with its incomplete and subjective and frequently self-serving interpretation of some small select subset of that infinity of data we construe to be a life. I often prefer to disagree with them on this topic, but the reasons I disagree are, to be sure, illogical, and our disagreement may be said to amount merely to a question of degree.

For one thing, I believe that a *reader* can sometimes come to know quite a bit more than an *author* appears to tell. For another, I believe that, in biography, "truth" is something closely akin to a defined benchmark, a narrative pole star serving as a point of origin or reference. In my experience, the writer who is given health and time and the right muse will often succeed in setting such a truth before the reader's eyes. It is also important to remember that *in the very first instance the author and the reader are always one.* An occasional author might set out to lie, yes. But if an author sets out to give a locally "true" picture of events, I hold there is no *a priori* reason to deny him or her hope of success. And if, on rereading what has been written, the author feels for one continuous month that a local truth has been told, then it seems to me it has. (Yes; perhaps I doth protest too much.)

The events that even here I have been postponing reporting to you could be radically condensed into two brief chapters. Both of those chapters in my life proved to be extremely painful, yet at the same time each of them also seemed to be strangely healing. In the first chapter, after another extended trip to visit my mother at Lake Tahoe, I returned home to my wife of seventeen years, and to certain precipitous events that led me to question the appropriateness of our continuing to live together.

In the second chapter, after finally deciding to separate from my wife, I discovered to my astonishment that in some sense this decision appeared to be rather long overdue to at least a few of the people who know me best. I was told, only then, that retirement did not seem to be suiting me, that for the past few years I had appeared to be getting progressively more distant and quiet, looking wan, worried, and preoccupied. I was astonished to hear this, as much because I had thought retirement was being particularly kind to me as by the fact that these friends did not at all reinforce the guilt that I was feeling. My decision to separate certainly *had* provoked dismay in a few of my friends. This fact added to the guilt I was already experiencing while living with Elizabeth's new pain and anger, and it added to the guilt coming from my own somewhat tarnished sense of what I had long believed constituted honourable and appropriate behaviour and "sufficient justification" for ending a marriage.

When a marriage dissolves, there can be many casualties. Even others who have been through the trial themselves somehow feel the need to withdraw some portion of their affection from one or both of the partners now that the "couple" is not available and the relationship with each party appears to require a more narrowly focused expression. I had expected that the great majority of our friends, Elizabeth's and mine, would find it hard to accept my decision and actions, not knowing its full range of causes, and that for this reason they would be lost as friends of mine. Ironically, this expectation may yet prove to be ninety-five percent wrong because currently there are only three sets of old friends who still find it hard to forgive or to communicate with me. I like to hope these friends, too, will one day resume their comfort with my company and will accept what they cannot understand or now change. In any event, the casualties among my friends have so far proven to be fewer than I had feared they would be.

Lost friendships were not the only casualties that I had expected on taking this sharp, uncharted turn off the map of my presumed life's course. I had also expected to lose my retirement home, the unique retreat on Kootenay Lake that has meant so much to me since 1989 when we purchased the land, when I first saw the possibilities of creating the staircase down to the lakeshore and of creating a Gatehouse, and when I first planned the location of the main house. To sell this treasure after only three years of residence in the house, a few months after finally being able to furnish my tower office and library there, seemed as great a potential threat to my continuing mental and physical health as did undertaking the dissolution of my habitual, if cool, life with Elizabeth. And yet this loss of my home was also a risk, a likelihood, a great price, with which I found I soon made my surprising peace.

It now appears that, in the end, I may not lose this home. In the separation agreement that was painfully forged between us during this long spring and summer of mutual frustrations and delays, I have been given a few years in which to buy out Elizabeth's interest in our property. For the time being I hold the title to this treasure while in turn Elizabeth holds my mortgage. Meanwhile, Elizabeth has arranged to move to the warmer and more stimulating harbour city of Victoria where the possibility of financial security and climatic comfort has for some time seemed to her to be much more likely. A sea change then. A sea change for which neither of us had ever planned.

And then, as if these changes were not complicating enough, there are two additional (and much happier) changes in my life that have occurred. First, in two weeks' time my common cold book is due to be published in Canada under the title *In Cold Pursuit: Medical Intelligence Investigates the Common Cold*. I had thought that the stress of my marital situation might prevent me from the timely completion of both the needed revisions of my manuscript and also the creation of the index for this book. But to my surprise, solitary work on the book manuscript all this past year became a welcome diversion and something of a tonic for my dissolving sense of identity. It also helped greatly that my editor, at Stoddart Publishing back in Ontario, was so very good at her job, making my work all the more satisfying. Thus, my own sea changes included experiencing, for the first time, the process of turning a manu-script into a published book.*

Stoddart's editorial offices are in Toronto. I still have friends in the Toronto area, including a woman I have known and admired for nearly thirty years, a woman with whom I used to have lunch once or twice a year, depending on her travels and my own. Her name is Lorraine, and she is an executive with Random House Canada. Lorraine's insights into the publishing process were to prove particularly helpful as my own publication date drew near.

While consulting briefly with my editors at Stoddart late this sum-mer, I was, for the first time, a guest at Lorraine's rural home. Another significant sea change for me is the decision growing out of that visit that I will spend this coming winter with her in Ontario. There I will be better able to help with publicity efforts for my book and to search for some necessary part-time employment, either in the classroom again or in some other consulting capacity. And while during this winter I will miss my mountain home, I hope to enjoy the companionship of a very remarkable woman and the hearth of a particularly peaceful home.

There is, of course, much more that I know about the past year that I will not tell here; only parts of which would I withhold out of respect for the privacy of others and my own privacy. There is just too much to tell and too little need for the reader here to know. And, too, it seems likely that there is still very much that *I* don't know about these events and their role in my life after retirement.

If I am to keep my home in the Kootenays I am going to have to come out of retirement; that much has now become clear. Had I not been such a novice at retiring, I now see that from the begin-

---

* A year after writing this, the interesting perspectives I noticed while producing my first book index would unexpectedly lead to further indexing projects, with some surpris-ing and happy consequences.

ning I should have been referring to this past four years as "my first retirement" rather than referring to a singular retirement. Many of my friends, knowing my love of classroom teaching, had been sure I would be *psychologically* incapable of staying retired. In that respect it turns out they were mistaken. But for the time being at least, I am no longer *financially* capable of staying retired. And what will I miss about retirement if I do undertake a spell of full-time work? I will miss most the generous time I now have for reading the variety of books that Lorraine has begun introducing into my library. Books such as Alain de Botton's charming and helpful little tour-de-force *How Proust Can Change Your Life.*

Which brings me back to the question raised before: Is there realistic hope of a writer ever achieving capital-T Truth? Can Truth be captured in language, in text, in memoir? In de Botton's book I found a telling remark about the difference between what it is that an author sees and what it is that a reader sees when each arrives at the same spot in their lives or in their world. On the penultimate page of his book, de Botton has occasion to observe that "a genuine homage to Proust would be to look at *our* world through *his* eyes, not to look at *his* world through *our* eyes." An author, a painter, a composer, and a reader—each sees the world from a different perspective, framed by different experience. Some perspectives are more screened than others, and some are more distant. Viewpoints and elevations differ, as do the existing lighting conditions. The natural tendency is for us to test various truths and other viewpoints by examining them only from our own current perspective. But where an author like Proust, or de Botton, truly can bring us closer to the truth is by offering us a different perspective and a better view of where *we* ourselves really are now, not a view of where some *other* really was then.

Yes, memoirs purport to tell the truth about their author. I would now agree that in many respects they do not. But memoirs, like novels, can offer us a clearer truth about the world in which we as readers live and move. Still, the first reader *is* always the author. Each author, too, has the right to claim at least a piece of the truth.

For myself, the sea changes in my life since my father died, the renewed doubts and disapprovals of myself that sometimes surface, plus my renewed awareness of the limitations of reason wherever it meets human emotion or examines itself in the looking glass of memory, these sea changes make very precious to me those people who have found the secret of acceptance of others—people of good heart and a forgiving nature—people generous with their *self*-acceptance, who then give it freely to others. If retirement can be given a proper job description, surely the cultivation of a loving acceptance, of oneself, of others, and of the natural world, belongs in the opening sentence of that description.

18 | *Removals from Office*

*S*ome retirements are dictated and unwanted. The unlucky retiree is pushed unwillingly from office, rather than pulled by a wish for leisure or new challenges.

The news this week is full of the U.S. Senate debate over the utility of a forced retirement for William Jefferson Clinton. A majority of American voters seem to have made up their minds about a Clinton impeachment and have turned their backs on the debate, waiting to see if their preferences will or will not be vindicated by the verdict of the Senate.

But for some, me included, the debate over impeachment is proving far more personally significant and more complex than it appeared at first to be.

Did Clinton actually commit perjury or not? If he did, was it a "high crime" under the U.S. Constitution? Mightn't one argue that perjury was perhaps "forced" on him "unjustly" by questions that should never have been allowed during an inquiry into other unrelated matters? Are there some perjuries that are heinous and some that are not?

These are not the sorts of questions that normally would interest me, and I'm not sure I understand why they do now. I only became interested in the impeachment proceedings while visiting my mother at Lake Tahoe in Nevada. This occurred last month, when the House Judiciary Committee was considering a recommendation for articles of impeachment. Each evening we watched the news together, lying atop her bed, while privately I anguished over my ever more complicated relationship with my mother: she the elder American Republican of strong views and I the retired Canadian holding some conflicting and strong views of my own.

Before I initiated this ten-day visit, there had been some talk with my brother, and with Lorraine, about the wisdom of my going. I had wanted to see my mother while I still had the opportunity, to see if I couldn't achieve a greater acceptance of our troubling differences, especially the two differences that touched me most deeply at the time, concerning (1) my evolving life with Lorraine and (2) my mother's troubled relationship with my brother (and, to some extent, more recently with me).

To date, my mother has not met Lorraine. They talk briefly and cordially when Lorraine happens to answer the phone. But that is rare, and my mother does not mention Lorraine when talking to me. She has never asked to meet her or learn more about her. If I bring up Lorraine's name she responds with minimal signs of interest. The closest she comes to asking about her, or showing any interest in my life with her, is to ask wistfully when I will arrive back at my home in British Columbia and thus be closer to her at Tahoe. True, my mother had never been particularly interested in any of the women in my life. When Elizabeth and I separated, and after my mother and I were finally able to discuss the event, she said she now understood, and thereafter she said no more about it. My mother is the only remaining member of my close relatives and friends who has *not* asked to meet Lorraine. Those who have met

Lorraine have been charmed by her and have forged immediate warm relationships with her on their own. Even my brother, Scott, whose direct manner often left the women in my life more or less uncomfortable, left Lorraine feeling warm and welcomed.

When we were youngsters, Scott and I had many terrible fights. At the same time, even then, we were frequently very close. Despite the rivalry between us, it generally seemed to me that my mother's fierce disciplining of my brother (who challenged her often) was undeservedly and counterproductively severe. In high school, I began having my own strong clashes with my mother. But for the most part she always seemed somehow fairer in her dealings with me, and more often ready to be loving. Compared with Scott (who is younger), I was certainly far less of a challenge to and for her, and far more the dutiful son while growing up. For the past twenty-five years, however, I have grown to respect and love my brother still more. Privately, I find myself supporting his cause and his view of matters in his continuing difficulties in relating well to our mother. It hurts me to hear her periodic criticisms of him when I visit her. Say whatever I may in his defence, there appears to be no changing her opinions or perspectives about his perceived failings as a son. Or, for that matter, about my own similar failings.

Thus, before bad-boy Clinton eclipsed our other discussions as we lay watching the news on her bed, mention of my bad-boy brother was often a stimulus that would cause me to go silent. But now I was again being permitted to suppose that my mother had raised two bad boys, not one. In the turmoil following my separation from Elizabeth, and the beginnings of my communications with Lorraine, although my mother had been careful in her turn not to say very much, she did say that under no circumstances should I inform my brother about Lorraine's existence. When I revealed that I had long since informed him, the conversation between us temporarily ended upon her response, with some disgust, "Oh no! You didn't!"

So later, while watching the televised news each night, the American president and his behaviour became (if only for me) something like a cipher for encoding discussions about bad boys and their moral failings. My mother was very clear that the president had lied under oath and that this perjury rendered him unfit to continue in office. I tried to suggest to her that the questions put under oath about his personal life during his recent time in office were irrelevant to the court case dealing with matters that had occurred well before he took office. (They had been confirmed as irrelevant by an earlier trial judge.) And I argued that his evasion of these persistent, hostile questions, giving answers that were evasive white lies, was not as immoral as was the prosecutor's continuing search for, and publicizing of, prurient personal material meant to shame the president for behaviour that was none of the public's business.

Surely, I thought, any lies told by Clinton about his private life were far less a threat to the U.S. Constitution and Government than were the lies told to Congress by Presidents Reagan and Bush, Sr., when they denied all knowledge of, or any role in, the covert sale of arms to Iran and/or the illegal support given to the Sandinista rebels in Honduras by the CIA. Those apparent lies would constitute direct subversions of the U.S. Constitution and Congress. Clinton's evasions would not. But my mother apparently required her Republican presidents to commit necessary perjury for the protection of "democracy" while Democrat Clinton needed to confess all and to resign at once because democracy was never at stake as an excuse for his perjury.

Politics or religion can always be counted on to provoke an argument between two people who are avoiding a discussion of the unrecognized issues that truly separate them. How sad then that between a parent and her offspring (let's not call this retiree her "child") there can remain such old sensitivities and psychological scabs. All my professional life, until quite recently, I accepted the traditional clinical teachings that communication, dialogue, and insight are the prerequisite medicines for curing interpersonal disagreements and for discharging family tensions. But lately I have begun to suspect that those medicines do not generally work, even when both parties to a family dispute are willing to swallow them. Something more is needed. I now believe that this something *starts* with acceptance. *First* there is acceptance. *Then* can be undertaken a healing dialogue and a new understanding.

Tradition and theory also assert that to accept another person one must first achieve a full *self*-acceptance. Should this happen to be true, retirement may not be the best time to achieve any such self-acceptance. Yet often retirement seems to be the only time that we have. Prior to retirement we tend to make our self-acceptance dependent on our productivity and usefulness, and/or on our level of public esteem or power. The "self-acceptance" that we seek and monitor prior to retirement appears to shroud a working persona or a parental persona. But these are incomplete personas, and the shrouds that veil them can and should dissolve with the onset of retirement.

How to create in oneself an acceptance of another person, acceptance of them just as they are, is tricky business at best. There are few guides for how to achieve it, and I see little sign that the methods often advocated for achieving it are either efficient or generally effective. Perhaps it *is* true, as some still say, that to accept another person one must first achieve self-acceptance. It concerns me, however, that like my mother, so many older people, in their pain and increasing isolation, appear to get increasingly less tolerant of both themselves and others rather than more tolerant. Is it true that some of these people resent their bodies for letting them down? Could it be true that such resentment is projected too easily onto the inhabitants of other, younger bodies?

As for learning to accept others as they are, perhaps such acceptance can come most directly from a belated recognition of our deep ignorance about life, including the unrecognized magnitude of our ignorance about that familiar, troublesome, other. Certainly President Clinton has become a complete cipher to me. As am I, sometimes, to myself.

We appear to be so much more than we are ever likely to be able to know. Maybe, then, the legend over the entrance to the fabled groves of Academe, the one that reads "Know Thyself," should be retired in favour of a more accessible legend reading "Know thy Limits and the Horizons of thy Ignorance." Ignorance does not excuse us from acting. Nor does accepting our limits and ignorance lessen the pain that is caused to us by their existence. But I think an increased recognition of our limits and our deep ignorance does lessen the pain of feeling that pain.

As for my mother, however, it is a safe guess that she would not agree. She would probably advise me to pull up my socks, sit up straight, and think again. That, at least, would make me laugh. And laughter is indeed among the best antidotes we have to pain.

19 | *Rushdie's Sentence*

There is much to be said for having unhurried breakfasts alone, with ample time to read deep into the morning paper. This is particularly true on a lovely morning like today, after I stumbled on an article written by the novelist Salman Rushdie, an article that helps me (against my so-called better judgment) to appreciate him.

There is much to be said, as well, for having time each evening to relax in bed with a good book. It happens, however, that the book I'm reading these evenings sometimes makes it harder (in one sense) to enjoy the paper in the morning.

This book happens to be a pre-publication manuscript that Lorraine brought home a few months ago as part of her Random House homework. It has what at first I impetuously judged to be an awful title: *The New American Spirituality*. But then one of the interesting themes of this book is that we all need to look more directly at our ubiquitous human "judgmentalness," including its many double standards.* That theme speaks to me these days. And somehow the "double standards" rampant in the columns of the morning paper seem even clearer on reading this book. Its author, Elizabeth Lesser, also happens to treat a number of additional themes that speak to me right now. There is the usual list: Death, Virtue, Egotism, Meditation, and, of course, that questionable but mesmerizing topic called the Pursuit of Happiness.

Though the topics in this book are interesting, I find the unedited manuscript itself is hard going, particularly at those times when perhaps it strikes just a little too close to home. I notice that I haven't stopped reading it, however. Sometimes I go out of my way to find fault with the prose, or the line of argument, or the strange and almost random order of its chapters. (Yes, I know what you are thinking.) Nonetheless there is much that works well in this prototypic self-help book, despite its many daunting and different lists of Ten Steps for Pursuing Personal Growth.

One reason I keep being teased along in reading Ms. Lesser's self-help biography is that I keep finding new and wonderful quotations in it. Many of these quotations belong to wise others, but some belong to Ms. Lesser herself. This is not to say that all these quotations are wise. Last night, for instance, the following gem leapt off the as-yet unedited pages of Ms. Lesser's manuscript:

> One of the reasons that pop-psychology can come across as such drivel is that what actually goes on behind the therapist's door is very difficult to describe. Each time that I would emerge from a powerful [therapy] session and try to explain what had happened or what I had learned, I would hear myself sounding like a self-help book.

---

* This book was edited and then published in June 1999 by Random House USA. A paperback version was published in the fall of 2000 under the title *The Seeker's Guide*.

Life is full of so many ironies, deliberate and fortuitous, recognized and unrecognized. What happens between a therapist and a patient (off the pages of a self-help book) is indeed much more than can be painted with words. But of course it is different for every pair of protagonists and for each different therapy hour. Therapy, like life, even includes its share of drivel, not that one should expect or seek that. Although for my purposes Ms. Lesser's manuscript currently has many rough edges and spaced points of interest, last night I came on one section in which she describes at some length her reaction to sharing the dying days of a close woman friend. Here Lesser is quite eloquent, and to me at least, here her writing sings. That is why, this morning, mortality is on my mind. And that is why Salman Rushdie's article in the morning paper was able to touch me at last.

It is easy to dislike Rushdie's writing, at least for those of us who haven't yet learned to relax in the presence of a large and loud ego. But then I know so little of Rushdie's writings, and none of what he was known for prior to that famous second death sentence (the first death sentence coming when he quickened into life), the sentence that was pronounced over him by Muslim militants. That second sentence, and the large reward still offered by an Iranian foundation to anyone who becomes Rushdie's assassin, depress me beyond words. But my need to halt such injustice, that is my problem, and writing this today will hardly meet that need. If, however, the Muslim mafia ever do succeed in giving new meaning to Rushdie's "retirement," if they take it into their hands to confirm his mortality, it seems very likely they will thereby ensure that lasting attention is paid to the very work of literature that so offends them, the work that they so desperately hope to extinguish.

There is a sentence in Rushdie's article today that reads: *"Wherever my books find themselves—by a favoured armchair, near a hot bath, on a beach or in a late night pool of bedside light—that's my only home."* In one

sense this is Rushdie's way of confirming that now he has no home
other than in those mental hollows where his textual shadows fall. But
in what sense could that constitute a true home?

I see in Rushdie's attitude about this home further expression of an
unhelpful ego: wanting many readers, wanting to persuade them to his
often admirable (if judgmental) points of view, wanting never to die to
the world of historic literature. The irony is that these memoirs of mine
are clearly packed with much the same family of unhelpful motivations,
however much I sometimes try to exorcise such motives from the page
or from my thoughts. At least in Rushdie's case one may choose to approve that many of his prejudices are frankly paraded by him, where so
many other writers would try to persuade us under cover of reporting
objective news or providing simple entertainment.

It has been said that genes seek to endure. That viruses seek to endure. Even that *ideas* seek to endure, insofar as ideas may be construed
to be the children of genes. What then do we know that does *not* seek
to endure? Yet what do we know that could have any reasonable *hope* to
endure? I agree with Lesser, who, if I understand her correctly, reminds
us that nothing endures forever. We who are older, who are often sharply
aware of our pursuit of happiness, learn to look for happiness through
acceptance. Acceptance of the moment. And acceptance of the past. As
for the future, the retiree is sooner or later helped to let go of that, once
and for all. And what a surprising gift letting go turns out to be.

Rushdie, it seems to me, wants his future back: a future he never had
to begin with. He wants his eternal home in the literature of the future.
He, too, wants to affect eternity. Will Homer, or Plato, or Shakespeare
affect eternity? (I'm sure they will. Like every other person, they already
have.) And will their writings last more than six millennia? (Very probably not.) The day will come when Homer's prose goes extinct, just
as did those first transcriptions of his work. It seems far more likely
that the various publications of Rushdie and Ms. Lesser, or my writ-

ings, dear reader, or yours, will not last one one-hundredth as long as those of Homer. Rushdie's "home" in print is just as temporary as was Homer's Troy. As transitory as all things that live in time.

Rushdie was long ago sentenced to live completely in the wondrous now. My heart goes out to him, and to the rest of us. If only he could begin serving his sentence instead of doing time. If only we all could.

20 | *Weighing the Probabilities*

THURSDAY JUNE 24, 1999
KASLO, B.C.

*I*n my financially constrained state right now the normal queue at the cash register in Kaslo's drugstore takes on a new light. I used to be amazed at the number of people ahead of me who were standing patiently, holding no purchase in their hands, simply waiting for their turn to select one or more lottery tickets. Seeing them ahead of me, I would chuckle at the memory of that wonderful line: "To the first seven decimal places, the probability of winning the lottery is the same whether you buy a ticket or do not." And yet, as the sight of my friends in line now reminds me, life does not stop with the seventh decimal place.

Prior to retirement I was often assigned to teach statistics, which I quite enjoyed doing. Still, as a teacher, I had to wrestle long and hard in repeated attempts to overcome the difficulties of explaining probability theory. Ironically, my biggest difficulty was to keep students from reifying its theoretical worldview when they suddenly began to catch on to its simple (and persuasive) underlying logic.

I remember my own early years when the "laws" of probability first took on the appearance of incontrovertible facts. As a youngster living just inside Nevada, I became fascinated by both the mathematics and the psychology underlying that state's gaming industry. That gambling could be addictive was quickly clear to me. But for me it was very hard to understand *why* gambling would be addictive given the mathematical obstacles standing in the way of winning. Even harder to understand (as a youngster) was the fact that the ideal world to which probability theory applies, and the real world in which we live, may not be the same worlds, even if and after well-intentioned and superhuman efforts were made to merge them.

When something is extremely hard to understand, something that seems like it ought to be merely difficult, it is often the case that multiple phenomena are occurring, having various causes, each disguised as the same single phenomenon having but a single cause. Common colds certainly fit this pattern. They are of many different types and they arise in various ways. I'm sure that most addictions fit the same rule of multiple types. Even "single" phenomena generally have multiple causes, however, and according to chaos theory, chaotic phenomena (today's local weather, for instance) have an unlimited number of potentially significant prior influences.

Probability theory rests on the generally accepted assumption that the world to which it will be applied is not chaotic but instead is random. The difference is that two random events are completely independent of each other, and they share no jointly determining causal impulses trickling down from some common ancestral source. But chaos theory (at least in my imperfect and oversimplified understanding of it) assumes that tiny ancestral causal events may have some effects that *can* trickle down, practically forever, occasionally with their original effects being amplified as they go. And whereas probability theory describes events spread out across the infinitely long run, the real world seems to be filled with events in a finite and crowded lifetime run. In short, somewhere out beyond the seventh decimal place, probability theory may not apply to the world in which we live.

Probability theory certainly works effectively enough in most of the real-world situations to which it is generally applied, including most lotteries and games of chance. Similarly, many other approximate models of reality work well in their own limited domains: for instance, Newton's model of planetary motion. But limited functional utility does not equate with universal and literal truth. With Newton's model, somewhere out beyond a proverbial seventh decimal place, or when applied to moving objects approaching the speed of light, the model starts going noticeably wrong. It no longer agrees with observation. It is out here that Einstein's relativistic model still does seem to work. Einstein's model is "truer" in that sense.

By the same token, in my view probability theory starts going wrong somewhere out beyond its own proverbial seventh decimal place. A tiny gap starts to open up between the expectations of the theory and the observed frequencies of the very rare events being predicted by the theory. On those infrequent occasions where this discrepancy has been noticed, it has always been assumed that true randomness (true independence of events) was not achieved, and that is why the theory seemed disconfirmed. Moreover, it has also been assumed that true randomness could have been achieved with just a bit more effort. I agree that complete independence hasn't been achieved in these settings, but lately I have come to doubt that it ever could have been achieved.

Standing in the queue at the drugstore, with my financially challenged state much on my mind, I still feel no temptation to buy a lottery ticket. This is true despite my new appreciation for the near uselessness of one's last dollar, particularly if it is framed by the thrill of hope that, if put to risk, it might buy many new dollars. Nor am I tempted to buy a lottery ticket by my conviction that the random number generators that are used to produce the winning lottery numbers each week can never produce "truly random" output conforming to (and confirming) the ideal assumptions of probability theory. For while these lottery devices may not be truly random, they are practically random, out as far as, say, that sixth decimal place. They make the money they are expected to make, even if that amount is always a few unnoticed dollars different than the predictions of the formal theory.

The way I see it, there is a wonderful paradox here, but even the new teachings of chaos theory have not made that paradox apparent to students of probability. The paradox is this: Truly *understanding* randomness appears to be extremely difficult, yet, with effort, it is easily possible. Meanwhile, truly *achieving* randomness looks to be very easy, yet, however great the effort, in fact it is likely to prove impossible. Moreover, even if it were possible, it might yet remain impossible to prove that it had been achieved.

Meanwhile, I am getting ready to play medication roulette. When it is my turn at the drugstore cash register I will pay for a placebo called vitamin C. This is to ward off any incipient colds that I might feel coming on this summer. You see, I know from considerable reading of the research examining the effectiveness of vitamin C in preventing or curing colds, that invariably it averages no help at all, except when and if the research "blind" happens to be broken so that the research subjects figure out (from the taste, usually) whether they are receiving the placebo or the real thing. Thus, any observed vitamin C effect seems to be all placebo effect: It depends on believing that you are getting some effective acidic stuff. But that's fine. I happen to believe the label on the bottle that I hold in my hand. I believe I'm going to find real ascorbic acid in this bottle. So I reckon it should work for me. The odds appear to favour that anyway.

21 | *The Ritual of Retiring*

After a long vacation from television, Lorraine and I elected to spend the stormy evening yesterday with a hot cup of tea watching an inspiring videotape. From out of her personal brown paper bag, filling slowly with its own retirement treasures, Lorraine pulled one of Bill Moyers' interviews with Joseph Campbell, part of the PBS series *The Power of Myth*. This episode was about ritual and about its functions in helping us move through life. To my surprise, Campbell was soon talking about his own retirement years. But what he was *not* talking about was any ritual that accompanied his retirement. Could it be that he, of all people, experienced no retirement ritual at all? That certainly seems to occur frequently in this day and age.

Campbell was also talking a great deal about psychology, about human development, and particularly about the Big Questions we encounter as we go through life. He was talking about major life changes and some of the ways we attempt both to understand and accommodate to those changes. He had occasion to observe that human cultures have often used rituals to reveal the best ways to live, and to address the main anxieties of life. The best rituals, then, are wise teachers that prepare us for what is coming next.

Campbell notes that, death being our greatest source of anxiety and wonder, the first rituals for which we have unambiguous historical evidence were funerary rituals. But evidence for ancient rituals of initiation comes a close second. In Campbell's view, these various rituals, and most of the myths and religions for which we have good historical evidence, offer somewhat similar answers to those Big Questions. All their answers posit the existence of a transcendent truth, one that is beyond the reach of language yet not beyond our knowing. This truth has no location in space or time, being (as it were) everywhere at once, both spatially and temporally. The pathway to this truth, and even a reflection of it, is said to be given in consciousness. Full realization of this truth, full connection with it, brings a great peace and clarity about life. Campbell suggests that short of that full enlightenment, however, an inspired ritual can help bring a needed confidence in the new directions so often taken by our lives.

Still, according to Campbell, truly powerful rituals appear harder to come by today than ever. Even the Roman Catholic Church has deritualized most of its services and sacraments, and there is little in modern Western life (save perhaps in some inspired books and works of art) to help us find our path during a dark night of the soul. This is why Campbell was particularly grateful that our libraries still record many of the ancient myths that can act as our guides whenever we encounter another sharp bend in our life path, or whenever we arrive at a place where such a bend begs to be created.

Now it is hardly my contention that retirement constitutes a dark night of every soul (least of all my own). Yet I cannot help but wonder if retirement doesn't deserve its own powerful rituals and mythic stories to help us meet the terrors it already inspires in some, and to warn against the complacency of those others who do not recognize the impact that retirement certainly will have on the journeys that they have yet to complete.

What are our formal rituals for marking retirement? At worst, and typically, the answer seems to be that there are almost none. In India, however, Campbell tells us that many retirees deliberately don a new form of dress, take a new name, and pursue a new vocation. That new vocation is the one I mentioned in an earlier chapter, the religious vocation, a search for enlightenment.

Somewhat to my surprise, my own retirement experience is now beginning to look more like a dilute version of that Indian model than I first realized. Looking back, I see that from the day I retired and moved away from Toronto, my dress changed markedly. Gone were the tie, the dress shirt, the slacks, and dress shoes. In their place came wool shirts, jeans, and hiking boots or moccasins. Gone, too, were the professional names of "Professor G." or "Dr. G." and instead, to the friendly faces in Kaslo, I enjoyed being simply "Barney." Although this suited me just fine, I was never sure why it did. Could it be that my new Kaslo identity was a partial and satisfying substitute for not having undergone a properly profound retirement ritual?

All this is not to imply that my retirement went unremarked. I enjoyed two retirement events back in 1993. One was a dinner given by University College for a few of the college retirees, and one was an afternoon cocktail party given by the department of psychology. At both events I and others received a bit of personal roasting and some comforting praise. Gifts were presented. Not the gold watch of Victorian tradition, but in my case books—splendid books—to help fill my brown paper bag.

At my departmental party various comments were also made about the unseemly haste with which I was rushing into retirement, long before the sanctioned age of sixty-five. Some of these comments were only thinly disguised as humour, and it came as something of a surprise to discover that among my friends were some who appeared to be frightened at any implication that they, too, might soon have occasion to abandon the comfortable life. They seemed distressed that I had actually elected to abandon it. I wish now I had known to point out to them that, on the contrary, it is the comfortable life that consistently abandons us. I was only trying to welcome it in my own way.

Today, then, with the echoes of Joseph Campbell's observations still in my head, I'm beginning to think that retirements could profit from rather more ritual than we currently employ. I believe that, ideally, retirement ceremonies should be held for just one person at a time. I envision a ceremony at the beginning of which the retiree is formally requested, by an entry-level colleague, in front of the entire corps of co-workers, to address those assembled and to speak unhurriedly of four things: (1) his or her personal odyssey through a life of work, (2) remarkable changes in the local work world that he or she has observed taking place throughout those years, (3) personal perspectives and speculations about what might have been better ways for things to have been done during those years, and, by extension, in the future, and then (4) to end with a public statement of the retiree's intention now to let go of working life, together with some hint or public declaration of the path to which he or she will next turn.

At the close of this talk, one or more recent retirees from the same workplace, returned this day for this precise purpose, should rise to speak, praising the courage of the retiree, reiterating the public vow that he or she has just made to turn to new things, and offering encouraging words for success in this endeavour. The new retiree should then be well and ceremoniously dined.

Finally, all during the following (and final) week before full retirement, the retiree should receive a formalized series of individual office visits from his colleagues, allowing each of them to say goodbye, to talk about the retirement speech, and in every case to depart using the same ritual formula, one that would go something like this:

"As your former colleague, I now take my leave of you, and with me I take your former responsibilities here and your devotion to them."

(Exit the visitor.)

I can imagine Joseph Campbell's reaction to such a ritual. He'd probably say:

"By god, that ought to reduce the retiree to tears! And well it should!"

Indeed. And well it should.

22 | *A Beginner Again*

It was probably Alice, from the musical *Alice in Wonderland*, who crooned those sad "will-I-*ever*-learn" lyrics of the song that begins:

> *I give myself such very good advice*
> *but I very seldom follow it.*

I can no longer remember how the song continues, but no matter. Life is full of repeats, and some of them get transposed into a minor key, however hard we may try to be the sole composers of the music that is our lives.

The press of continued financial need recently induced me to accept an encore engagement in a Toronto classroom after a retirement sabbatical of seven years, there to teach a course in developmental psychology. I hadn't taught that particular course in over twenty years. My new course met just thirteen times, one evening each week, for a punishing three-hour time period. Last night it finished. As I was driving home, I suddenly noticed, to my surprise, that I was humming Alice's lament about not following her own good advice. And I had to laugh. Still, in order to change this insistent refrain, I also had to turn on the car radio to CBC 2, there to discover a timely broadcast of Beethoven's Pastoral Symphony. Alice had been hitting just a bit too close to home.

The last lecture in each course that I have taught has usually been among my favourite two or three of the year. Not because the course is completed, but because I feel a certain permission to philosophize in this final lecture, and to place the course in a much broader context, addressing some of those more personal questions with which my students may be wrestling. At least, that is how I have previously interpreted my pleasure and my nervousness over the preparation of an impending final lecture. But last night it hit me that in fact these final lectures, which always border on being preachy, are more than anything else directed at myself. They are "very good advice" for me, and only possibly very good advice (which is to say, workable advice) for some of my student listeners.

In these various final lectures that I have given (and in these pages, too), there is a curious tension between that preachy streak I recognize, one that tries at times to micromanage my own life using a faintly Calvinistic interior monologue, and a far more gentle voice, one that urges patience and forgiveness in all of us, but particularly in myself. Some of my students, I am sure, could hear this second voice in what I said last night, and some, alas, could probably hear the first. However, many of my students probably heard neither, because they are beginners at the unfolding art of listening, just as I am a beginner at the art of speaking to this younger evening audience, and a beginner at learning to bridge a new age gap between us that I had not felt prior to retiring.

My message last night, then, concerned a lesson that can be learned from a close study of child development and child psychology.

The lesson is that beginners face certain inevitable handicaps, among which is a crucial form of ignorance. Recognition of the mere fact of this ignorance can go a long way toward easing the difficulties it creates. But we have to do two things: (1) We have to realize that we are beginners, which is not nearly as easy as it sounds, and (2) we have to be willing to work patiently through the time it will take us to gain the knowledge we lack as beginners. Speaking for myself, this latter willingness can sometimes be very hard to come by. And it is all the harder if, during that time of waiting, we are impatiently telling ourselves that the years are quickly slipping by and our mental powers are ebbing.

Last night I didn't mention any of these latter thoughts, however. The years appear to stretch far ahead of these students, even if their looming final exam currently has some of them believing that their own mental powers are also ebbing dangerously. I began instead by reminding them of two concepts that we had met earlier in the course when looking at the psychology of four- and five-year-old children. One of these concepts is that of egocentrism. The other is the concept of realism in children's thinking.

Technically speaking, egocentrism is defined as *ignorance of the relativity of one's own point of view*. As such, egocentrism is quite distinct from egotism. Egotism carries implications of a pride and social self-centredness that are no part of egocentrism. Few four-year-olds are truly egotistical in the way that a fourteen-year-old can be. But few fourteen-year-olds are as pervasively egocentric as is the average four-year-old. An example will help make the distinction clear.

There is an experimental procedure in psychology that requires two participants. The procedure is called the Referential Communication Task. The two participants play the respective roles of communicator and recipient. They are seated so they cannot see each other but can easily talk to each other. Each one has in front of him or her the same set of nonsense shapes, sometimes called random shapes. These shapes have strange outlines and interior lines or curves, similar in some respects to the shapes that clouds sometimes take, or to those nameless shapes that sometimes substitute for profanity or pain in the balloons of a cartoon strip. The communicator finds these shapes laid out in a certain linear order, from left to right. But the recipient has them all jumbled up in front of him or her. The task is for the communicator and recipient, working together, using speech only, to get these unnamed shapes into the same order on the desk of the recipient as they are in front of the communicator.

It's not easy being a beginner at this task, but generally adults quickly learn to have fun with it, inventing all sorts of wonderful discriminating descriptions for what they're looking at. The communicator might say, for instance, "Now the next one looks something like two side-by-side elephant legs with a snake falling off the top of the leg on the left." The recipient might reply, "Does it have a couple of half circles at the bottom of the leg things?" And the communicator might say, "No; I see the one you are thinking of. That one will be the last one." And so it goes.

After they solve the task, the roles are reversed and same shapes are put in a different order in front of the former recipient, who now becomes the communicator. And this change of roles switches back and forth with each different order on each new trial. Quite soon, however, the two participants fall into a shorthand code that enables them to solve each new order in no time at all. The communicator may simply have to say: "elephants, circles, lightning, hydrant, periscope," etc. and the task is finished in jig time.

But with egocentric four-year-olds the scene is far different. The story has it that the very first pair of young children asked to do this task (given much simpler shapes) had the experimenters wondering why they had even bothered to try the experiment on young children in the first place. The communicator took the first shape in his hand, and speaking to his invisible partner announced, "The first one is *this* one."

The unfazed recipient picked up the top shape on his desk and said aloud, "You mean *this* one?" And the communicator replied, without so much as a glance in the direction of his invisible partner's voice, "No, not *that* one. *This* one!"

This is pure egocentrism: Each child shows a complete ignorance of the relative nature of his own knowledge state and its dependence on his personal point of view.* Egocentrism brings along with it certain other mental attitudes and illusions, and one of these is the tendency to "realism," or "realistic thinking," the second of the two concepts I recalled last night for my class.

Now in the jargon of psychology, "realism" does not mean at all what it sounds like it means. It does *not* denote thinking that is accurate and in accord with reality. It denotes thinking that is in accord with *appearances*, or with *first impressions*, rather than with reality. The "realistic" point of view, in this sense, is that everything really is exactly and only what it first appears to be. In my course I illustrate realism of this kind with a number of stories.

One of them is a story about the three-year-old daughter of a friend who refused to take her first airline flight with her parents, screaming in terrified protest at the airport because (it was later discovered) she knew that the airplane would soon go up into the sky, where, experience had already taught her, the higher it went the more it would shrink in size, until it would become so small that anyone inside would necessarily be crushed to death. For this "realistic" child, airplanes really do shrink.

Another story, illustrating the "realism" in a child's thought, is that of the youngster who lay in his hospital bed while the nurse at the nursing station tried again and again to speak to him via the intercom over his

---

* Another fine example of egocentrism is given in a "moron" joke of old. Two morons face each other across a wide and busy highway. One calls over to the other, "How do I get to the other side?" The other answers, "You moron! You *are* on the other side."

bed. Finally, in exasperation, the nurse said, "Come on, Bobby, answer me. I know you're there." After a slight pause a very frightened little voice asked, "W-w-whadda you want . . . wall?"

If it *seems* like the wall is talking, then indeed it *is* the wall that is talking. This is mental "realism" in action.

The way the psychology textbooks are usually written, egocentrism and realism (together with some related mental strategies of childhood) soon fade out, to be replaced with much more logical forms of thought. It would be easy to imagine that we are never again bothered by them after about the age of nine. But in fact all these early mental habits remain with us, and, I argue, they are still there to see in adult dreams and during states of exhaustion, illness, or great stress. Even aging can bring a return of realism and egocentrism. And, as I tried to suggest last night, being a beginner surely does, too.

We don't like to think of ourselves as beginners. Especially with a lifetime of experience behind us. Yet one lesson that the study of developmental psychology teaches is that we are *always* beginners. Being a beginner never stops. We find ourselves beginners at a new school, at a first job, after each promotion, upon marriage, when the first child comes along, when the very different second child arrives, when the children leave home, when our parents die, when we retire, when we cannot drive anymore . . . the list is endless. It doesn't generally seem endless, but in fact it is.

At each beginning, we have to learn the many surprising new things that relativize our experience. At our first job we have no hint as to how very much our experience depends on the recent history of the company, or how our experience would be different if new employees were easier or harder to find, or if the boss was happier or less happy at home, or if the economy was stronger or weaker, or if the country was or was not at war, etc. When we become parents, we have no hint as to how different our experience might be if we lived in a different neighbourhood, or if our baby had a different temperament, or if the pediatrician were a different person, or if our father-in-law had just retired, or if the country had different laws governing immigrant labour, etc.

We are ignorant of the relativity of our special point of view. We suffer from beginner's egocentrism. And this means suffering, at times, from some very convincing illusions. Which means in turn that a certain amount of pain and confusion will soon be inevitable.

This is what I told my class last night. I said that as beginners we cannot fully understand the relativity of our unique points of view and personal experiences. We don't recognize all the significant things that we are not understanding, even if we sometimes are made painfully aware of a few of the significant things that we don't understand. Beginners have no choice, then, but to simplify their world and their worldview. Which often means they oversimplify. And because beginners oversimplify, they also overgeneralize at first. What works the first time, or in one situation, is taken to be a law that should work every time, in all situations. But typically it turns out that the world is not simple and the apparent "law" will often fail to work as expected.

Beginner's egocentrism is always supplemented, I think, by what I call developmental realism. Developmental realism takes simplified appearances for the reality. It produces the illusion that development really takes place the way that, so often, it first looks like it is taking place. I distinguish four aspects of developmental realism.

First, it often looks as if development occurs as an abrupt change, or qualitative change, against a normal background of static equilibrium. Thus, changes in our lives often feel discontinuous, and unusual. Change is experienced as risky, and, other things equal, as if it probably should be stopped. It is rarely seen as normal and natural.

Second, at the same time, when change is successfully negotiated, it is usually experienced as being progressive and for the better.

Developmental realism makes it appear as if change and development proceed from the inferior to the superior, from the immature to the mature. Whatever is mature appears to be best. Once change is behind us, it often looks like things are much better than they were. (Oh yes, we *do* love to keep score, don't we?)

Third, it appears at first as if development is typically goal directed, as if it is intended to achieve some final, normal, ideal. It appears as if development will stop when this goal state is reached. Then there will be nothing further needing change, nothing further to say about it except perhaps that timeless and formulaic silence we all once learned: ". . . and they lived happily ever after." But if, god forbid, the changes don't stop at the imagined apex of development, then of course any further changes appear to represent a "decline" or loss.

A fourth and final aspect of developmental realism is the common illusion that the changes we are experiencing now (or will experience next) are the biggest changes ever, and, if only they can be successfully negotiated, they are likely to be the last significant and difficult changes that we will face for a very long time to come. It is as if each developmental hurdle is seen as being the final one, and, of course, the highest and most difficult one of all.

Yet the reality seems to be that life is continuous change, unchanging change. History is chaotic. It never truly repeats itself. The context of change is always new because history is deeper, older, and richer than it was before. Personal histories are no exception. We come to each new day something of a beginner in a newly changed world. But rarely can we appreciate how much our beginner's status affects our behaviour and our unrealistic expectations of ourselves. And without that appreciation it is hard to do very much about it.

There is a lesson in all this—more than one lesson, in fact. But the primary lesson, it seems to me, is that we need a great deal more patience in the world, greater tolerance of our status as beginners, greater recognition that we may be wrong in what we imagine to be true, yet willing to call it true for now, while we must, as we gather the experience that will help us discover what may be truer. It is not a failure to be a beginner, to be egocentric, to be discouraged, to suffer from illusions. That is the human condition. But the human condition brings us joys and successes, too. And so last night I ended my lecture by saying:

> What is important is how we react to our human condition. And how we react *depends*. It depends very much on the meaning we assign to our experience. It depends on whether we tell ourselves that we are failures, or merely beginners who can still do better. And just what is it that we are assuming would *constitute* this "*better*"? Because we also have to recognize that we may be beginners at knowing what *better* might truly be for us now, at this time of life. *Better* might not be what our realism is telling us it is.
>
> If we can just learn to recognize our beginner's egocentrism and all that goes with it, then the experience of growing wiser can be much more satisfying. Let us try to be patient with ourselves. Let us try to avoid the illusion that says we know something only if our grades are high, or our income is high, or if we are granted great powers or public praise. The important thing is to try to really know ourselves. And that requires both tolerance and time.

Well, I do think I gave myself some very good advice there. But even for me, hearing it again after these early years of retirement, it still isn't clear how one achieves the intention to *follow* that advice. So I had to laugh when a number of students came crowding up to speak to me afterwards, each of them with questions about . . . their upcoming final exam! And I stood there answering cheerfully, all the while unconsciously humming the tune that Alice sings so poignantly: "I give myself such very good advice . . ."

Thank goodness for Beethoven's Pastoral Symphony. Yes, retirement represents another opening movement, and, happily, it sometimes deserves Beethoven's opening notation to that sixth symphony: "On awakening to feelings of joy in the countryside."

23 | *The God of Old Age*

*U*ntil 1993 I had long assumed that, among its other pleasures, retirement would be filled with reading. Reading the classics and reading fine recent fiction would make the afternoons glow with pleasure, or so I imagined. However, as with so many other preconceptions, it has turned out rather differently. There have been major periods over recent years when I didn't—even couldn't—bring myself to read any fiction. The long shadow of my cardiac scare, my father's death, the dissolution of my lengthy marriage, all combined to drain away the playful reader in me, the one who enjoys the mental stretch and travel occasioned by reading good fiction. Instead, when I did read, it was invariably the non-fiction that I picked off that pile of Christmas and birthday books that Lorraine so generously gives to those closest to her.

Recently, however, all this has changed following the unexpected receipt of a gift from a friend who lives abroad. She sent me a copy of her favourite novel, one that I had promised to read but never quite

170

managed to get around to starting. Out of a sense of duty I set about reading this book, and in the end, naturally, I loved it. Afterwards I wanted to give her one of my own favourite novels. I had been urging her for some time to read *Fifth Business*, by Robertson Davies. For a time, twenty years ago, this book had been my favourite novel in all the world. So I purchased a paperback copy of it and prepared to post it back overseas, with thanks for the very enjoyable book I had received.

But just before posting the novel I was tempted to read the first page again. And then the second. After which, there was no turning back. I read it all through again. There was so much that I had forgotten, and so much pleasure remained in the story, even though a few of the stunning surprises late in the book were no longer surprises.

I discovered during this reading a scene that I had quite forgotten, dealing with the return of Christ, a scene that reminds me of the famous *Grand Inquisitor* chapter in Dostoyevsky's *The Brothers Karamazov*. Davies is not Dostoyevsky, nor is he trying to be. His suggestive passage is far shorter than that book-within-a-book Dostoyevsky wrote. In *Fifth Business* the protagonist has met a charming, aging Jesuit priest with a particularly flamboyant temperament. In return for providing his new friend with gourmet food and drink, our hero is treated to some remarkable conversation and philosophy. Here are the passages that leapt off the page as I read. (They have been selected in such a way to help preserve one of Davies' plot secrets, and to keep to my topic.) The Jesuit, Padre Blazon, is speaking. He says:

> You know that Jesuit training is based on a rigorous reform of the self and achievement of self-knowledge. By the time a man comes to the final vows, anything emotional or fanciful in his piety is supposed to have been rooted out. I think I achieved that, so far as my superiors could discover, but after I was forty I began to have

notions and ask questions that should not have come to me. Men
have this climacteric, you know, like women. Doctors deny it, but
I have met some very menopausal persons in their profession. But
my ideas—about Christ for instance. He will come again, will He?
Frankly I doubt if He has ever been very far away. But suppose He
comes again, presumably everybody expects He will come to pull
the chestnuts out of the fire for them. What will they say if He
comes blighting the vine, flogging the money-changers out of the
temple one day and hobnobbing with the rich the next, just as He
did before? He had a terrible temper, you know, undoubtedly inherited from His Father.

But it happens to be aging that most concerns old Blazon. Soon he goes
on to say:

My own idea is that when He comes again it will be to continue His
ministry as an old man. I am an old man and my life has been spent as
a soldier of Christ, and I tell you that the older I grow the less Christ's
teaching says to me. I am sometimes very conscious that I am following the path of a leader who died when He was less than half as old as
I am now. I see and feel things He never saw or felt. I know things He
seems never to have known. Everybody wants a Christ for himself and
those who think like him. Very well, am I at fault for wanting a Christ
who will show me how to be an old man? All Christ's teaching is put
forward with the dogmatism, the certainty, and the strength of youth:
I need something that takes account of the accretion of experience, the
sense of paradox and ambiguity that comes with years! I think after
forty we should recognize Christ politely but turn for our comfort and
guidance to God the Father, who knows the good and evil of life, and
to the Holy Ghost, who possesses a wisdom beyond that of the incar-
nated Christ.

For Dunstan Ramsay, our protagonist here, age is not yet a focus of concern in his life. He is more concerned with another issue. Blazon gives him some further advice about that, and then continues:

> I can see what is in your sour Scotch eye. You think I speak thus because of this excellent picnic you have provided. "Old Blazon is talking from the inspiration of roast chicken and salad, and plums and confectioneries, and a whole bottle of Beaune, ignited by a few brandies," I hear you thinking. "Therefore he urges me to think well of myself instead of despising myself like a good Protestant." Nonsense, Ramezay. I am quite a wise old bird, but I am no desert hermit who can only prophesy when his guts are knotted with hunger. I am deep in the old man's puzzle, trying to link the wisdom of the body with the wisdom of the spirit until the two are one. At my age you cannot divide spirit from body without anguish and destruction, from which you will speak nothing but crazy lies!
>
> You are still young enough to think that torment of the spirit is a splendid thing, a sign of a superior nature. But you are no longer a young man; you are a youngish middle-aged man, and it is time you found out that these spiritual athletics do not lead to wisdom. Forgive yourself for being a human creature, Ramezay. That is the beginning of wisdom; that is part of what is meant by the fear of God; and for you it is the only way to save your sanity . . .

These passages are found on pages 176–78 of my Penguin Canada paperback copy. There is an echo of them, found much later in the book, on page 242. Perhaps it will not be giving too much away to quote this much of that echo here. The speaker in this case is "Ramezay," [i.e., Dunstan Ramsay] and he is speaking to an over-achieving childhood friend of long-standing, one who is fighting off something like his own climacteric.

. . . You want to pass into oblivion with your armor on, like King
Arthur, but modern medical science is too clever to allow it. You must
grow old—you'll have to find out what age means and how to be old.
A dear old friend of mine once told me he wanted a God who would
teach him how to grow old. I expect he found what he wanted. You
must do the same, or be wretched. "Whom the gods hate they keep
forever young."

Now to me this splendid fiction provides stronger drink and a richer
feast than any of the recent non-fiction I have been consuming, with
the possible exception of Hofstadter's original book *Gödel, Escher, Bach*,
which I recently reread. (Well, no, of *course* I didn't reread *all* of GEB—
but all the good parts, yes.) Not to say that Davies' fiction is wholly digestible, or that it ends up with all the right answers. But I submit that,
for a retiree, *Fifth Business* asks all the right questions and offers some
very helpful leads to finding personal answers. If some Lorraine doesn't
give it to you for Christmas, perhaps you might give it to yourself, as
I inadvertently did.

As for finding any "god" who will teach us how best to grow old,
it is hard to imagine one god preaching to a multitude on that topic.
Growing old is too much an individual matter, and finding the gracious
pathway probably means doing one's own continuous daily search. Let's
not forget, however, that the right work of fiction can help. And it can
help a very great deal if the mental soil has first been well prepared.

For that preparation, then, perhaps we can look to near non-fiction.
Or, perhaps, to certain of our friends.

24 | *Naps and Maps*

*R*etirement offers many opportunities for naps. And naps, in contrast to our deeper sleeps at night, more often seem to bring dreams that one can remember on awakening. This afternoon I slipped into a nap while reading Sharon Butala's soft little booklet *Coyote's Morning Cry*. It was more by accident than anything else that I recently picked up this book, during a rest stop at a potter's studio *cum* book and tea shop in Eastend, Saskatchewan, while Lorraine and I explored our preferred yellow-brick road across Canada, from Kaslo to Terra Cotta. But accident or not, *Coyote* turned out to be a very happy purchase. Like that other of Butala's wonderful books, *The Perfection of the Morning*, it shares with its readers a great deal that is personal and thought-provoking.

    Coyote is a series of meditations on aging, although it doesn't exactly claim to be that. Rather, it claims to be a report on one person's search for inner truth. Maybe that's what aging is—a search for truth. I'm not sure. But for me, aging, like retirement, seems more involved with the creation of personal maps, maps that chart the discoveries of our searching, maps that point us in the direction of inner truth even if, by themselves, they do not yet take us there.

Dreams, too, may be helpful in mapping the route to inner truth. That appears to be Butala's view. On at least two important occasions in her book she examines a significant dream that she has had, and she alludes to other dreams that seem to have helped her find her way in life. Although she and I appear to have different theories about the origin and significance of dreams, still, her somewhat Jungian interpretations of her own dreams seem very appropriate in the circumstances.

Some dreams certainly are memorable, far beyond their mundane contents or illogical plot lines. I believe these particularly memorable dreams, with their auras of special significance, do finally justify what we "learn" from them, whatever may be their ultimate sources and however imperfect may be our existing tools for their interpretation.

For me, memorable dreams are the canvas on which we more or less successfully attempt to paint the interpretations that our deepening wisdom next requires. I suspect that other canvases could serve almost as well if only we believed enough in them. In fact, my guess is that if some random dream of someone else were written down, and if (perhaps via hypnosis) I were successfully led to believe that this other person's dream had actually been my own dream (previously written down and forgotten), then my attempts at interpreting that exogenous dream could help me learn as much about myself as would any similar attempt to interpret an earlier dream that truly had been my own.

Be that as it may, influenced by Sharon Butala's dream prose, by the gloom and rain of an equinoxial afternoon, and by a certain heavy uncertainty about what inner work I may now be in the process of trying to carry out—I fell asleep. And I had a dream.

This much of it I remember: My young love and I arrive at the edge of a wilderness area, there to rendezvous with half a dozen other young people. We will spend the night in (for me) uncomfortable youth-hostel accommodations, and then in the early morning we will all set off for a beautiful three-day trip in the park. Our sleeping arrangements here are curious. Three of the others are bedded down on one long narrow shelf, with pairs of legs straddling either another's head or another's legs to make all three fit. My love and I are on the nicest "bed," still very primitive, close by. We have no privacy and little comfort.

What happens next is very vague. I go outside to see if something better might be arranged, but once outside it is now the next morning, and our guide seems to be gone. Something has happened and it looks like we will be unable to take this trip because of the guide's disappearance. At about this point in the dream, as I am looking for the guide around the complex of buildings in the area, I note (in passing, on a wall) a large topographical map of the wilderness park we had expected to visit. But I am in too much of a hurry to stop and study it closely, and I fail to get a good fix on where this map is pinned up so I can return to it. I note only the myriad of wonderful lakes dotting the map before continuing on my way.

It soon becomes clear that the day is rapidly passing and we are now definitely too late to take the three-day trip even if the guide does return and even if the now scattered group of young people could be found and brought together. My love passes by, and I see she is not feeling nearly as warm toward me as before. But from her I learn that our trip was to have taken us in to see Lake Claux. (She pronounces this name to rhyme with "blow" but I confirm its correct spelling with her, having somehow understood all along that it was to be spelled "Claux.")

At once I determine to win back her love by finding that lake on the map and guiding just the two of us there in the time remaining. But then I am unable to find the map, and my mounting frustration leads me to have a kind of panicky tantrum. My love becomes even more annoyed with me because of this, and I feel guilty to have acted so "childishly."

The dream is interrupted very soon after, when I wake up. But by that time I am now pronouncing "Claux" like the English word "clue." And there is a residual aura of smarty-pants pride that I feel at knowing how the name should be properly spelled.

A reader versed in the traditional literature of Freudian dream interpretation will doubtlessly "recognize" at once that this dream, with it's many "clues," was apparently "made to be interpreted." Given my reading matter when I slipped into my nap, it was very probably a dream about dreaming, or about dream interpretation, or about the significance of dreams, or all of these together. And when I awoke, curiosity about this dream was fresh in mind, a rare state of affairs for me.

Of course there are other, more personal interpretations that may be pursued: references to "my love," to "childishness," to "mounting" frustration, to "guilt." Lovely oedipal doors, those, for the believer to open and walk through.

But what struck me most about this dream were the many allusions to a journey with others, younger others, and the allusions to maps, guides, and clues. Or perhaps the allusions are to decipherment. Whatever they may be, in the dream my guide disappears, and my map cannot be found.

Where are we going here? We appear to be going nowhere without a guide or a map, and young love is annoyed by the waiting. Is this then a dream of impatience? Retirement as "the waiting room"? Retirement as the time of renewed dependency on others? Retirement as a crossroads devoid of any signposts? (Which, pray, is the road that will not simply lead us back to Rome, back to Caesar?) Time is short. There seems to be so little time left in which to reach the distant goal. And how very disappointed, even censorious, will my conscience be if I don't reach that goal and complete my chosen journey.

The literal journey that is uppermost in my mind this week is the journey just completed: the journey from Lake Kootenay to the

Caledon Hills outside Toronto; the journey through Butala's remote corner of Saskatchewan and east through small-town and francophone Manitoba—Lorraine as my co-driver, and the finest maps that money can buy lying open on my lap.

But that journey is now over and today I am at a fork in the road on a more figurative journey: the writing of this "journal." (*Le journal*, in French.) And now, suddenly, it hits me—all the French connections behind this dream: those first canoe trips with my friend David Watson in Algonquin Park. Mock "voyageurs," the two of us. Our affected French accents. His "Jacques-Louis" to my "Jean-Bernard." Is this the heritage leading to Lake Claux? "Wilderness" as a youthful Eden to which we fear we will never return? The wilderness of yesteryear, with two voyagers discovering its secrets and mapping its beauties?

There is much about the inner wilderness that appears to be anything but beautiful. Or should we say, much that has an unfamiliar and as-yet-unrecognized beauty? Words, exactly like our maps, fail to capture the terrifying, discontinuous topography of this inner wilderness. Here, too, we find dragons and monsters painted over those fog-filled regions where a great *Terra Incognita* meets our imagined *terra cognita*. The placement of such graphic beasts does nothing to reassure the inner voyager who may be feeling faint of heart. So in my dream I choose to explore this realm with others, lending and receiving moral support and guidance as will be needed. Yet somehow, exactly as fairy tales have always foretold to us, our companions will drop away and we will become separated from the group. Our loved ones will leave. Our guides will disappear. We appear to be left with no choice but to forge on into the beckoning wilderness, alone, carrying only a map, parts of which may already be washed an indistinct gray following the spill of earlier tears, indecipherable, a map that is itself aged, and now stamped "out of date."

It is not just naps and dreams that might help us to chart some of the key spaces on whatever fogged map we carry with us. Books can help, too. The challenge is to find the right book for us, and the right pages in it, and the places where those landmarks will be found that match what we see when we open our interior eyes to spy out the landscape there. Maybe it *will* be on *this* page. Or . . . maybe on the next.

25 | *A New Page*

*L*ate last November, Lorraine and I adopted a six-week-old Border Collie puppy shortly before this puppy adopted us. Her name is Page. Why? Well, because she is black and white, and because she can be so hugely entertaining to read. Her breeder, Margaret, seemed to think that Page might be rather a wimpy name. But she was calling this puppy Pretty Little Girl at the time, so in that respect at least we didn't feel particularly threatened by her apparent disapproval.

Margaret seemed very keen that we choose this puppy and not one of the other eight in the same litter. There is no question that she knows more about Border Collies than we will ever know. But at first it wasn't clear to us that Page would be the puppy we wanted, especially because at age five weeks a couple of the other pups seemed so much more interested in adopting us.

Margaret's reasons for wanting us to choose Page had a lot to do with her estimation of how well or poorly we might fare in the inevitable tussle for Alpha status that would occur as we raised our pup and he or she shaped us. When, one week later, we finally overcame our resistance to Margaret's implicit directives and admitted to ourselves that "Pretty Little Girl" was actually the puppy that we also wanted (despite our perceived lack of much remaining choice in the matter), we had little thought or concern for who would become the Alpha member in our new family pack.

Page weighed only five pounds when she arrived home, and at first she was in no mood to do much more than eat and sleep and follow us lovingly about the house.

Now Margaret herself appears to be very much the Alpha in her relationships with her clients, and certainly with her dogs. (There are probably only six ways to raise a puppy: five wrong ways and Margaret's way.) Like her dogs, Margaret is slight of build and full of energy. Her dogs jump when she says jump, and some of her clients would be hard-pressed not to do the same when so ordered. (I know because I jumped.)

Page came home with us in a small crate (a cat crate, actually) that Margaret lent to us pending our purchase of her recommended standard-sized crate. It was arranged that we would return this borrowed crate a month later and would bring along Page when we did.

When the time came, Lorraine and I were both ever so slightly nervous, and just a bit puzzled as to why we would be nervous. Page was turning into a pretty great pup and we had made (we thought) good progress in socializing her.

Page was on a leash when we brought her in to see Margaret. She no longer recognized Margaret in the unfamiliar setting where our meeting took place, and when Margaret approached her, she immediately showed her a submissive belly. Margaret's first words to us were: "Oh, she's much too heavy. How much have you been feeding her?"

During the next few minutes we were instructed to cut down on Page's food, to get her into a puppy school right away, to tighten her collar, and to make sure she starts meeting other dogs soon. To us Page looked trim, happy, and well socialized. But Margaret somehow neglected to add anything positive about her.

A couple of days later we had a date with our neighbour and friend, John, who is also our veterinarian. I mentioned Margaret's concern about Page's weight and in response I got a marvelous illustrated lesson in how to assess the proper weight of a dog. John used Page to show how the ribs should be invisible but easy to feel, how the waist should tuck slightly in, and how to assess other subtle signs of perfect weight. Page was, that morning, a fine exemplar of the perfect profile of a healthy dog.

"How much are you feeding her, then?" John asked.

When I told him he said just what Margaret had said, i.e., that it was already time to cut down on (and soon cut out) the middle meal of the day. We should soon feed Page only two-thirds of what she had been eating during her peak growth period. But as long as we were giving her lots of exercise, there was little chance she would ever get too heavy.

This all took place two months ago, when Page was three and a half months old. Quite recently, however, just before we were both to be away on business, Lorraine and I decided that in our absence the best place for Page might be back at Margaret's. Knowing that Margaret currently had a small home full of dogs, and a new litter due while we would be gone, plus a different litter of Jack Russell pups not yet fully dispersed, we doubted that Margaret could or would consent to board her.

To our pleasant surprise, however, she did agree.

And then she cheerfully asked: "Is there anything you'd like me to work on while she's here?"

We were delighted by the generous offer, but not quite surprised.

"Well, yes, Page still needs work on the command *down*," we told her.

And from that moment, chez nous, we began calling Margaret's home Margaret's Happy Boot Camp.

On the afternoon before our departure I drove Page out to Boot Camp. As instructed, I brought along her spacious new crate (her bedroom while at Margaret's) and a seven-day supply of dog food (a small cup's worth for each of fourteen feedings, plus one more for good measure). When I walked in, Margaret temporarily ignored Page and immediately tried to sell me on the charms of her one remaining Jack Russell puppy. I was in no position to submit, because this is not a breed that I have learned how to love. I excused myself, set up Page's new crate, but then didn't see Page anywhere around. It turns out that she blended right in with the other Border Collies, each of whom was watching me at work assembling her crate from Margaret's apartment block of stacked crates. When I left to drive home, no mention had been made of Page's superb weight.

That evening, Lorraine phoned Margaret to add to my meagre list of things on which Page might need "work." This time Margaret immediately had us on the defensive, complaining of Page that "she doesn't know her name!" We were later to discover that, initially, when Margaret called Page by name, Page was either not listening or was ignoring this unfamiliar voice. Margaret immediately reverted to the call that weeks before had always brought Page and her eight siblings running: a high-pitched "Puppypuppypuppy!" Page showed complete insensitivity to Margaret's feelings, if not also a seriously flawed intelligence, by continuing to ignore her. Margaret was not amused.

Still, we were relaxed during our trip, knowing that Page was in fact in the best possible hands, and, moreover, that she was socializing with her maternal grandparents and other Border Collies, all of whom had the run of a large fenced yard.

The morning I went to fetch Page home, Margaret reported, to my great delight, that Page had fit right in, that she had made a dear friend of one of her two-year-old aunts, and that she hadn't been any trouble. Margaret was a bit sleep deprived that morning because the newest set of puppies had only just begun arriving the night before. Her praise of Page was all the sweeter in the face of her strain. Just before I departed I was handed the remaining bag of the dog food I had provided. I had to stare. It was still half full! Trying not to be obvious about it, I ran my hands down Page's ribs and decided that while she was certainly thinner, she was not yet undernourished.

It happens that Page is the first dog for which I have shared responsibility in over thirty years. The cats that I have cared for, like Sophie, always assumed their own responsibilities and/or were the responsibility of the woman in my life. But Page came clearly identified as our joint responsibility, the proverbial child of the childless Lorraine and Barney.

Lorraine's response to this heavy responsibility was to buy six books on the proper raising of a pup. All six agreed with Margaret's apparent belief that a firm if loving rule is needed to avoid becoming the Beta dog in one's own home. So when our would-be Alpha dog eventually took on the retired psychology professor, who was going to prevail? (Who had damn well better prevail!)

I have read, and you probably have, too, that seniors who have pets live longer and on average show less stress than do seniors without pets. It has the ring of truth to it, this myth, but I know of no persuasive data to support the idea that adding an animal to one's life really does add years as well. Maybe it is the other way around. Maybe those who are brave enough to be lion tamers or dog trainers are going to live longer anyway, and that only they are likely to have the courage to add animals to their lives, animals that may reflect badly on them in a boot camp world, a dog-eat-dog world, a world red in tooth and claw.

There can be no question, however: Reducing stress is important. Personally, I am trying more and more these days to live a life of relaxed scepticism, a life that accepts that all I still *don't* know could trivialize or negate my worldview and each of my cherished working theories. This acceptance is supposed to bring me calm and patience, and it is supposed to bring my friends and loved ones comfort.

But now I see it can take its own kind of toll, too. It can lead on to certain "dirty secrets" and to an apparent indifference to what others hold dear. For yes, currently I harbour a new and uncomfortable secret. I, an aging expert in the history of psychology (including the historical work on animal learning that is the basis of most current dog school dogma) believe that the "pecking order" semantics of Alpha owner and Delta dog are of restricted utility and questionable validity. Thus I find that I am a traitor to fashionable dog psychology and to those six books on puppies that we have dutifully read.

I want Page to become an individual, one whose potential "mistakes" are not mine to minimize, let alone mine to forbid. To my way of thinking there is no danger whatsoever that Page will not be devoted to me and to Lorraine whether we are lax or strict. I think it only fair that we each take our turns now and then as the Gamma and Beta in what others insist on seeing as our family pack. I don't want to risk Page's life allowing her to chase cars, and I won't offer her the chance to elect such a risk if I can help it. I do want her to come, or to lie down, on command, and I will ask her to figure that out. But she deserves the free choice she always has to put her priorities elsewhere.

Or so in secret I continue to think. Whatever her genes, I don't think Page's psychology resembles textbook pack psychology at all. I think she's a complete, if charming, mystery. And damn smart to boot. Because she is so smart, the learning theory they apply at puppy school is working well on her. Because she is smart, she *elects* to do exactly what others still believe that Pavlov promised she would do like a robot.

We are in love, she and I and Lorraine. We each obey the dictates of our hearts. We all are stressed, not by the prospect of becoming Betas in our own homes, but by seeing other family members in pain. So our hearts bid us to come when invited, and to lie down when invited. And perhaps that is one of the nicest aspects of being retired. You can always accept a new invitation to lie down. Happily.

26 | *Why Read? Why Write?*

SUNDAY NOVEMBER 11, 2001
TERRA COTTA, ONTARIO

*I*t is Remembrance Day today, two months to the day after 9/11. All the glory has left the trees here and rain has leached the forest floor a uniform, translucent bronze. The air today is filled with tiny seeds of corn snow thoroughly confused over which way is down. If we were going to be home this afternoon there would surely be a fire in the fireplace. But we are not. And so there isn't.

I have been at loose ends for some weeks now. Recently I was laid low by a third cold in what seems like as many seasons. My watering eyes made reading a great effort. My unfocused thoughts made writing seem hopeless. And then today I picked up the most recent issue of *The Economist* and found there, almost by chance, a review of a forthcoming book of essays by Susan Sontag. The reviewer quotes her on the topic of why essayists like Roland Barthes write, saying: "The point is not to teach us something in particular. The point is to make us bold, agile, subtle, intelligent, and detached. And to give pleasure."

This may or may not be why Barthes wrote, or even why Sontag writes, but it certainly has a seductive and exalted ring to it. A writer might well aspire to "make" readers into something closer to Sontag's heroic image, however "bold" (yet unsubtle) that image may prove to be. Still, I doubt that writers can bring it off. Only readers can hope to do that. For themselves.

This is not to say that most writers don't *aim* to entertain, educate, persuade, and change their readers. I'm sure most do. Writers of fiction, of non-fiction, even memoirists would each like to "make a difference." By which I think they secretly mean, "make my reader more like some better parts of me." Some *fiction* writers are modelling their aesthetic vision for us, some are modelling their psychological vision, some, their moral vision. Many *non-fiction* writers are trying, with varying degrees of subtlety, to teach and/or persuade. Or they are trying to create a privileged point of view, or to propagate some meme that lies close to the author's heart. And the *memoirists*, presumably, are motivated by some combination of the same motives that drive the writers of fiction and non-fiction. (Certainly memoirs appear to have their fictional aspects.) But let us not forget Sontag's tag line. The writer writes for whatever reasons: "And, to give pleasure."

Now I would word that slightly differently. I would say the writer writes "to *share* pleasure." For again, successful writing itself is the first pleasure. A pleasure given only to oneself. It is the joy of finding the right words, of achieving and capturing what could so easily have remained tantalizing and evanescent and out of reach. It is a joy that may partake of narcissism or pride, or one that may be something quite different, being mostly a grateful and surprised delight. The gift of a new muse.

Sometimes the *act* of writing remains the only pleasure, but for most writers a special reader, or a multitude of readers, is always assumed, always hoped for. For most writers, a sharing is wanted. I see their motives long since present in infancy, in the child who enthusiastically exploits her new skills at directing a parent's gaze. Her urgent pointing. Her fervent invitations to look. This need to share experiences seems to be in our marrow. Artists, most of them, appear to feel it particularly. The painter, the composer, the writer, each wants to share the pleasures of their creations, the surprises of their experience, the wonders of the things they love.

To be sure, there can be other reasons to write. Sometimes I write to clarify for myself what I think, or even to discover what (perhaps) I might wish to think. Yet sometimes, as during the nine weeks since September 11, I would like to write but cannot. I can only read and be grateful to those few journalists who are writing especially for me, offering some of their readers useful insights into the confusing nature of these times. With any luck, these writers help me understand part of why I am so distressed by the amplified rhetoric and sad politics of so many good nations and inspired citizens currently in the process of refusing to be *good*.

By which, today, I mean refusing to be *compassionate*. And *honest*.

A lot of what appears to be a refusal to be good these days may well be the product of different strategies for coping with current uncertainties. In the search for more security and for "justice," some strategies focus primarily on not doing further harm, at the risk (later) of not having done enough good, while other strategies focus on not doing too little, at the risk (now) of doing much further harm. Some strategies focus on a perceived need to act quickly, but they do so at the risk of acting rashly, while other strategies focus on the need to understand before we act, at the risk of acting too late.

Such views about competing strategies assume that all involved are good people who have understandable differences in their perceptions of strategic risks. But unhappily I can't bring myself to believe that all the people currently taking warlike actions, or even all those opposing warlike actions, are good people in that sense. I suspect that they want to be good. But I think that rather a lot of them are unable to be good because of various worldviews they have invited into their lives, and various bridges they have burned behind them in the past.

Of course it doesn't really matter what I think. I know that. And I wonder just how "good" I would manage to be, were I in their shoes right now. The confusion I feel these days probably does matter, however. Readers who can remember Remembrance Day in 2001 may very well recall having shared similar feelings of confusion themselves. Feelings that seemed to promise they might go away if only the right words were to be written down somewhere, and then found, and read. And when retirement offers us increased opportunities to read, it seems we have the greater duty to go find such words.

Maybe our feelings promise too much. Perhaps it is the human condition to live always at risk, always feeling uncertainty. The deeper we go into retirement, and the less reliable become both our fitness to see into the heart of things and our ability to act skillfully, the greater then becomes our need to find calm in the face of increasing risk and deepening uncertainty. One place I can find some of that calm right now is among friends. That is why it is so reassuring for me to know that late this afternoon we are about to drive into Toronto for a dinner, in front of a fire, at the home of Lorraine's welcoming relatives. And perhaps, in the glowing embers of that fire, I can begin to read some further answers. Provisional answers, yes. But calming ones all the same.

27 | *Shadows of Doubt*

*M*uch depends on what, each day, we are able to know. And yet there is always so much we still don't know. Very probably, over a lifetime, we will never be able to intuit even the smallest portion of this as-yet-unimaginable unknown. How that fact compromises what we think we know! How completely it must relativize our supposed wisdom! Reading the histories of ideas, of religion, of technology, and of science, one is tempted to say about those earlier times: "If only they had known about X ... how differently they would then have seen the world; how differently they would have behaved." Yet today, how often do we pay a proper respect to all that remains completely unknown to *us*?

This week, while I navigate among various mental shadows cast by (1) a recent book review giving me a clouded window into a patient's earthshaking experience of aphasia following a stroke, (2) my reading of the complicated history of changing Christian doctrine and theology detailed in the book *The River of God*, and (3) thinking about my mother's mental state (and my own when my time comes) as she suffers incapacitation from congestive heart failure and various pulmonary complications, I again find myself thinking about our imperfect knowledge. Not as any limitation on what we might or might not believe we know, but rather as a limitation on what we can or cannot doubt.

So many things seem to depend at least as much on what we are able to doubt as on what we are able to believe.

For instance, for some unknown reason I can quite easily doubt the common theory that tells us our minds seek to maximize comfort, the theory that tells us beliefs and doubts are there to help us avoid discomfort, whether this be done consciously or unconsciously. Clearly, the mind does both avoid and seek certain things, or so it appears, but whatever may be the states we seek, they are so variable and so personal, i.e., so different for different people at different times, that I question whether psychology can soon even glimpse them, let alone accurately describe them, or confirm their existence. Why do others find this evidence so hard to credit, while I find it so easy?

One might be tempted to say: "We are the prisoners of our past, prisoners of just those beliefs we can credit today; we have no freedom to doubt certain things, and no freedom to believe other things that seem to falsify what currently we do believe." Yet even that statement declares its own article of faith, one that I may doubt for a time, then later be unable to doubt. However much volition and choice may play some role in how I choose to act, they play no apparent role in what I can and cannot doubt.

We are not born doubters. Quite the contrary. My filtered past, the sources of the "light" of understanding that I currently use to "see" my world, helped me, slowly and painfully, to learn how to doubt, helped me slowly to create a largely uncensorious scepticism about the many and varied public theories of the way things are and the way things work. It took quite a while for me to accept that even science cannot provide us with lasting truths, and I don't recall ever being taught this initially uncomfortable idea by any of my science teachers.

This apparent fact about the apparent limitations of all human knowledge began for me as an unexpected hypothesis, one that only slowly gained my acceptance while I watched psychology attempt to find the laws governing mental life during the years between 1957 and my first retirement nearly forty years later. Psychology has long wished to emulate chemistry and physics, as if at least these disciplines have forged some final answers. But even the histories of physics and chemistry offer no assurance at all that the final major revisions of teachings in these fields are forever behind us.

Just as Gödel was able to show that in order to "prove" the consistency and truth of any proposition in a logical system one must always appeal to a stronger, independent (i.e., "higher") system to accomplish the proving, so too it is quite possible that to "understand" the human psyche may require a knowledge device that is more powerful than the brains we must use to achieve our understanding. And thus, all our theories may well prove to be imperfect. Paradoxically, however, I would not wish any such hypothesis to discourage or interrupt the work of science in general and research psychology in particular, even if this hypothesis were somehow known to be true. For even imperfect theories have their utility and constitute advancements on ignorance. It would just be nice if we didn't encourage students to believe in imperfect theories quite so literally, and quite so unshakably, as both we (and they themselves) so often have been helped to believe.

I sometimes think about what we *know*, as being analogous to the effects of penumbral lighting. It's as if there is a brilliant light source, only a very thin edge of which is not eclipsed, able to illumine our consciousness, however dimly. The deeper darkness of earlier times feels banished by the new light flooding our thinking. Yet we remain deep in penumbral shadow still, to a degree wholly unrecognized. And if the waning of our eclipse is continual and very gradual, we would not even notice how what we can "see" is subtly changing. We would not have any reason to hypothesize that we are still located deep in a penumbra. Our "beginner's realism" would not let us consider that what we already suppose to be a full and final brilliance probably still falls well short of an even greater brilliance denied to us by all that remains eclipsed in a residual shadow of unsuspected ignorance.

Of course eclipses can proceed in either of two directions. Sources of light may become less or more eclipsed over time. As can sources of pleasure. A month ago I was visiting my mother and I was struck by how hard it is becoming for me to want to be with her. It was not very long ago that I felt I wanted to spend large parts of my retirement time with her, while I still could. But our relationship seems to be dimming along with her declining strength, and with that dimming, my confusion about how and when I want to visit her grows. My visits and phone calls seem to release in her a general annoyance with the world and often some more particular one with me. Rarely now am I given any suggestion that she appreciates what help or companionship my visits do provide. My suggestions for bettering her deteriorating situation are met with annoyance and with multiple "reasons" why those suggestions are unworkable—"reasons" that to me seem irrational or off topic.* My suggestions for making my visits easier for me, and thus longer, are also met with multiple objections. And she soon interprets such suggestions as further proof that I am not happy while I am with her and as further evidence that I do not really love or have much interest in her

---

* A few years later I have been struck with a different perspective on this apparent annoyance and resistance of hers. I find that I am starting to act similarly whenever and because I am very tired, and so I grow frustrated when I cannot find the words that used to come so easily, words that would explain and nicely rationalize my differing point of view. And with that frustration comes an undeserved and unwelcome negativity.

and her well-being. Moreover, each time I leave her for my home, her anxiety and annoyance at the perceived brevity of my stays (which now are "only" seven to nine days at a time, with two further days of driving, each way) make me feel annoyed in turn. There must be a way to break the cycle of eclipsing love and respect, but I haven't found it.

I can almost doubt that my mother's declared wants and expectations reflect her true needs. But she fights my incipient doubt vigorously. I can almost doubt that her own assertions of the best ways available to meet her perceived needs are accurate and complete. Yet those alternatives that I seem to see, alternatives that appear better for meeting the most important of her needs, she insists are totally unworkable or totally unacceptable.

I can almost believe that the consequences of these differences in our viewpoints mean that I am required to do much more for her, sacrificing for her as in my childhood she so often sacrificed for me. Yet somewhere in the penumbral gloom of my thinking I am still able to doubt that. It feels like it is what she *cannot* doubt that divides us even more than what she *can* doubt. Still, what shapes our perspectives most of all seems to be the full pitch-black umbra of our unknown ignorance.

And so, what *is* the proper respect to be paid to all that remains completely unknown to us? Perhaps it is the respect of a persistent and gentle doubt of what we do imagine to be true, a doubt that must be tempered with an acceptance of life in a world that requires us to dwell in penumbral shadow. And where might such an acceptance be found? Beyond doubt it is beyond words. Or, just maybe, perhaps not.

28 | *Conscience and Small Things*

*T*hese are indeed stressful times. Could it be that all times seem (and therefore become) stressful?

Once again I am away from home, visiting my mother who has her own medical and psychological challenges. But back home, in Kaslo, we have recently lost our only doctor (to retirement) at the same time that we have suffered the enforced closure of half of our nearest full hospital (in Nelson), including almost all of its attached medical specialists. Those specialists have been given no choice but to retire or to move elsewhere.

Severe government cutbacks, imposed from afar, are taking a considerable toll. Suddenly, a badly broken bone or serious burn, a suspicious pain or an attack of pneumonia, will lead to a different kind of treatment and a more stressful removal far from any family. Now the provincial government has decided that for any significant medical care, we are all to travel to Trail, more than two hours away by car or perhaps only two-thirds of that same travel time if done at high speed, via ambulance . . . in good weather.*

The bureaucratic justification for this radical break with local service and tradition is said to be financial. However, local citizens who are fighting this centralizing disease have been able to show quite convincingly that financial savings are highly unlikely under the circumstances, unless these savings are achieved at the personal expense of those who fall ill and/or at the non-monetary costs of much greater stress for local medical staff, paramedics, patients, and their respective families and caretakers.

Naturally, the wisdom of this sort of governmental policy in action depends entirely on how you look at it. At the moment I am looking at it from the point of view of Janice Gross Stein's recent book *The Cult of Efficiency*, and from the bedside of my invalid mother in Nevada. I am led to wonder, where is the operation of conscience, or something like the golden rule, in politics today? It feels as if only "efficiency," turned into a synonym for Reduced-Spending-at-Any-Cost, is the concern of modern bureaucrats. But what has happened to the greater social "efficiency" derived from health promotion, from compassion, fair dealing, and the long view? The disregard of all but limited financial efficiencies seems to trouble almost no one in government, and too few in commerce. I feel as if government itself has almost become a form of commerce, and that politicians have become would-be CEOs in pursuit of ideal and inhumane profit indicators rather than being servants for the public good.

What has happened to our public servants and to our public conscience?

---

* A few months after writing these words we were to learn that an attack of appendicitis would not be treated in nearby Nelson either (although a surgeon had volunteered to treat such cases there), nor even in far off Trail, but much further still, in the town of Grand Forks, over a long high snowy summit to the west of Trail. This decision was justified as representing fiscal efficiency and wise budgetary management.

In a paradoxical way, it is the smallest things that have the greatest symbolic impact, offending my sense of what is right. For instance, Lorraine recently received an itemized electric utility bill at our Ontario home. It was distressingly higher, this bill, than any previous one, although we had been living in British Columbia all during the billing period and in Ontario our hot water heater and refrigerator had been turned off along with almost everything else in the house. This bill had been estimated, for the third month in a row, and it was based on an assumed rate of power consumption far in excess of any previous reality, a rate very favourable to the utility. Yet to me the most distressing part of that whole bill was an inconspicuous line itemizing the Goods and Services Tax applied on a new surcharge for Ontario Hydro's "Debt Reduction," i.e., a tax collected by the federal government on the interest and loan payments that the provincial government utility must pay on the large public loans it took out when its nuclear generators were built more than a decade ago. Are we then soon to be taxed on all our other loan payments and on our mortgage payments each month? Are all loans now to be called "services?" Are they commodities, i.e., "goods?" Where is the conscience in such treatment of fellow citizens?

Small things such as this seem to multiply lately. They are the "hassles" that balloon into "stressors" that become signs of the end of my world. All of which probably says more about how easily one can become fatalistic and hopeless at times when one is suffering sleep deprivation or compromised health than it says about the true state of the local world.

For indeed I am not exactly sane this week. My mother needs help, and while I am at her home, temporarily providing almost all the help she needs (even if not all that she expects), I will only be here a few more days. But no potential caretaker has yet been found who is willing to meet her conditions of employment that are clearly designed to minimize any financial cost to her and any need for her to allow vacation time to her caretaker "employee." She wants just one person here with her all of every evening and night, as indeed she managed to have for most of this past summer. And this she achieved at minimal financial cost to herself since the older woman who applied for the upstairs room and downstairs responsibility worked at a summer day job and was able to save the cost of her rent by staying free with my mother.

As someone who once expressed the wish to spend more time with my aging parents, my conscience again bothers me. And unless I miss my guess, my mother is counting on my conscience, and hoping to amplify its message while I am here. Given all the restrictions and conditions she puts on those who would help her (today I might say "serve" her) and given the stresses she experiences, stresses that seem to preclude any expression of reliable appreciation for what she receives, only a family member is likely to take on the caretaker role.

Twice so far during this visit I have raised the matter of her savings (she prefers to call it "capital") and the many years that those savings could assure her comfortable home care were they to be applied to that end. But she has come this far (age ninety-two) by "preserving capital" as best she could, and she tells me she is not about to "dip further" into her "capital" at this late stage.

My distressed mood shows, of course. And again she seems to be interpreting my frustration at our discussions and at my nagging conscience as signs of boredom with her, or worse, as signs of my lack of love or caring. And again, it is small things that lead her to these large conclusions. Yet there are times even now when she is a delight to be with. (That would surprise her to know, I'm sure.)

It is true, however, that for me such times have become rather rare, and no less precious for being so rare. More and more she seems to be critical: of herself and of the physical body that won't stay fixed, but also critical of those who remain among her caretakers and neighbours, who have also let her down. They don't clean her house properly, nor buy the proper fruit, nor cook food that is easy to swallow, nor do they put things where they belong, i.e., where she can find them. When I am here in her house it is hard for me not to feel let down, too, notwithstanding the large measure of empathy I feel for her condition. But I am bedevilled by the small frustrations deriving from her defences and her insistence on rigid control over her house and our daily routine.

My mother has a completely different eating schedule and internal clock than I do. She plans, for instance, that I will drive her somewhere in the morning after breakfast. But her breakfast finishes at 10:30 a.m., three hours after mine, and she is not up and ready to go out until almost my lunchtime. We depart for what I am told are two errands: the grocery store for five items and then to pick up a prescription. As the chauffeur (and not the son or old friend), I discover by the time we get home that much more than two errands had been planned and it was more than she had the strength to accomplish. Yes, it is true that I do get bored waiting for her to decide that none of the fruit will suit, and most of the meat is too expensive. Her list of five groceries turns into ten, and those ten take fifty minutes to purchase.

And when we get home after all the other stops, I am suffering (as is she) from a fatigue and hunger that eclipse any satisfaction I might enjoy for having been of some help. And she has had no pleasure from what help my being with her may have brought. The unfinished business we bring home, the items still on her private list of errands, leaves her annoyed. Or is it perhaps anxious?

These are small matters when viewed from a distance. They are small compared with my nagging conscience and her disappointment over the unfinished business that always seems to remain each time I leave Tahoe to drive home to Canada.

But here in this house small things can loom very large indeed. I am no beginner at trying to solve problems presented by my mother's situation and her personality. However, retirement has yet to give me new insights for finding solutions to these problems. It is becoming clear now that I had expected retirement would facilitate finding such solutions. And so, as stressful as are all the factors I have already mentioned above, I am further stressed by the dawning perception that retirement, with its time to reflect and to act in new ways, may never produce the insights and solutions I feel should be within my grasp.

The stresses that I feel today appear to be caused by matters offending conscience and/or justice and/or reason. But looking over the above, I am now struck by how much of today's complaints seem to touch on money: how money is and isn't spent. Or is it more one's energy and health: how that is or isn't spent? So far, I have been spared a health crisis and an emergency trip to far off Trail, B.C. I have my energy. But my conscience isn't well. Here at Tahoe it could use a small tonic.

29 | *The Frye Affair*

*Y*es, it turns out that retirement does not signal an end to acquiring new friends, new ideas, and some healthy changes of heart. I guess I feared that it might, however, reflecting perhaps an unnoticed contagion of similar fears observed in certain distressed colleagues who couldn't imagine why I would want to retire, and particularly to retire early. Yet in retirement I find myself happily doing things that previously I would never have dreamed I might do. Moreover, I find that such doings offer up to me the occasional surprising pearl of great price.

For instance, in order to supplement my pension, instead of listening closely to psychotherapy patients, as once I did, I am now listening closely to forthcoming books in need of an index. And the work of producing an index for such books, however it may appear to the uninitiated, turns out to be anything but dull. In one sense it is the ultimate way to absorb a text. It forces close attention to themes, to the links between them, and to how different readers might have different questions to ask of the book in question. As a consequence, indexing brings unexpected new perspectives that often prove to be as helpful as they are interesting.

That is not all this work gives to me. It also introduces me to some very interesting authors at a very interesting time in their lives, i.e., in the delivery room, while giving birth to their current baby. It was just one week ago, in fact, that I had the pleasure of a business lunch with the author of a forthcoming book, production of the index for which has lately been occupying me. The author was J. Edward Chamberlin, and his new book explores stories and the various ways that each culture's stories define and constrain it. This is a wonderful book, with many layers of meaning. It is proving to be a challenge to index properly. And like the author himself, it is a book I hope I may encounter frequently again in the future.

At our lunch I happened to ask Chamberlin what had brought him to Toronto in the first place, and to my surprise his answer included a mention of Northrop Frye. Quickly, habitually, I changed the subject. Call me oversensitive after all these years, but any mention of Northrop Frye continues to haunt me.

It all began many years ago (you could look it up) when the *New Yorker* magazine published a review of John Fowles' newest novel *Daniel Martin*, a review to which I happened to take great exception. And thus was set in motion a series of events culminating in another of that small set of life experiences, any one of which might reasonably qualify for the title of "my most embarrassing moment."

Stories and their powers being uppermost in my mind this week, let me share with you the story of that series of events, or mishaps, or failings. Since it happens that I am the sole surviving witness to the events that I will recount, I have the advantage of telling my story any way I like. (I have chosen the way that lessens my embarrassment.)

Frye was a man thoroughly familiar with irony and humour (even when unintended), while at the same time he was one who could appear, when sitting silent and impassive, to be suffering fools less than gladly. This is the story about how, apparently, I was a fool. Or, perhaps not. (We shall see.)

There would be little point today to looking up and rereading the *New Yorker* review that started all this. I suspect the reviewer was as renowned as was Professor Frye, and having now forgotten who the reviewer was, I suspect that I've grown to admire him or her again. If true, it would be nice to leave things that way. What matters to my story is that the reviewer was absolutely certain that *Daniel Martin* was a failed novel in more ways than one, and he or she severely criticized the work for each one of its imagined failures.

It had not been long since I had finished reading *Daniel Martin* when the *New Yorker's* review arrived in the mail. The primary reason that I was appalled by the review was that it attributed to Fowles multiple motives and goals that seemed to me quite orthogonal to his true intentions in creating that work. I thought the novel was wonderful, brilliantly conceived, and very effectively realized. For the reviewer to presume to dictate to the author (as I saw it) the different book that he "should" have been writing, seemed to me to give a black eye to the whole charade of literary criticism.

At this point I heard in my own psychotherapeutic ear, spoken in the rumbling tones of the crusty old grandfather from *Peter and the Wolf,* a voice saying solemnly, "This is all very well young man, but WHAT do YOU know about literary criticism?" The voice continued at some length, the implication being that I was not fit to read criticism, about the traditions and conventions of which I clearly knew nothing, particularly if I could so misunderstand a review of which the editors of the *New Yorker* had clearly approved. In short, the voice hoist me on my own petard, asking what business I had in presuming to know what reviewers should and shouldn't do or say?

It was a clash of cultures perhaps. My clinical culture said that one should never presume to have correctly understood, let alone censure, another person's motives until you have considerable first-person evidence for what those motives truly are, and, more importantly, until you have deep insight as to how these motives have been developed. My culture said different beliefs and different stories and different environments are helpful to different people at different times. My culture did not accept any "one-art-fits-all" definition of what is good or recommendable, beautiful or praiseworthy. Quite simply, I considered the published review of Fowles' book to be egocentric, cruel, and destructive, without any visible justifications for so being.

But it also had to be admitted that there was a culture that approved of such definitive and assured reviews, a culture that felt very foreign to me. If I were going to criticize that culture, it behooved me first (given my own cultural bias) to try to understand it better. Which is where Northrop Frye came in.

I was teaching psychology at the same Toronto university where the world's acknowledged expert on literary criticism taught English. Frye was said to be a literary critic's literary critic. I had never met the man, but his reputation was for being a great teacher as well as an original thinker. "Great teacher" conjured up for me visions of a patient, insightful mentor, the sort of man who might say to students, or to colleagues such as me, words like:

"*Ahh, yes, yes my boy. This is a common misperception you have. Here, have a look at this small book. I think it will answer to your need. I have another copy of it somewhere. Bring it back when you like, and let's see if that helps you out of your dilemma.*"

And so I determined not to be like those shy undergraduates I knew (and once had been myself) who were chronically reluctant to "disturb" their teacher, to confess to their confusions, and to seek pointers toward understanding. I would seek out Professor Frye and ask him by what convention and what justification a critic could presume to fault John Fowles, and his motives, for writing *Daniel Martin*.

It turned out that Professor Frye was indeed a busy man. An appointment would be necessary to see him. His secretary must be consulted before the man himself might be. She asked for the nature of my business. I recall being less than fluent, trying to save that answer for the man himself. Finally (and I had the sense, reluctantly), his secretary gave me an appointment many days hence, which I dutifully recorded in my calendar and proceeded to move on to other things.

When the day came for my interview with the professor, I made my way through the gates of Massey College and negotiated a small labyrinth of doors and hallways that led past his secretary and into the den of the master critic. He gestured me in and bade me sit opposite his desk, and asked me my business. I remember very little of what happened thereafter. I took some time to explain why I had come, and, not having rehearsed my side of this intended dialogue, I was less than efficient or effective in my choice of words.

When I had finished, and had begun waiting either for his *"yes, yes, dear boy"* or perhaps for his *"what can I say dear boy . . . the review was egregious . . . hardly what one would call true 'criticism',"* I began to notice the silence growing longer. And longer. And rather quickly I began to feel a fool, one who was not being gladly suffered.

Frye did finally have some words. And I had a few more, too. My impression was that his words were carefully chosen to avoid any continuation of my topic, while mine were less than helpful in changing his mind about the general weight of the questions I had brought to him.

I will never know what Frye thought of the young associate professor who crossed the cultural boundary to come from the realm of the social sciences to speak with the titan of the humanities. As for me, if I thought that he was less than humane with my quest, it was only for a moment. Almost at once, and for the second time, I thought I had been a fool, and that Frye had seen me for one, and that indeed I had much to be ashamed of. I recall (probably quite incorrectly) that I said nothing to anyone about this meeting for a very long time.

Now it happens that this morning's *Globe and Mail* contains a telling Thought du Jour, one that I discovered over breakfast. This thought is one of the two things that have led me to recall this story and to tell it here. What's more, I think it has also eased some of my earlier shame. The *Globe* quotes William Phelps, who said: "This is the final test of a gentleman: his respect for those who can be of no possible use to him." Northrop Frye was clearly a fine gentleman. Yet on that obscure afternoon in history, that one day when our paths crossed, it seems to me now that he was also able to be other than a gentleman.

Or was it rather that the culture clash between us was even larger than I could see? Did each of us see the other as "not playing by the rules" (or the roles) that happened to be all we knew? I ask this in light of the book I finished indexing yesterday: Chamberlin's forthcoming *If This Is Your Land, Where Are Your Stories?* Nowhere have I seen normally invisible cultural divides mapped in such interesting and helpful detail as in this book. And today I have to wonder: What would Frye have made of Chamberlin's book?

30 | *Desert Springs*

Twelve days ago, on a day of local sunshine and outdoor ease, the first weekend in spring and the first of the unsettling war on Iraq, I called my mother and discovered her again to be in failing health.

At age ninety-three her cycle of ups and downs, of one damn thing after another, has generally left her mood sour and pessimistic. Lately, however, she had been blessed with much less of that anxious annoyance so long familiar to those who know her well. I attributed her improved spirits to the antidepressant medication that her cardiologist, "Dr. Tim," had finally persuaded her to add to her confusing bloom of other pills.

And despite her current setback, which sounded to me like a lower intestinal infection of some sort, she managed one or two chuckles during our talk.

A few days later she wasn't chuckling quite so easily when I called to learn the diagnosis of her latest troubles. When he was finally able to examine her, Dr. Tim had discovered that my mother has a classic case of shingles. But she is game. And even during this phone call, there was the occasional chuckle during her description of her current state.

Despite the predictable evaporation of our recent false spring, already only a memory, my thoughts are beginning to turn to my long drive west for the summer at my home in B.C. This time, however, I am driving not to B.C. directly, but instead I will first go to Lake Tahoe, the sooner to see my mother. All winter she has had two caretakers staying in her only guest room, two young sisters from Australia who are ski instructors by day and assistants for my mother by night. But the Tahoe ski season will end very soon, the sisters will return home, and no one has yet been sought to come replace them. Into the breach I am to go: across the Michigan border at this time of U.S. war-anxiety, across prairie states I have never before travelled (Iowa, Nebraska), over the Colorado Rockies, and on to the deserts of Utah and Nevada.

To me this desert war in the Middle East, with its inevitable risks and carnage and divisiveness, feels like a tragedy that need never have occurred. Rightly or wrongly I find myself blaming a virulent hybrid of rapacious corporate culture and religious fundamentalism and xenophobia for the American need to war, the need to offend, to pre-empt, to spurn international cooperation. I will be driving with Canadian licence plates, never before any concern to me, but enough Canadian criticism of American policies and of this particular American Government has come to the attention of the U.S. citizenry that I do worry some about possible vandalism while I travel.

The themes evoked by the concepts of desert and war also seem to blend in my recent dreams and reveries with the concepts of garden, of wilderness, and of home. I was once in Iran during a sabbatical trip around the globe. My goal was to reach Persepolis, recently turned five thousand years old, site of the ancient Persian palace of Darius and Xerxes, and conquered by Alexander the Great. The Persepolis ruins lie alone in the middle of a vast dry dust-filled desert. At that time they could be reached only by a long hot bus ride north from the town of Shiraz. It was the early 1970s and westerners were not exactly welcomed in Shiraz. The town itself was a dry and dusty place with ruined walls and shimmering heat.

Somewhere in this town, searching for privacy and shade after returning awestruck from Persepolis, I stumbled into a small enclosed rose garden, one that had obviously seen better days. The garden, too, had its share of dust everywhere. But in this place, with the town and desert walled out, I was unexpectedly enveloped by the scent of some struggling roses and the cool of an enduring fountain. Here, suddenly, I understood for the first time the symbolic power of the rose-garden image, particularly amid a desert. Here was Sanctuary. Here was Home.

Different people seem to grow into very different homelands, places that call to them when they are away and that offer sanctuary and contentment on their return. My forthcoming U.S. detour back to B.C., tracing two sides of the triangle joining homes that have signified adulthood, childhood, and retirement (Ontario, Lake Tahoe, and Kootenay Lake respectively) partly amplifies my recent curiosity over our ideas of home. But so does my recent work on Ted Chamberlin's book dealing with stories of homelands, homesickness, and diasporas. Moreover, Chamberlin's book also deals with deserts, wilderness, and, yes, even gardens—all evocative settings since the dawn of storytelling. Two weeks after finishing work on his book I still notice echoes of its ideas.

On page 68 of the book, while speaking in general about our disparagement of nomadic cultures, but in particular about dams on the Columbia River, Chamberlin has written:

[These dams] were manifestations of one of the venerable parables of agricultural settlement: turning a wasteland—sometimes construed as a wilderness—into a garden; making the desert bloom. There is a powerful Judeo-Christian rhetoric at work here, in which the land that brings forth plenty is deemed to be blessed by God, while the land that does not is cursed. One of the markers of divine disfavour is the barren land. In Islam, too, which like Judaism is originally a religion of the desert, the waterhole is a blessed place.

And, I would add, so is the rose garden. The great natural beauty of the open desert, or the truly wild, is invisible to the "civilizing" eye. Instead, the desert is the hateful place of satanic temptations. A cultivated garden is what the civilizing eye finds beautiful: the home, the sanctuary, the land that has been tamed, subdued, arranged, and uniformly greened. The wild and empty lands, the unfenced and trackless plains or deserts, regions where the winds push hard and the weather is king, hide their beauty from the runaway children of the city or the family farm. But the children of the desert or the tundra or the steppes or the children of the island seas look with different eyes, and they see a different beauty in their vast homelands.

Deserts come in a great variety of forms. There is the clean and sandy Sahara, of course. But there is also the dusty emptiness around Persepolis. There is the scrub and sage of Nevada's basin and range. There is the blooming desert of Death Valley after a rain. There are deserts of alkali, of lava, and of ice. There are flat deserts and mountainous deserts and canyon deserts. There are even oceanic deserts. Each of them is a place of extremes. Each of them is a place conducive to fear. They appear hostile and dangerous on one hand, while being open to infinity and liberating on another. Deserts reintroduce the *possibility* of awe. A garden offers the *possibility* of ease. Life needs both awe and ease. Put a small garden in the middle of a vast desert, and both seem the richer thereby. Put bombs and soldiers there, and the desert seems violated.

Now, of course, the deserts of Persia are in the headlines each morning. As I read the war news, my thoughts still carry echoes of my reading in Chamberlin's book and echoes of some of his meditations on desert cultures. Those cultures are dying, and they are dying in ways that seem as unnecessary as they are unnatural.

It happens that my forthcoming route to see my mother will pass over an extension of the desert where the very first manmade nuclear explosion took place. And it will pass directly through the deserts (in Utah and Nevada) where the radiation from a long series of subsequent atomic tests still ghosts the hills. Among those hills originated the loud crack and prolonged rumble that I can still remember hearing as a boy at Lake Tahoe, the sonic boom from pre-dawn nuclear tests conducted hundreds of miles away in southern Nevada.

And when I arrive at Tahoe, now so very changed, no longer a natural garden and no longer my home, what will I find? (Hopefully, I will find my mother still able to navigate her home.) The lake itself is inexorably losing its crystal clarity. Its shoreline has become a continuous carpet of cars and roofs. Many people, far too many, now call Tahoe home. Yet the irony is that I can no longer imagine what they feel for it, and what about it still is home-like for them. This is another sign of aging, I suppose, one of the little things about which we are not told, or, one of the little things we do not *hear* when we *are* told. Gradually, and all unnoticed, change overtakes our eroding skills for assimilating it. At such times, stepping into the desert of old age, we risk becoming complainers, sour voices in that new sort of wilderness that is no longer (perhaps never was) the different (friendly) wilderness that we imagine we can remember from our childhood.

Is it in this sort of desert that I will find my mother wandering?

I hope I can avoid turning into a complainer as I age. At Lake Kootenay I still am blessed with a personal oasis and a metaphoric rose garden. And whenever Lorraine and I are alone I still find sanctuary. These are true blessings. My mother has had many blessings, too. But now I see her feeling betrayed by her aging body, willfully determined to reform it. Her complaints all appear to have a moral basis and each of her physical trials seems to be experienced as a rank injustice. She wanders in her desert of the aged, apparently receiving temptations in the form of promises of renewed mobility and restored control over her life, in return for … well, for what?

Perhaps for stoicism. Perhaps for survivorship.

It is something of a mystery to me why she is so focused on pulling through and living another fifteen years in the face of all the evidence that such is not to be. Yet something tells me I had better not cast stones; that I, too, may find myself in exactly the same mental place, hearing the same apparently diabolical temptations when my turn comes.

Is there no way to be prepared? One might try to flee a desert war, but there is no true flight from aging. Apparently that is how it is meant to be. I wish I understood why. Or, if not why, then … *Why*.

31 | *Demons*

*D*uring the year since last I wrote here I have been stressed by my mother's prolonged decline. Three more times now she has been in hospital, twice on the point of death. And yet for the past three months she has been at home, with hospice supervision, under the full-time care of a remarkable young Peruvian doctor named Rosa who is in the United States studying for a medical licence in that country.

My mother can no longer swallow safely, so she is fed liquid meals via a tube that leads directly through her abdominal wall into her stomach. Her voice is often barely audible. But until this week, despite her chronic bedridden state and hospice care, she has remained insistent that she was soon going to be getting better. She has been expecting to be able to fend for herself much more, to be able to drive her car again after more than a year, and to be able to restore her house to the state it was in before that unfortunate time when control over it passed into my hands and those of her full-time caregivers.

This week, however, my mother was again told by one of her hospice nurses that she is not likely to get much better, and in fact will likely soon die of pneumonia should she recklessly continue to try to swallow little treats (like ice cream) that could "go down the wrong way." Because she is generally hard to hear and slow of speech, I am never quite sure I understand her now, never quite sure if she actually remembers and is denying what she has been told about her short life expectancy (due primarily to her chronic congestive heart failure, not to her poor swallowing) or whether she has simply forgotten again.

Whatever may be the reason, at age ninety-four she clearly expects at least two or perhaps six more years of life, much of it enjoying more mobility than she has known at any time during the past two years. In revealing these unrealistic expectations she may well have been just protecting me (or herself) and keeping her knowledge of her frail prognosis under wraps. It may all become clearer when again I will see her, soon after Easter, and can be present each time the Hospice nurse makes her regular visits.

I was surprised that my mother's dominant will to live proved as effective in preventing her death last winter as one might have known it would. To see her so immobilized now, and so weak and in such continuing discomfort (even her shingles are no better), is hard for me each time I am visiting. I am unable *not* to wish for a peaceful release from her compounding trials of advanced aging, but at the same time I am frankly frightened by any construed wish that she should die. (My conscience will not even accept that "peaceful release" euphemism, and it strongly disapproves of my having referred to it above.) Moreover, the uncertain financial implications (to me) of the timing of my mother's death also hover in the background, leading to their own potentially dangerous and unspeakable accusations and fearful threats.

And then this week's *Economist* magazine arrived with a major section devoted to the impact on societies of today's markedly aging world population. Apparently there has been a dramatic increase over the past ten years in the proportion of people who are more than one hundred years old. The focus of these articles was on the doubtful economics of funding pensions and health care in such a world. And in my current state of uncertainty about the reliability of both my personal income and of health care in rural British Columbia over the next twenty-five years, this reading has only served to increase my level of concern.

One other thing, too: A few days ago I learned from Elizabeth that immediately after the spring equinox a judge in Victoria finally signed a final divorce decree between us. I have yet to receive any official word of this judgment, which I had been told to expect some time ago. It is not as if I had any special plans for remarrying, or for making some other use of the divorce decree, but the long delay in achieving this closure, and, having forgotten that it has been in the works for many months now, this unexpected surprise concerning the divorce has further added to my recent stress level.

The combined impact of all these uncertainties and disagreeable thoughts has produced a kind of shutting down of my abilities, and a life focused on just getting by until my darker, viscous moods finally drain away. But my mental demons have a life of their own and they do not leave when invited to do so. They have long kept me from this keyboard and they have taken their toll in a variety of other ways.

I notice that I stick closer to home these days. I seem to be less selective as a reader, spending more time fretting about current events and local politics than enjoying good books and widening perspectives. I am happiest these days when completely focused on my curling game, or allowing the dog up on the bed for a morning greeting, or walking the land with Lorraine. These little pleasures of retirement, pleasures my demons seem determined to portray as undeserved, unearned, and unproductive, are sweet indeed. Sometimes the psychologist in me can even manage to laugh at my awkward demons of conscience, at their effective (if also pathetic) attempts to unmake me. Still, such demons do have a certain *emotional* intelligence that reason needs to respect. That is part of their continuing power over me.

The Jungian, James Hillman, knows quite a bit about the demons that come with aging and solitude. He appears to have learned how to relax in their presence and to recognize some of the good they might do. I keep meaning to get and read his recent book *Character*, which has much to say to the aging retiree who is visited by demons, but I still procrastinate carrying out this undoubtedly appropriate intention. I know about Hillman's book from Marilyn Powell's wonderful *Ideas* radio essay on the CBC called *Growing Oldness*, a CD of which I added to my brown paper bag last year after hearing the broadcast. The demons of old age serve a purpose we are told, one that is both knowable and unknowable. Insofar as *part* of their purpose may be knowable, it behooves us to attend to and learn from each demon.

It is night demons that Hillman speaks of when interviewed for "Growing Oldness," the ones that visit older people in those wakeful hours when all the clocks have stopped and dawn is still far away. They bring regrets at all the might-have-beens of our youth if only we had been wiser and more skillful. They bring regrets at all the pain we have sown, e.g., as a consequence of our ignorance about those crucial personal histories that shaped the lives of our parents, of our classmates, and of our colleagues at work, an ignorance or lack of understanding that produced in us corresponding absences of compassion and forgiveness.

It is strange about demons: They seem to do everything in their power to prevent our forgiveness of and compassion for their own harsh words. But patience to hear them out, compassion for their angry natures, and forgiveness or humour in the face of their accusations probably are the only ways to really learn the lessons their words may be able to bring us. Sadly, demons appear to be rather like teachers who do not wish us to learn, despite the evidence that their mission is to teach. Perhaps such teachers need to be taught that their world will not collapse if at last we pass their tests and graduate. Perhaps demons may find that even their own graduation may be hastened thereby.

32 | *Winnowing Memories*

SUNDAY JUNE 13, 2004
KASLO, B.C.

There are earnest cognitive psychologists and breathless young journalists who make it their periodic business to announce that by age seventy (if not well before) we all have noticeably compromised brains, brains with ever-expanding vacancies where once resided permanent memories. Sometime during the past week (and I can't quite remember when or where) I have seen two new media reports again suggesting that, among retirees of a certain young age, cognitive decline is inevitable. "Senior moments" of memory loss are said to be the hallmarks of that decline.

Such pronouncements always seem to be presented as statements of unquestionable new truth and universal generality. I suspect that the cognitive psychologists know better, while the journalists don't, but why is it that the media reports never seem to qualify these pessimistic assertions? Why do they not ask if perhaps the failures they trumpet are quite temporary or situationally specific in some interesting and special ways?

Yesterday, for instance, Lorraine and I attended the open house held to inaugurate the new wing of Kaslo's old Victorian Hospital and to celebrate the long awaited arrival of our newest temporary doctor who is just starting a one-year locum in Kaslo.

Our health facility is no longer allowed to call itself a hospital, however, being yet another casualty of the provincial government's preference for business school theory and the politics of power over the conservation of working local medical institutions. So our new facility is now called The Victorian Community Health Centre of Kaslo. (As if there were Victorian Community Health Centres located anywhere else in the province.) Kaslo's rare and wonderful medical legacy from the venerable Victorian Order of Nurses had been the last, and one of the oldest, private hospitals left in British Columbia when recently it was metamorphosed into our health centre. It was a leftover from earlier days when inadvertent self-amputations by working miners and loggers needed fast local repair, and travel by paddle-wheeler could not be counted on to get an emergency case to Nelson in time to save life or limb.

As we walked the loop of new offices and surveyed the sunny new rooms, I encountered half a dozen old friends I hadn't seen since last fall. Two of these friends did not have names that would respond to memory's call; nor were these the two that I knew least well. One of the names came to me very soon after we began talking, but the other, curiously, came only much later, in the car as we drove home. Both the names came, though. They were not gone and erased. And while the names were temporarily unavailable to me, there was still very much I knew about each of these people: e.g., that one had lived near my stepmother, Helga, had a dog I admired, had played that special role in the local Gilbert & Sullivan production two summers ago, and drove a blue pickup, etc. The other was the one who had voted the "wrong" way on our referendum to create a volunteer fire department, who once had helped me move my canoe, who had told me where I might find the right type of rock for a rock wall I wanted to build, etc.

These sorts of memory lapses, these increasingly familiar senior moments, are well known phenomena. Nor are they unique to seniors. Psychology still does not know why on one meeting a name is not available when wanted and at another it is available. Nor does neurophysiology know. Nor does biochemistry. And when one or all of these disciplines does discover apparent answers for why, those answers are unlikely to explain why we forget where we last put our gloves, left the keys, or placed the note we made about that important appointment. I do not deny that cognitive function changes with age, nor do I deny that it gets less fluent at carrying out many tasks. But cognitive function seems to me to continue to get better at certain things. (Well, sometimes. In some people.) Despite which, the latest "news" is always about decline: about how aging is to be feared.

Brains are subtle things. They have many ways of accomplishing the same wonders. People who recover functions lost due to strokes are but one proof of how resilient brains can be. And, how mysterious. Whenever I read one of these journalistic revelations offering new reasons for hopelessness in otherwise contented retirees, I try to remember these wonders about brains. I try to look at potentially happier revelations still to come about brains.

All of which has led me to reconsider a "winnowing memories" theory of aging. You can get something of the flavour of this theory from the story told about David Starr Jordan, a famous ichthyologist who became the first president of Stanford University. Jordan was renowned on campus for his ability to remember the names of students, and he would greet many of them by name as he crossed the campus. When asked how he did it, the old fox is said to have answered: "I don't know what the secret is. I only know that for every student's name I learn, I forget the name of one fish." (Not all his students were amused.)

I don't think Dr. Jordan was being entirely facetious in his remark. It seems to me that Jordan was re-evaluating his priorities after he became president of the university, and it's a little bit as if he was then winnowing his memories, separating the new wheat from an older harvest, one that had permitted the new to come into being. Perhaps Jordan had become a different sort of fisher, a fisher for student minds, and no longer a fisher for ichthy-nomenclature. Perhaps one of the skills that helped make him such a successful ichthyologist was now placed in the service of making him a great mentor.

Similarly, perhaps the retiree's brain is ready to separate older, drier kernels, kernels that once had produced the bread of a working life, from the new kernels that might produce a loaf of something approaching wisdom and contentment. Whatever the reasons, priorities do change in retirement. Names become less important with age, while relationships become more important. And most important of all may be improving the narrative of our own lives: understanding what we have handled poorly and what we have done well and why. All in the service of helping more people to go right and fewer to go wrong, starting, of course, with ourselves.

You see, it is distinctly possible that an adult brain, one that is tuned for remembering names, is poorly tuned for doing the better work of the aging retiree. It is possible that a senior brain may be in fact well tuned for the work of re-analysis and re-emphasis that comes with increasingly noticeable intimations of mortality. Whatever may be the proper work of these later years, when age is most advanced and cognitive function looks to be most simplified, perhaps that work requires a reorganization of memory. What then *is* most important to remember? What *is* most important to know? And (now pay attention): What *is* it that may be most important that we *forget*?

In short, I wonder if in fact we are not meant to winnow our memories as we grow older. And by "memories" here I include particular

derivatives of memory such as our perceptual biases, habitual attitudes, and long-standing set ideas. We probably need to forget a certain
amount of these memories in order to renew ourselves. We cannot look
ahead if the view ahead is occluded by large, multiple, rear-view mir-
rors. Earlier I argued that we need to doubt more than generally we do.
Perhaps forgetting is the aging brain's way of facilitating new doubts,
helpful ambiguity, and new wonder.

I wonder in fact if we are not meant to wonder more, in the same
way a young child can wonder at the marvel of life's daily surprises. If I
could die full of that wonder, how wonderful that might be. Pain is the
likely problem, of course. Anxiety may be another. As near as I can tell,
pain and anxiety are quite incompatible with feeling awe and wonder,
let alone with everyday good mentoring, or with building life anew.

My mother seems to experience little wonder, and strong periodic
anxiety, as she deals with her failing powers, her failing independence.
Thinking of her, I cannot help wondering yet again if such a fate awaits
me in the years to come. But more of that kind of wondering (worry-
ing by another name) is surely unhelpful. It is unhelpful for many of
the same reasons that articles about fading memory and compromised
brains seem unhelpful. Such articles focus on only a small piece of the
whole picture and so cannot predict what as yet they don't see.

I hope journalists will remember that, the next time they set out
to report the latest pessimistic research "news." Still, if I am destined to
forget my own good advice, I think they might be forgiven when they
do, too.

33 | *Meeting the General*

*W*hen I was still in my twenties I remember making a list of the friends (or perhaps I should say the professions of the friends) that I intended to cultivate over the course of my life, friends whose expertise might help me to test my own impressions of political and economic and jurisprudential and ecological and military reality. Thus, my close and wise friends would need to include an experienced Diplomat, a highly placed Politician of broad outlook, a respected Economist or three, a highly placed Judge, a highly placed Director of an international NGO such as Greenpeace or the Red Cross, a highly placed General, and also a longer list of more frequently encountered professionals, including doctors and lawyers, but also liars and poker players.

As it turned out, most of these hoped-for worldly friends were never met, except in books and occasionally in passing in a few select magazines or television documentaries. My academic colleagues in psychology were sometimes wonderful substitutes, however, and toward the end of my teaching years, when I was cross-appointed to University College and after I moved my office to the college tower, I came as close as ever to filling out my list of experts at the regular morning faculty gatherings over coffee in the Old Senate Chamber. There, a group of splendid foxes, each from a different discipline, would debate and inform each other on subjects ranging from baseball to foreign policy and far beyond. However, even in the armchairs ranged around the fireplace there, we did not have a General.

Had I met Lorraine's family much earlier than I did, I might have known just the man to fill the bill. Lorraine's father, Lt.-Col. Lee Symmes, served six years abroad on active duty during World War II, and then for a time taught military tactics to officers after returning home to Canada. At the time of his early death from melanoma, he still carried shrapnel from wounds in his head and neck acquired in close encounters of the mortal kind. The more I've learned about him, the more I regret that we didn't get a chance to become both friends and relations.

My interest in befriending a General originated while I was first living in residence at Stanford. Freshmen there were grouped on long dormitory floors containing about thirty men each. I was assigned to the first room on the left as one entered our particular hall. Far away in the last room on the right was a quiet young man on scholarship who already had planned a career in the military and who was angling for a place at West Point after graduating from Stanford. (Or so an unreliable memory insists.) I liked him, but in the end we never became close friends and I don't know what ever became of him. Still, I remember that I grew to hope that he would become my General.

It was my first (mandatory) world history course at Stanford (everyone called it "Western Civ") that piqued my interest in the military, its politics, and its psychology. That and my existing draft status during this time in the years between Korea and Vietnam when the potential dangers of military service were uppermost on many of our minds.

War had long been a frightening thing to me. I can still remember my air-raid anxiety during 1942 and 1943, living near San Francisco in a neighbourhood where the homes had no bomb shelters but where each home was fitted throughout with mandatory blackout curtains. We had air-raid drills from time to time and I remember at least one frightening (and happily false) air-raid alarm that occurred late one night. I can also remember childhood nightmares following Nagasaki and the end of the war, nightmares in which an atomic bomb exploded near our house.

Probably because of this fear in my youth, for many years I had little interest in the history of battles or military strategy. In particular I had no interest at all in the great Civil War that America still remembered and relived, a war that had been far removed both in geography and time from where I grew up. Years later a close Canadian friend happened to mention his interest in some of the great battlefields of the American Civil War and he was surprised that I seemed so actively uninterested in them. I was surprised in turn by his surprise, and by his interest. I did not want to look at the mass slaughter that was the Civil War. That was for others. That was for the Generals.

Still, in that first Western Civ course at Stanford, the importance of understanding military psychology had dawned on me, and my attitude toward my dormitory hall-mate quickly began to shift from amazed incomprehension that he could want to go to West Point to an understanding of how it might be important and interesting to have the knowledge that West Point graduates appeared to have. It might be helpful to make a friend of a General. But as I say, it appeared this was not to be. And yet, something almost as desirable seems to be happening now, in retirement, long after each profession on my list was to have been checked off.

One of the splendid serendipitous benefits of my new retirement career as a book indexer is that I've been given a kind of second chance to meet some of the people on my long languishing list. Although I still haven't met a General, I have now "met" someone with most of the same wisdom and insights that I had hoped knowing a General might afford to me. This is by way of saying I have almost finished indexing Gwynne Dyer's new revised edition of his 1985 book, *War.*

War is a stunning read, I think, and it gives a thorough and helpful perspective on how it may be possible to manage some of the risks associated with military conflict in a MAD world of "mutual assured destruction." The optimist and the pessimist will each find much to justify their prejudices in this book.

It was from this book, in its role as my General, that I have just learned something that as a psychologist I had never guessed: It is hard to make a soldier willing to kill, even when his life is at stake and he is experiencing severe battle conditions. Studies carried out during World War II uncovered the fact that during the "modern warfare" of that time, when soldiers were no longer massed in phalanxes, and where the soldier closest to you often could not see exactly what you were doing, only an average of fifteen percent of soldiers fired their weapons in battle. Rare was the circumstance when more than twenty-five percent of soldiers would "do their duty" and shoot to kill. These studies and this discovery came as a shocking surprise not only to the officers of those men who were studied, but also to the eighty-five percent of guilt-ridden soldiers themselves who imagined that they alone were not firing their weapons during fire fights.

Soon after these studies were carried out, evidence was rediscovered to suggest that even on the massed battlefield at Gettysburg during the Civil War, the same phenomenon had been occurring. Dyer reports data from a study of more than twenty-five thousand abandoned muskets, picked up after the battle, revealing that

> ... over 90% were loaded, although the nineteen-to-one ratio between loading time and firing time would logically argue that only about

5% of the muskets should have been loaded and ready to fire when their owners dropped them. Indeed, almost half of them—some twelve thousand—were loaded more than once, and six thousand of them had between three and ten rounds loaded into the barrel.

For Dyer, the conclusion is clear. He continues:

> The only rational conclusion is that huge numbers of soldiers at Gettysburg, both Union and Confederate, were refusing to fire their weapons even in stand-up, face-to-face combat at short range, and were presumably going through the act of loading and perhaps even mimicking the act of firing when somebody nearby actually did fire, in order to hide their internal defection from the killing process. And very many of those who did fire were probably deliberately aiming high.

Moreover, it doesn't end there. Dyer reports:

> This conclusion, counterintuitive though it is, applies even to the shoulder-to-shoulder formations of the eighteenth-century infantry that blasted volleys at each other from close range: the "kill-rate" was far lower than it logically ought to have been, given the accuracy of those weapons at those distances.

It has always been true that both the basic training of soldiers, and the speeches given to troops about to enter battle, dehumanize the enemy in an attempt to override the moral aversion to killing that is present in most soldiers. Thus it isn't persons that a soldier will be killing, it is "vermin" or the equivalent.

But modern basic training techniques have gone much further to address head-on the reluctance of soldiers to kill. During basic training, killing is now practiced in ways that become progressively more realistic. Killing is celebrated consciously and justified extravagantly. By degrees, the recruit is brought to a place where guilt need not follow.

In an age of ever more violent computer games, games that in some ways resemble the modern techniques of military basic training, the cultural prohibition against killing would appear to be waning among the very recruits sought by the military. And yet, the high rates of post-traumatic stress disorder seen among veterans of the current military tragedies in western Asia make me wonder if guiltless killing has in fact been achieved.

Perhaps it might be different if the "enemy" today didn't look like civilians, and sometimes even like children. But particularly today, people who are the "enemy" are impossible to tell from civilians for the very reason that they are, and always have been, just people, not vermin. Surely, continued recognition of this fact by soldiers is a very good thing.

Now that I have "met" my General, by indexing his book, I see that things are as complex and mysterious in the realm of military matters as they are in the realms of psychology or economics. There is a sense, I now think, in which understanding any topic, and every profession, really involves understanding just its own special aspects of psychology. Without greater progress in understanding human psychology, we may soon reach the limits to progress in most other areas. Still, "progress" is perceived in the eye of each beholder and I would personally regret, for instance, any progress being made in helping people achieve greater ease with acts of killing.

We have already come rather too far in that direction technologically, with powerful atomic bombs that weigh less than one hundred pounds and that can fit inside a car, and with virulent biological agents of devastating lethality. For us to add to this mix a greater psychological comfort in more and more killers appears truly suicidal, yet as a species we don't seem too concerned about our own inadvertent suicide.

It should come as no surprise, then, that today the extinction of "lesser" species breeds almost no concern at all.

What, then, is to be done?

It is not hard to understand how many people can and do become fatalistic when looking at the risks humans face in a world of shrinking size, rapid change, and uncertain threat. It is easy to conclude that, as an individual, there is nothing we can do to change the odds for the better. But any such conclusion makes no allowance for the huge unknowable effects of our efforts. Again, we have to remember that each of us affects eternity: We can never tell where our influence stops. For instance, my new General, Mr. Dyer, doesn't know he has prompted the writing of these words today after my time spent working on his book.

Today, as I record them, I have no reason to think that these musings of mine will even leave their first electronic home, let alone be read by anyone else. We mustn't let the voices of doubt, of fatalistic resignation, stop us from trying to contribute what may next be needed, whatever part of that it might be within our unsuspected power to contribute. If we are to be stopped from acting, then it is the voice of conscience that should stop us, that should always be encouraged to stop us, whenever our actions may increase the risk of doing harm to others. Conscience yes, but fatalism-induced-passivity, never. Doubt, disappointment, and earlier failures should not be allowed to stop us from trying to make things better. Human survival depends on this every bit as much as it depends on military wisdom rather than military might.

34 | *Ritual Goodbyes*

*S*hortly after 11 a.m. on the warm Tahoe morning of Sunday, August 1, my mother died from an overwhelming infection that appears to have originated, of all places, in a scraped knee caused during a fall. Her passing was anything but unexpected, yet so long had she resisted succumbing to her various ills, and so minor did her knee infection originally seem to be, that the timing of her death left me quite unprepared. Still, I was at her Truckee hospital bedside when she died and had been with her for the three previous days as it became increasingly clear that again she was gravely ill.

In her will, my mother had specified there was to be no funeral service or memorial service and that she was to be cremated. But she did not specify any special arrangements or disposition for her ashes. Seven years earlier, at the time my father had died, he had already arranged his cremation, but he, too, gave no specification about any memorial or ceremony, nor did he tell us where he wanted his ashes to reside.

A month or two after my father's death I had participated with Elizabeth Colby (who was his loving partner during his last few years of life) in our own furtive and satisfying ceremony, saying goodbye to my father while we entrusted his ashes to a lovely spot at the high-tide mark on his favourite ocean beach in all of California.* My brother, Scott, had been with us both before and after my father's death, but he was not able to return for our impromptu ocean-side ceremony.

Among the various similarities between the deaths of my two parents was the fact that I was present in both instances. In both cases I arrived a few days before the end and I had a chance to talk with each of them before talking became impossible for them. Moreover, in each case I was alone with them in the few minutes just prior to death. My mother had been moved to the hospital after I arrived at her home, so that we might better control her pain from the septic knee that apparently was spreading disease throughout her body. In the last moments of her life her full-time home caregiver, Rosa, entered the hospital room to see how she was doing. Immediately afterward my mother suddenly clutched my hand very tightly, half turned toward me, raised herself slightly off her pillow, and died.

For the next few minutes, Rosa and I sat stunned. Rosa (I learned later) had never before seen anyone die, even though in Peru she is a doctor. Soon, I left the room briefly to inform the nurses of my mother's death. They came and confirmed the event, turned off my mother's IV and oxygen, etc. closed the door and left us alone again.

Rosa and I each seemed to be struggling, perhaps trying to find the right ceremonial acts to mark the magnitude of the new situation each of us faced. Rosa was suddenly unemployed, and prematurely forced to face a major crossroad in her life. I had suddenly just become a true orphan and the likely trustee of my mother's home with its many atten-

---

*   Furtive, because it involved trespass.

dant legal responsibilities. It was also a palpable mystery to me what, if anything, this irreversible loss of my mother's long life may have been meaning to and for Rosa.

It was past noon when I left the hospital, dazed. For the next three months most of my waking hours were suffused with thoughts about the myriad of arrangements necessary for settling the estate, executing the will, and administering the Family Living Trust into which my mother had long before placed most of her assets. And while there were very many helpers who made succeeding in these varied arrangements far easier than I had feared, there were also some unexpected difficulties as well. One such difficulty centred on the form of ceremonial goodbye that should be made (if any) to mark my mother's passing.

Part of what made this a difficult decision was the fact that she had specified there should be no funeral, but she had not said what she might prefer by way of any other form of remembrance. Another difficulty was that I was pretty sure that my brother, who had been so very warm and supportive of me for the past few months, might find fault with any plan I suggested for a family ceremony, given the long and sometimes rocky relationship he and my mother had with each other. Thus, for a month or more I postponed all action, hoping the right ritual might somehow suggest itself.

I had flown down to be with my mother as soon as word had come that she seemed to be worse again. A week after her death I flew back home and then arranged to drive back down to rendezvous with my brother: to inventory, clean, and dispose of many of my mother's personal effects. Lorraine joined me on this trip, and Scott's wife, Carole, joined him. We met, stayed, and worked at the house together. The four days we overlapped were very productive yet also sometimes tense. The ghost of my mother and her belongings hovered over our work, and the nature of that work meant we were all working alone, often in different parts of the house. It was decided that before it could be sold the house was going to need major and professional cleaning. Scott and Carole agreed to bring two friends (expert cleaners) to Tahoe later in the month to undertake this work.

On the day before we all departed, tired and stressed, a disagreement arose among us, one that left me even more concerned about approaching Scott concerning arrangements for any possible memorial or ritual to mark our mother's passing. I received criticism from him for being insensitive and overbearing, and our absent mother came in for even stronger criticism, much of which I privately felt was justified. We all departed the next day, after awkward and formal goodbyes. I still faced the upcoming time when Scott would be returning with the two cleaners and I would be returning there, too, to move a piano and my other bequests from the Tahoe house to my home in Canada.

For nearly two weeks there was no further communication between my brother and me. I didn't know what to say to him. And I certainly didn't know how to bring up the sensitive topic of any ceremony for dispersing our mother's ashes. I could only hope that whatever pain had triggered that examination of our mother's perceived failings, and my own, that pain would ease with time.

And then a close Kaslo friend happened to ask me if any goodbye ceremony were planned to mark my mother's passing. I said none was yet planned, and I went on to describe some of what had happened on the most recent visit to Tahoe that had me feeling that the topic was still too sensitive to discuss with Scott. When I had finished, my friend remarked with a smile: "But surely those criticisms your brother expressed were his ceremony."

Perhaps this friend was right. It's an interesting possibility. If our final goodbyes need to be ceremonial, if they need the presence of other people (and I believe that in large part they do need others), then perhaps this was Scott's best honest chance. Perhaps it was mine, too, although I failed to take proper advantage of it. He said things about our mother that wouldn't be easy to say or to hear at a memorial ceremony with her friends present. He said things about her that I could hear but could not begin to say myself.

If retirement ceremonies need to be reconsidered (as I have previously argued here), then so, too, do various other ritual goodbyes, of which funerals are the most final.

But it is interesting: We do not make it easy to say critical things at a funeral ceremony, and some there may be who feel the need to include the mention of particularly critical things. With anyone, and particularly with a parent, it is easy to feel that somehow they "should have known better" with regard to certain hurts we may have suffered in their presence. It is common to have felt unjustly treated, particularly in those early years before one's egocentrism wanes, as well as during stressful periods thereafter when one's egocentrism has been induced to reappear.

I believe that with some people there exists in the shadows a feeling that they are "owed": owed an apology, owed justice, owed overdue love, owed recompense, even owed regrets on the part of some other. That feeling of being owed brings with it a corresponding hope: hope for vindication, hope that we may receive at last what we believe we have long been owed. But the death of any person from whom we had hoped to receive recompense destroys that hope permanently. And with that loss our whole approach to the future becomes forcibly altered. No longer can we live waiting for our vindication to come. If we are able, we must learn at last to live in today's present, rather than in an imagined future when vindication might become ours. Yet the loss of hope, for possible vindication and for justice, can amplify those same feelings of victimization and anger that earlier had made learning to let go so difficult.

All of which leads me to wonder if there isn't a better way to say funereal goodbyes, one that could facilitate the process of dissolving a perception that we were and still are owed something, a perception that the deceased could and should have acted differently toward us: They should have "known better" or "acted wisely" or "seen the error of their ways." These are pernicious perceptions and great emotional handicaps. Where are the rituals that might meet them head on and assist in dissolving them? Or am I missing something: Are these in fact helpful perceptions? Would their dissolution bring harm?

Not everyone who might harbour feelings of victimization will recognize them or admit to them. The ritual I am seeking here would at least encourage a recognition and examination of any such latent feelings. Somewhere, unknown to me, so-called bereavement counsellors may have rituals they use for just this purpose. Yet it would not surprise me if they don't. Different people almost certainly would benefit most from different rituals. But I had to invent my own ritual in the case of my mother, after my brother graciously deputized me to act alone, an event that occurred in the last minutes before he and the cleaners left Tahoe a few weeks later.

My ritual began with the distribution of my mother's ashes at three locations: half of them at the spot near her home where family and friends agreed she had been the happiest, a second portion of them in the garden of the home where she had been happiest, under aspen trees that she had herself transplanted and nurtured, and the remainder of them at a nearby overlook of that whole Tahoe geography that had meant the most to her in the final eighty years of her life. It was not easy to know what to say as I carried out this ritual. And in the end it was almost all said silently. None of it was critical of her. And yet none of it felt adequately loving either. I invented the script as I went along and felt only marginally satisfied at the outcome.

Some echoes of my goodbye ritual continued episodically during the following weeks, as I responded to friendly expressions of sympathy from friends. My replies to these people (I noted later) all seemed to stress apparent justifications for my feeling relieved and calm following my mother's death: how she had suffered in the last months of life, how I had worried about her, and therefore the blessing that was represented by the end to her increasing pains and worries. Even as I said such things, however, I actually became more stressed, hearing a dissonance between what I was saying aloud and memories of my mother's long-lasting unwillingness to accept dying. I was beginning to wonder if her final spasm, and the look on her face at the moment she died, had signalled anger and terror at being betrayed by her body, her doctors, and perhaps by me. They haunted me: those memories, and such questions.

And, to a degree, they still do today. Perhaps a public funeral or memorial service would have made things different for me (and even for my brother), particularly if my mother had not been the last of her cohort of good friends to die. But almost all of those who knew her best and who were near to her in age were already gone, a fact she often mentioned and lamented.

I still cannot guess what memorial ritual would have been best under the circumstances. Maybe after all the one that I did undertake was best at the time. Or maybe my writing these words today constitutes a better ritual. I hope so. Clearly, however, you, dear reader, will need to invent something even better if and when your time comes, assuming that you have not already done so. And perhaps one day every retiree who writes a will can also bequeath to his or her loved ones the memorial ritual that may be best for them. That is a very tall order, I know. One word may help considerably, however, if it is spoken more than once, and with heartfelt acceptance. That word is: *Amen.*

Postscript, added four years later

With the death of my mother, I became the oldest surviving descendant of my four grandparents. Almost at once I repeatedly found myself thinking, "Now I'm the next in line to die." As I write today, that death could still be a score of years away, yet not all of those years are likely to be healthy years. Moreover, the temporal inflation that comes with aging means that any optimistic "score" of remaining years will probably *feel* like something closer to just five years.

This inflation effect is heightened for me by the familiar rhythm of a lifetime framed by a long series of academic Olympiads, beginning in grade nine. These Olympiads were marked by cohorts of fellow students (and later by student friends), each of whom arrived at my schools, grew up quickly over the span of four accelerating years, thence to graduate and disappear over the horizon. Those Olympiads unconsciously became the ticks of my personal metronome, setting the tempo of my life, and in one sense they still do so today.

So time seems shorter now than ever it did back in the first Olympiad of my retirement. That fact alone has been sufficient to turn my thoughts in new directions, and to change somewhat the tone of the chapters that follow.

Part Three

Arabesque

35 | *Sound Advice for Our Advanced 'ears*

WEDNESDAY AUGUST 10, 2005

KASLO, B.C.

*L*ast night, after a string of hot days and uncomfortably warm nights, a surprisingly violent thunderstorm blew in from the west, its sudden approach hidden until the last minute by the Selkirk Mountains behind us.

I had just gone to bed, outside on the sleeping porch, and had tuned in late to that night's *Ideas* broadcast on the CBC. Above the rising shriek of turbulent wind and the lake's crashing waves came a woman's voice exploring environmental themes. The speaker appeared to be very well informed and, yes, she was rather eloquent.

Yet somehow it wasn't *what* she was saying that most impressed me, rather it was something about her warm voice, her tempo of speech, and a certain open, relaxed, and unselfconscious charm in the way she spoke that held my attention. The rising noise of the storm could not help but cause me some concern—Would a tree blow down? Would our outdoor furniture blow away?—yet the sound of this soothing voice overrode and neutralized all such concerns.

When I think about it now, I would say that almost at once I had fallen quite unconsciously in love with this voice. But soon afterward I was able to fall asleep and so I quite forgot about all that, until this morning when I was unexpectedly reminded of it while reading our *Globe*.

Now it is a fact of Kaslo life that to read the *Globe and Mail* newspaper one must go into town to buy each issue at our drugstore, and that paper only becomes available after noon on the day following the day it was initially published.

This is why it was only this morning that my eye happened to fall on a well-placed quotation from last Monday's Facts & Arguments page, the quotation that suddenly reminded me of last night's broadcast. The quote was attributed to Thomas Fuller and it read: "Choose a wife rather by your ear than your eye." What a strange yet wonderful thought! And I asked myself, "Can that be done? Is it a good idea? Isn't it possible that many people do this unconsciously anyway, and not always for the better?"*

Psychology seems to supply many examples of largely unnoticed aspects of a situation that have strong and unsuspected effects on how people react in that situation. I've never thought much before about the impact of voices, their timbre, their tempos, their pitches, their overtones, and undertones. And yet as a former psychotherapist I realize that some of the hypotheses I once formed about my clients came from exactly this source: a notable hesitation, a cool and clipped way of pronouncing certain words, an exhausting rush of words, or a slow and dreamy searching for a word that was different from the one this person would normally have used. "Listening with the third ear" it used to be called. I would say that when used effectively it is actually more like listening with the heart.

---

*   A synchronicity here: I learned at the end of last night's broadcast that I had been listening to the lovely voice of Alanna Mitchell, a writer for the *Globe*.

But what about voices in more prosaic contexts? Do people fall in love with voices, or take an instant dislike because of a voice? Were Roosevelt's fireside chats so effective (for the moment I am assuming here a retiree reader of considerable years) because Roosevelt's voice was more reassuring than his words? And those speeches by Winston Churchill, was it something infectious and reassuring about his authoritative basso or was it only his choice of words that made one love to listen?

"Voice" is often very important. We all seem to know somehow what the true voice of conscience sounds like, and how it is different from the sound of the true voice of respect, the true voice of injustice, or the true voice of contentment, or repentance, or forgiveness. We may find occasions to say: "Don't use that tone of voice with me, young man." Or: "You don't mean a word you just said." Clearly we sometimes know how to listen very carefully to the "voice" that carries the words. Soft and soothing versus soft and cynical: the difference is striking. Loud and worried versus loud and thrilled: The voices are completely different.

Last night's voice was soft, yet not "quiet." I appreciated that. As I age, I'm noticing that "loudness" is generally more and more discomfiting. It is a problem for me in movie theaters, during TV commercials, at parties, or on city streets. Hearing loss probably would be very frightening at first. But it also seems that hearing loss may have some partial compensations. Nevertheless, the loss of the ability to hear *nuance* would be (will be) one that leaves me considerably diminished. And, if I were aware of that loss, it would leave me considerably uneasy in the company of strangers.

There was a famous (perhaps infamous) experiment done on hearing that social psychologists and ethicists often recall, often with disapproval. The experiment was carried out at Stanford, probably in the late 1960s, by Professor Philip Zimbardo. No, this isn't his jailer-prisoner study that so surprised and shocked the study's experimenters, some participants, and many who heard it described. This was a study in which temporary deafness was induced using post-hypnotic suggestion so the student participant was unaware of the reason for his sudden hearing loss. Zimbardo was pretty sure that deafness will often trigger paranoia, and in this experiment apparently that is exactly what happened. (Or so the rumour has it. I don't think the study was ever published, in part because Zimbardo did not wish to subject any other people to that degree of discomfort, however temporary.)

Deafness deprives one of auditory nuance, and my hypothesis is that it is this that leads newly deaf people to feel in the dark, out of their depth, and at least a little paranoid. In its more psychotic manifestations, paranoia invariably includes a persistent delusion that one is constantly being talked about behind one's back. And with this delusion comes a corresponding compulsion to overhear everything that suspicious looking others may be saying. Moreover, with our curious human psychology that so often links simultaneous opposites in one and the same personality, paranoia will often include the hearing of hallucinated voices, sometimes distinct, menacing, and inescapable, from which the paranoid would like to flee, or possibly to end, even by killing the presumed speakers if necessary.

Here I am reminded again of Julian Jaynes' remarkable discourse on the central role of hearing and language in human psychology.[*] His thesis includes the idea that prior to the achievement of human self-consciousness, the Gods of yore were heard speaking to almost everyone as vocally hallucinated commentary, somewhat like voices in a dream. A commanding voice was, in those times, the most important ingredient of authority. And, as it remains today, voice was and is the key vehicle for all human

---

[*]   Jaynes, Julian, *The Origin of Consciousness in the Breakdown of the Bicameral Mind*. University of Toronto Press, 1976. Don't let the title put you off. Few books are as readable as this one.

language, the vehicular basis for the bulk of human intelligence.

Early humans, Jaynes suggests, were *told* what to do, what to say, by "voices" they heard in their brains, i.e., by their own emerging thoughts not yet understood to be such. Moreover, these various inner voices were recognized as (learned and heard as) being those belonging to certain Gods, or Kings, or familiar Masters, Teachers, and other authorities. Parents might die, but their children continued to hear their voices speaking to them.

Such events are not uncommon today. No wonder that "life" after death (even "life" after the radio is turned off) remains a familiar and enduring hypothesis. If Jaynes is right, we have evolved to pay particular attention to the human voice and its many nuances. For Jaynes, that is a key factor determining why we have become conscious beings, and why we have come to conceive of ourselves as beings with particular human natures.

Whether or not Jaynes is essentially correct, what we don't always recognize is how very different our various perceptions are about the "true" nature of human natures. We rarely suspect how differently two people have come to perceive their own psychologies (and those of most others). Sadly, psychology itself often misses these important individual differences in perceived human nature, or so it has seemed to me.

There is that old saying: "Never judge another until you have walked a mile in his shoes." Sometimes I wonder if this is even possible. The "shoes" of few other people will fit us comfortably, very possibly because their understanding of human nature does not fit our own. If we walk in another's shoes, distorted first to fit our own understanding of human nature, then those shoes become not the other's but a second pair of our own. His blisters stay his, and our blisters stay our own.

It is rather like our own voice and the voice of another. Our hearing of our own voice is very different than the voice others hear from us, and vice versa. Perhaps you can remember the first time you heard your own recorded voice played back in high fidelity. Perhaps you remember the shock at how different it sounded from what you "knew" to be the "true sound" of your own voice. Distort a familiar and beloved voice, particularly if it is your own, and a great deal of anxiety is immediately provoked. Yes, the voice does matter. A lot.

It is interesting that the stereotype of seniors includes people who often talk aloud to themselves. Often the stereotype includes someone who complains that others are always mumbling and won't speak clearly, yet that same person may mutter aloud to himself or herself more than ever before. These people talk to themselves throughout the day. Children can often be observed happily doing the same thing, rehearsing the roles of authorities, directing their own behaviour. It is as if there are times in life when we need flight controllers to guide our pilots through life, times when our brains are fogged, and our reactions are slowed. At such times we turn to the familiar voices coming in over the "radio" of our interior minds: voices to bring us through.

What does a retiree's voice say at such times, and more particularly, how does it *sound* when it says it? Does the voice sound light and forgiving? Does it chuckle? Is it confident? It certainly could be. That would be worth aspiring to, such a "voice."

Schopenhauer once gave some very sound advice to people suffering from distinctly inconvenient infatuations. He said something like: "Treat each of the temptations of your sensuality as if it has been a prank planned against you, but one about which you have been secretly informed in advance." Let's adapt this for today's retiree; we might say: "Treat the infirmities of aging (physical and social) as if they have been pranks planned against you, but ones about which you have been secretly informed in advance."

I like the appropriately light tone of voice in that advice. To be sure, without a sense of humour this advice is not easy to act on. And it is hard to keep a sense of humour when one is hurting. But it clearly helps to have a soothing voice in your ear, one that can say, in effect, "Don't you worry now; I'll help you take care of that, and here's what I want you to do first." Maybe that's why the best nurses and doctors are so effective: They have the right voice and the right heart for the job, not simply their sound advice.

Last night's storm blew over quickly. No trees came down. Nothing blew away. This morning, the welcome sounds of voices past reverberate warmly in my ears. Today I'll be listening with renewed attention to those special sounds.

36 | *Psychological Economics*

*R*eading Richard Parker's recent biography of John Kenneth Galbraith I came across the following remarkable sentences buried in the pages of the chapter discussing Galbraith's 1958 bestseller *The Affluent Society*. Parker writes:

> . . . capitalism generated its own powerful limitations on freedom, promoting as it did the coarse ideological claim that ever-increasing consumption is freedom. To Galbraith this was "a false ideal." He argued, or hoped, that given affluence, more and more people would come to realize that "leisure, free time and intellectual achievement are the real thing." (p. 303)

I construe this to mean that, for Galbraith at least, the ever-increasing accumulation of wealth and things is to be seen as a false good; that in fact it is a disguised ill. By contrast, early retirement looks to be a truer good, socially, economically, and (interestingly) morally.

But concerning retirement, there are two counterarguments that spring readily to mind.

First, retirement plans are becoming much less dependable, and one's retirement income is becoming much less predictable. However "good" retirement may actually be, to an increasing number of workers it is not a choice that appears to be readily or safely available.

Second, there seem to be many people for whom retirement really does risk being dangerous to health or happiness.

I am thinking particularly of the recent work of certain Japanese psychiatrists who have lately been diagnosing a great deal of RHS (Retired Husband Syndrome) among the wives of Japanese retirees. Apparently, having hubby suddenly home and irritable is destructive to marriage and to health in many cases.

And why should Galbraith's "good" of retirement provoke irritability in hubby? Because, particularly in Japan, hubby's closest friends have typically been his colleagues at work, who are also those with whom he regularly played when not working. If hubby was often away at business-related social events, sometimes including weekends or evenings, and if suddenly he is no longer supposed to join his business friends to play and get out of the house, he can become (not to put too fine a point on it) rather inconsiderate and a trial to be around. In such a case, retirement actually decreases rather than increases leisure time, and the time it does free up is rarely used for intellectual achievement or the pursuit of new interests.

When work is too much fun to leave, a forced retirement is no blessing. (Which is not to suggest that forced retirement would normally be a blessing, even in disguise.)

To a North American ear this may all sound a bit strange. And yet there are many people who are too happy at their work to want to retire. There was a great deal that I enjoyed about my work at the university before I elected early retirement. I have always said, rather habitually, that I was extremely lucky to have had my university career during the years that I did, and that I was extremely happy while in it.

If that were true, however, then there was and still is something rather dissonant about my eagerness to retire early and about my current love of retirement. I am suddenly struck by the thought that perhaps I have always protested too much about how enjoyable my life was as a professor. If it really were true that I loved academia, why then did I so look forward to sabbaticals, and why was I so sad when my sabbaticals came to an end? If I really loved my work, why was I feeling so very sad as I left Kaslo to return to Toronto each fall in the years immediately prior to my retirement? Even at that time I recognized these signs as reasons to consider retiring soon.

Maybe I felt, just as Galbraith apparently did, that it might be best if there were a ceiling on one person's production of goods and income. Or maybe I didn't realize that something about Toronto life, or my teaching, or my research work, was no longer the source of joy that I imagined it had always been. (Or perhaps, guiltily, some part of me did realize it.)

I do recall one notably disappointing event at the university toward the end of my career there, and that event probably did colour my feelings about continuing my academic teaching and research. Until now I have supposed that I had long ago shrugged the matter off. But today I am not so sure. Alas, that old disappointment rankles still. The event to which I refer was my complete failure to make the case that teaching (particularly undergraduate teaching) was being under-supported, and under-emphasized, in most departments at the university.[*]

---

[*]   I had the opportunity to attempt this as a member of a Provostial committee that was charged with examining the university's existing policies and actual practices for rewarding both teaching and research. In the end, this committee was not persuaded that existing practices deserved improvement, or that they undervalued good teaching.

I attributed the university's lukewarm support of undergraduate teaching in part to the undeniable difficulty in quantifying excellence in teaching, and also to the university's sleight of hand that generally gave lower weight to ratings of success at teaching than it did to corresponding ratings of research excellence. Both sets of ratings were combined as a basis for various general assessments of how well individual professors, whole departments, and the entire university had been performing.

In my view, the university had long sought to reward mainly renaissance men and women who shone both as exceptional researchers and as exceptional teachers, but with this latter virtue being treated as something of a secondary bonus, forgivable whenever it happened to be absent. There are and always have been very few such people, people who have been truly gifted in the lab, in the field, in the library, and also highly gifted when standing behind a lectern. The men and women perceived to be truly excellent in only one of the research or teaching realms, who had been perceived to be average or below average in the other realm (assuming here that we could *correctly* know that they were—an assumption I also have reasons to question), were regularly encouraged to upgrade themselves in their weaker area rather than being truly valued for their stronger (and in some senses, unique) contributions. More to the point, most professors were given above-average teaching ratings (because most were pretty good, it was said) while averaging only average for their research (because of the different way these ratings were quantified), though most professors were pretty good at doing research, too. Thus the more variable research ratings always carried significantly more weight in determining the rankings of overall merit once these more variable research ratings were numerically added to the more uniform teaching ratings.

I have always believed that quality should trump quantity in evaluating academic and scientific publications. And trumping both should be the *value* placed by future readers on various articles and books in the role such publications play as contributions to the reader's own understanding and the reader's own work in progress.

But here's the rub: (a) Future readers often won't be in a position to read or appreciate a publication until quite some time after it is published, and (b) they may never recognize how crucial their reading of that publication has been in "helping" them, and (c) almost invariably they will be in no position to provide any public acknowledgment of the value they received from reading that publication, acknowledgment that could have been used by others who may wish to reward that value. I hold that one seminal article published by an obscure academic, an article that leads to someone else's fruitful theory or brilliant experiment or advance in technology, deserves just as much recognition and support by a university or foundation as does either (a) that later achievement by someone else and/or (b) last year's rich publication list of that obscure academic's better-known colleague, no articles or books by whom have yet led on to any great advances.

In short, only time, and sometimes a very long time, too, can give the slightest hope of revealing the supposed worth or utility of a given piece of work and its place in the long-term evolution of ideas, culture, and technology. We should accept that ratings of academic publications (and by extension, every publication) cannot be reliable indications of professional merit, whatever may be our criteria for recognizing such merit.

The same is even truer of the work done by teachers. Teachers are publishers to the mind. Their unprinted words are spoken to the ears and hearts of students who are willing and enabled to hear. Their lesson plans are designed to awaken interest and insight. But again, there is rarely any reliable way to determine that a given teacher has sparked a fire in someone who in consequence is destined to accomplish great things later on.

Have you noticed the contradictions in what I have said above? On the one hand, I implied that my ego was bruised because my university undervalued (in particular it seems, underpaid) the work of its good teachers while simultaneously overvaluing and overemphasizing the work of its many approved researchers. But the university could do better only if it had a reasonable way of identifying its truly good teachers and good researchers. On the other hand, I implied that there *is* no reasonable way to define good academic work because only a long-delayed assessment of such work could have some validity, and even then only in the rare instance when the personal contribution of that work has been both recognized and also fed back to the university assessors could it ever be appropriately used.

I have to laugh (and hope you can, too) as I admit it: I want it both ways. I want a more reasonable method of assessing both teaching and research contributions, without the need to wait forever for those assessments even though no adequate assessments may ever be devised. Still, I will soon try to insist that it may be *possible* to have it something close to both ways. But first there is more to be said on the topics of popularity and status and power, and their places on the job, and during life in general.

When it comes to assessments of both academic teaching and academic publications, there are at least a few common factors used by universities and foundations, by editors and by granting agencies, in separating the presumed wheat from the presumed chaff. Popularity is generally the main such factor, whether recognized or not, and whether rated directly or measured indirectly. In the case of academic publications, popularity is usually reflected in (and assessed using) a count of the number of articles or books an academic has recently had accepted for publication, and later, sometimes, by the number of occasions any such publications have been cited as references by other, later, authors.[*]

---

[*] Citations are not always signs of approval by others; and citation rates are generally skewed in favour of research topics that are currently popular and active, rather than pointing to seminal articles that are helpful and "important" but may be on a topic whose time has not yet come or is incorrectly assumed to be past.

As if all publications can be counted as nearly equal, be they long or short, broad or narrow, on research that took days or years to accomplish, and whether they treat ideas that are simple or complex.

When assessing teaching, the *popularity* of a given teacher's courses, and student ratings of their enjoyment of, or satisfaction with, those courses, often weighs heavily in the assessments made. I have prospered considerably from such a popularity criterion because I was regularly blessed with teaching a fascinating topic (Introductory Psychology) to hundreds of students who really wanted to satisfy their curiosity about that topic.

But I also taught courses in statistics and in measurement theory, courses that are much less popular as a rule, but ones that happen to be very pertinent to our topic here of accurately assessing skills and performance levels, including attempts to measure academic excellence. These were not courses that a student would normally elect, nor normally find fascinating. In these courses, superior student course evaluations were much harder to come by, and they only came, when they did, by virtue of helping certain dedicated students achieve skills and understandings that did not come easily, yet nonetheless did come.

Even so, superior course evaluations in these classes often did not come at all. But then, on certain happy occasions, a rare letter would find its way to me after half a dozen years had gone by, a letter saying that what my correspondent had learned in that challenging class of years past continued to be more helpful and useful than they had ever guessed it would be, and, that they were very grateful for the effective guidance and help they had received in understanding that particular difficult topic.

Now that, to me, is the better criterion of good teaching, and equally of a good academic publication. Time reveals it to have been of significant help to those who follow. Still, this doesn't make for popularity, particularly not in the short run. Popularity is a flawed indicator of "making a significant contribution." Just as popularity is a flawed indicator of being a better person.

Of course, academia isn't the only workplace where popularity plays a large and often invisible role in decisions about awards of salary and/ or status. Most employers attempt to assess "merit" in their employees using a conveniently limited number of criteria to do so. Popularity appears to play a central role in ratings by managers of an employee's work. And assessments of the managers themselves are even more likely to come down to their popularity with those above or below them. Often, of course, this truth is so uncomfortable that ratings and bonuses for managers are claimed to be based solely on supposedly "objective" criteria, such as so-called productivity in their departments, their level of sales, their profitability this quarter, their success at meeting preset goals and deadlines, etc. Unfortunately, such successes (or failures) generally depend far less on managerial ability than they do on factors completely outside a manager's control, such as general economic conditions and limiting decisions made by those higher in the company's hierarchy.

Even while using supposedly objective criteria, assessors often have considerable leeway for adjusting the final assessment. This temptation is always present whenever the "objective" and the subjective impressions lead to different assessments, which is to say whenever the "objective" rating feels subjectively invalid. In short, aspects of popularity (friendship with; admiration of; the wish to be liked by; etc.) in someone being assessed have a way of subjectively invalidating an unfavorable "objective" assessment made of that person, the "questionable" nature of which is often easy for the assessor to "see." It works in reverse, too, of course: A favourable "objective" assessment, of someone who is not popular with the assessor, can often be rationalized away equally as easily.

Assessments of employees generally are made in the context of deciding on financial rewards for those employees. But financial and related benefits are not the only incentives that employers control and to which employees respond. "Status" and "power" are also important incentives, increases in which can be strong incentives for some. In fact all these factors (financial rewards, increasing power and responsibility on the job, and increasing status within the work world) overlap and cross-fertilize in many corporate and academic workplaces. There will be some who do not wish to retire until they have enjoyed rich earnings; some who do not wish to retire until they have achieved a high rank or status on the job; some who do not wish to retire until they have enjoyed the power to achieve certain changes or accomplishments in their organization or in the world. And (naturally) there will be some who seek and expect all three of the above before they even consider retiring. Moreover, there will always be some (getting back to Galbraith's insight) who will not recognize when enough is enough: that the appropriate time to retire has passed.

Who then does deserve financial reward, increased status, and more power? Who gets the bonus and who gets the glory? It is hard to argue with a reply that says: It is he or she who has exercised the greatest skill or ability who should be rewarded the most. But there are psychological costs even in what may at first appear to be a fair and unbiased meritocracy. Envy of the lucky gifted ones by those who are denied status and reward, plus the potential for unhelpful (yet common) discouragement and self-deprecation by these same people, are psychological costs that must not be denied or underestimated.

So how can I have it both ways? How can there be good assessments of academic performance (or any other type of performance) without access to the time and evidence that may permit those better assessments? How can the psychological costs associated with existing imperfect assessments be avoided?

I think the answer is to acknowledge openly the many existing problems in creating valid workplace assessments and incentives, and at the same time to stop pretending that it is somehow necessary and useful and appropriate to treat employees unequally when it comes to salary and status. Put very simply: We should use assessments of performance very sparingly, and except for decisions involving hiring, promotion (reassignments), or firing, we should not use the results of these assessments to create differences in salary, status, or power among employees. If an employee has a particular gift for any part of his or her job, that employee should be valued for that gift. Different employees bring different gifts to the workplace, each of which can contribute to the organization's overall accomplishment and productivity. These contributions should be appreciated and valued equally.

I recognize that our society was never ready for such a radical plan. And we enjoy competition too much to ban it from the workplace just yet. For some, the competition helps turn work into play. Without winners and losers, some people will feel cheated. (Many current winners will anyway.) But competition can be enjoyed in other arenas, outside the workplace. And my hypothesis is that when the psychological and economic *costs* of competition in the workplace are finally exposed to the light, they will be found to be surprisingly high. When these costs are minimized, my guess is that *Net Employee Happiness*, not to mention overall employee productivity (in academia: happier teaching and deeper thinking), will greatly increase. One day (not soon) perhaps Psychological Economics will be understood much better, and in consequence *Net Employee Happiness* and *Net Customer Happiness* will have their own more appropriate measures and their own contributions to make to a much less important *Net Return on Investment* or *Net Profit*. I say "not soon" because both psychology and economics are fields where outcomes are the products of hundreds of causal factors that interact in complex ways.

Meanwhile, I look out my office window at the lake and dream of Plato's ancient grove, where the only competition was to be the first to understand, and the first to teach. It sounds to me like maybe this is part of the dream that the wise economist, Professor Galbraith, had in mind, too.

POSTSCRIPT

SATURDAY JANUARY 21, 2006

CALEDON (FORMERLY TERRA COTTA) ONTARIO

Half-unconsciously, taking my retired psychotherapist's hat off the shelf and putting it on my head for a moment, I cannot help but be intrigued by the tentative suggestion at the start of this little essay that my early retirement may have been impelled by a disappointment over a matter of academic politics. (Perhaps it was, in some small part. But just how significant was all that?) One might ask what there was for this academic to be unhappy about, returning each fall to Toronto?

This particular memoir fragment begins almost at once to talk about marriages (in Japan) and difficulties with short-tempered husbands (in Japan) but then it diverts from that theme to talk about interpersonal academic relations, and social status, popularity and esteem, and finally about perceived self-worth. We are talking here about someone trained as a "developmental" psychologist, someone rather familiar with theories of "stages of development." Someone who, soon after retiring, appears on the surface to have elected the pain of a marriage breakup. Are we never to learn about this person's marriage, and how his spouse felt about his taking early retirement, and what he thinks it all meant to her? Perhaps he doesn't "protest too much," except when he says that he does. Perhaps he protests rather too little?

Returning my dusty psychotherapist's hat to its shelf, slightly amazed and taken aback, let me answer:

(1) I accept these questions and observations as valid, if a bit narrow and off-topic.

(2) The married retiree clearly does face a different retirement than does the widowed retiree or the single retiree, differences that deserve exploration and examination by those who have lived them.

(3) My marriage to Elizabeth, and particularly many of the events surrounding our separation and later divorce, I consider to be personal and confidential. I assume she does, too. I see no reason to elaborate on those topics further. And finally,

(4) "Stage theories" of development generally seem to me to be much too oversimplified to be particularly valid or helpful. Retirement is not a stage in life *per se*. I see it as a temporary goal, one that opens up choices among a variety of more interesting goals while we are playing seriously at the work of growing old.

37 | *Playing with Stones*

*O*ur culture has an interesting take on the work-play arenas, seen sometimes as a work-play dichotomy. How much of retirement is play? But then, how much of work was or still is play? Should retirement be all play?

People have always made a distinction between play and work. I was never quite sure if such a distinction was more help or hindrance in thinking about play. If play is coextensive with fun, work can certainly be playful when it is going well. If play is about exploring ideas, work can certainly provide further opportunities for that, too. If play is about practicing ways to achieve a goal, a lot of work involves such practice.

But if play is following your own whims and doing whatever seems enjoyable and interesting right now, perhaps work limits that type of play in ways that retirement does not, always depending, of course, on the state of the retiree's health and circumstances. Ask people what they plan to do after they retire and you will usually hear a list that may include things like "play more golf" or "play more bridge." Some plan to buy an RV and see the world: their retirement being seen as a last long vacation; travel seen as play; and here perhaps, play perceived mainly as any vacation from work.

There was a time, long ago now, when I was fascinated with children's play. I wondered why play is so absorbing to children, and what functions it might serve. I wondered why it appears to drop so much in importance among young adults. (If in fact it really does so drop.) For a time, play behaviour became my special area of interest and "expertise." My Ph.D. thesis at Yale was devoted to one aspect of children's choices among play materials. Today, play is still a mystery to psychologists. But I find that playing in retirement is no less important to me today than it was when I was a child. And it has now become more important than ever it was before I retired.

I stopped doing research on play behaviour, and stopped doing much thinking about the topic, soon after the journal that published my Ph.D. research declined to publish a better study that I had carried out two years later, one that was done in a natural setting rather than a laboratory setting, a study the results of which called into question some of the conclusions I had published earlier. The journal (and two others) declined to publish even a brief note to warn readers that there may be limits to the usefulness of my earlier published conclusions. My professional interests soon turned toward other puzzles, and particularly, at the end of my career, to the mysteries of psychosomatics and to those surrounding the causes of the common cold. Even so, I never completely stopped wondering about play.

As befitted a stereotypic academic-to-be, I was never very serious about (or particularly skilled at) sports in my youth. I played some basketball on school teams until torn knee ligaments (acquired while skiing beyond my limits) put an end to such fun for quite some time. As an adult, I got most of my exercise walking or bicycling throughout the city. And for whatever reasons, I did not anticipate more playing when I retired. Yet now I find myself playing much more than I ever had before.

As a young adult I generally played table games, both solitary and competitive. I played a smattering of solitaire and poker, some chess, but later I played mostly Go. Go is a two-person board game that eclipsed my interest in chess after I was introduced to it while at university. I soon understood why Lasker, the great chess grandmaster, had given up chess for good and played only Go once he had been introduced to the game. The rules of Go are much simpler than those of chess, the strategy of Go is at least as deep and challenging as chess, and unlike chess it is possible to handicap the start of a game of Go so players of unequal experience and skill can both have a challenging game without the handicap changing the strategy that each player will use to try to win. In chess, employing a handicap does indeed change a player's experience and some of the strategy of the game.

Go is played with small lens-shaped black and white "stones." Players take turns placing their stones on the intersecting lines of a grid nineteen lines by nineteen lines in size. Any stone (or linked group of stones) that is completely and adjacently surrounded by stones of the opposing colour is removed from the board. When there is no more room for either party to play a stone to advantage, the game is over and the winner is whichever player has surrounded the most territory, i.e., the person who has surrounded the greater number of the 361 locations where stones might be placed.

Simple though this game is to learn, Go players are still not easy to find, the way chess players are, except in east Asia where the game originated. As a result I took a very long vacation from playing Go sometime in mid-career after I had moved away from the few friends I had to play with.

My last game of Go was played many years ago now, in Toronto, with a younger Japanese man I had just met at a party. He invited me to his high-toned yacht club to play Go one weekend afternoon. Neither of us knew our relative strengths and so our first game was played without any handicap.

All of the Go games I had played until then involved a lot of thinking on the part of both players before making many of their moves, and each game took approximately three times the length of time taken by a normal chess game. But on that day my Japanese opponent gave almost no thought to each of his moves and within forty minutes it was clearly apparent to both of us that he would win by an overwhelming margin. I followed the tradition I had grown up with and resigned at this point.

Since the time remaining was still plentiful he asked if I'd like to play a rematch. I said I would, but I asked him if I might be given a handicap in recognition of the clear difference between us in skill level. He wouldn't hear of it. That would constitute an insult to me, his guest for the day.

In the long years that followed that day the only stones I played with were various beauties that I brought home from my travels. One particularly large and heavy stone, a miniature slate mountain, sat on my office filing cabinet in the decade before I retired. Visitors to my office would sometimes reach out and touch it, generally quite unconsciously. The old pun is apt: There is something very grounding about rocks.[*]

As a boy I used to hunt for flat stones to skip across the water, while playing for hours at the Tahoe lakeshore. Now, as a retiree, I've begun devoting equally happy hours to the work of "delivering" rocks and "sweeping" stones, in the hope one day of becoming a Skip myself. You see, since retiring I've discovered the sport of curling.

---

[*] As I write at my desk today there are at least a dozen stones within reach, and another dozen in the surrounding room, stones originating from places all over the world. I am constantly finding reasons to touch or heft or rearrange them.

It all began when I was trying to interest some of my newly retired Kaslo friends to learn to play Go. I was lamenting my lack of any success when my good friend Denis suggested (for something like the fourth time) that instead of playing a board game I should be joining him at Kaslo's small ice rink twice a week to take up curling. In my naiveté I had always thought of curling as "just shuffleboard on ice." Oh shame! Shame! Happily, Denis finally prevailed and I joined the senior men and women of Kaslo each Tuesday and Thursday afternoon for my curling apprenticeship.

Curling turns out to be far deeper and more interesting than it generally appears to those who have never played it. Eight stones are delivered (alternately) by each team during each "end" (a mini-game). The object is to finish each end with one or more of your own stones closer to the central "pin" at the far end of the sheet of ice than is the closest single stone belonging to your opponents. Achieving this is not easy.

Curling is at once very strategic, and very dependent on skillful teamwork. The skills needed to "deliver" forty-three pounds of polished granite (starting the stones on their travel down the ice) are simple skills to learn, yet they are capable of considerable refinement. So, too, are the skills needed to decide when and how hard to "sweep" the ice in front of a moving stone (thus straightening and lengthening the normally curved path the slowly spinning stone will travel toward its intended resting place). The various skills needed to "Skip" the team are particularly deep and subtle and these include:

(a) Deciding what upcoming arrangement of stones may be most favourable for your team.

(b) Choosing the destination and track for your team's next delivered stone.

(c) Knowing exactly where that stone should be aimed to allow for the curved path it will follow to reach the chosen destination.

The condition of the ice sheet is ever-changing, and it must be "read" and compensated for by all four team members as the game progresses.

It is particularly relevant to the novice retiree that one does not need a youthful physique to achieve impressive skills at this most enjoyable game. The oldest Olympic participant in the upcoming Winter Games in Turin will be a curler for the American team who is in his mid-fifties. Teenagers and seniors of both genders can and do become devoted curlers of great skill.

There is something else about curling that I find particularly wonderful. It still has a special ethos, almost universally respected, one that emphasizes friendliness in competition. The emphasis is very much on having fun while playing, not on outdoing someone else. This ethos results in taking pleasure at any difficult shot skillfully completed, whether that has been accomplished by your own team or by a player who happens to be an opponent. Compliments within and between teams are frequently given during the course of club curling games. Criticism, even self-criticism, is generally frowned on.

The respected tradition also includes this: Following a game the winners buy the losers a drink and all eight participants are expected to relax around the same table and socialize before departing. Curling, even played at Olympic and world-class levels, breeds an equality of spirit and a remarkable camaraderie that few sports can equal.

I deliver stones now, and sweep hard, as a pleasant way to keep fit during that half of the year when outdoor walks are not particularly rewarding. Energetic sweeping not only can pay off in "saving" an errant shot, but also it can leave one with a pleasant fatigue after the game. Even practice time, spent simply delivering stones, can leave one winded, and particularly so if you are of a certain age. But the satisfaction to be gained by successfully making a tricky shot can be delightful. And such satisfaction is even greater at seeing improvements in your game, particularly at a time in life where a diminution in skill levels is more generally the rule.

Even stepping onto an empty sheet of practice ice, flat and inviting, makes me smile now. And the long slide out with the stone, letting it glide ahead and gently curl out of my fingers, has a magic feel easily equal to that of skipping a perfect flat beach stone more than fifteen times.

In both cases, for a moment, time stands still. One is watching the stone recede, and slow, and curl. At the beach, a skipped stone quietly vanishes. On the ice, the gliding stone quietly anchors. In each case, it is a true wonder. And the feeling of wonder, I now realize, is primarily what turns it into pure play.

38 | *Angers Retired*

*I*f memory and my library can help me here, Erik Erikson once said of the retiree's "stage" of development (he called it the stage of Integrity versus Despair and Disgust) that these are the years when we "grow the fruit" of the seven previous life stages that he had discerned.

In Erikson's view the fruit of this culminating eighth stage includes a well-developed "sense of comradeship" with men and women of distant times and different experience. But should such fruit fail to materialize, if life has left integrity's early flower unpollinated by facilitating social encounters, experience, and life choices, then the result can be a quiet despair that lies hidden beneath what Erikson called "a chronic contemptuous displeasure with particular institutions and particular people."

To this I would add that "disgust" (and one form of "despair") may also be signalled by enduring anger, including silent anger, and perhaps visitations of wild Ate, and certainly by vengeful anger.

Because (a) there do happen to be a few particular institutions and

269

a few particular people that provoke in me something unnervingly close to contemptuous displeasure these days, and because (b) they have done so over modest recent timespans, long enough that others (oh, but never I) might decide to call these emotions "chronic," I do worry at times about my retirement mental health.

Thus I have lately decided I should refresh my acquaintance with Erikson's work, a project that I hope will soon involve rereading a book Erikson wrote late in life, with his wife, Joan, and their colleague Helen Kivnick, titled *Vital Involvement in Old Age*. My copy of this book, signed by Erik and Joan, who were friends of my stepmother Helga, still resides in my library nearly twenty years after Helga presented it to me. I hardly remember my professional first reading of it, but I am looking forward to reading it again, with rather different eyes this time, and through a new set of lenses.

It was at Stanford that I first encountered Erikson's ideas. Of course at that age I was particularly taken by his description of the adolescent stage where one nurtures a sense of Identity. In those days it was taking me some time (a) to settle on a degree major, and (b) to foresee a significant career deriving from that major, and (c) to achieve the basis for building such a career.

Today I find it puzzling and interesting that despite my eventual success in all three respects, I still exhibit (in part) an irrational disloyalty to my fine *alma mater*. There was so much good that happened for me at Stanford, and so much good that happened to me later because of Stanford, I might have expected to become one of the most grateful and generous of her alumni. And yet for some of the reasons hinted at earlier in my chapter "The Stanford Shadow," and for other reasons rather harder to see, I am currently unable to summon much generosity of feeling for and to Stanford. This is due in part to aspects of Stanford's Hooverism and to its part in supporting an increasingly vicious form of Republican capitalism: one that to me appears red in tooth and claw and moral ink. These tend to eclipse for me the prodigious virtues of Stanford's many thousands of thoughtful professors and graduates, of whom Steven Breyer[*] from my own graduating class is but one of many examples.

I find that I still cheer earnestly for the Big Red Machine whenever I discover the Stanford football team at play on television, but more often these days I am dismayed when the news shows Stanford's ex-provost, Condoleezza Rice,[**] propagandizing for a renegade Bush administration that has severely crippled American goodwill and good world citizenship, not to mention that administration's negative catalytic effects on American economics, American ecology, and world society.

Recently, *Stanford Magazine*, which is sent to all alumni, had a cover story that made me particularly uncomfortable and ill disposed to the university.[***] This article must also have provoked a similar response in many other like-minded alumni, for in the following two issues there were a large number of strongly critical letters to the editor about it. But of course, Stanford being Stanford, there were a dozen letters of high praise as well. I responded with a letter of my own, addressing a topic that had been indirectly introduced in the article, but one that none of the other letter writers addressed: the topic of enduring anger and how different people deal with their anger. My letter wasn't published, and I won't repeat it here.

Still, I would like to continue exploring, in somewhat more detail, the theme of enduring anger, and the dangers such anger can pose for individuals and societies. I suppose I am also hoping that occasionally grumpy retirees such as I may occasionally be spared a hasty Eriksonian diagnosis of contemptuous displeasure and despair. There is, I think,

---

[*]   A liberal U.S. Supreme Court Justice.

[**]   National Security Advisor, and later, U.S. Secretary of State.

[***]"Top Gun," by Kevin Cool, March/April 2006, pp. 42–49.

a proper place for controlled anger in our older years, but one that requires a close self-examination.

The article that sparked all the controversy was about the current president of America's National Rifle Association, a Stanford alumna named Sandra Froman. The article opened with a description of a night in 1981 when Ms. Froman was awakened by the sound of someone trying to jimmy the lock on her front door. She ran to the door where she saw, through a peephole, a man working away on her lock with a screwdriver. She banged on the door with her fists and screamed at the man, but he was not deterred. He straightened up and then went right back to work. She panicked, tried unsuccessfully to call a neighbour, then phoned the police who told her to lock herself in an upstairs room.

Unfortunately, there was no upstairs room with a lock. Thinking fast, she turned on all the lights, then opened the upstairs windows and blared her stereo at full volume to attract as much attention as possible. When the police arrived soon after, the intruder was gone.

Ms. Froman was understandably distraught by this experience. She reported, "I was scared and angry, and the more I thought about it, the angrier I got." The next day she drove to a gun shop intending to buy a gun for herself. She was advised to take a course on gun safety first. She did so that very weekend.

She was already a very good young trial lawyer. During her gun safety course she found out that she was also a very good shot. Soon afterward, she completed the purchase of her first handgun.

The article then went on to detail Ms. Froman's subsequent career and her growing volume of work in opposition to laws for gun control. "She carries a pistol in her purse or on her hip," we were told, "and occasionally has refused to enter establishments that wouldn't let her bring the gun inside." The article ended by quoting her as saying, "Everyone is safer when criminals don't know who is armed. I'm this five-foot-two middle-aged lady, but they don't know I'll shoot their guts out."

Twenty-five years after the event that first triggered her sense of helplessness and fury, the signs of her anger (and behind it, her fear) are still there. She reports feeling calm and safe now, with her guns close by, but it doesn't appear that her conserved anger has evolved into anything more generous or comprehending. As a retired clinical psychologist it seems to me that this residual unconscious anger, and the residual fears underlying it, constitute crippling psychological scars that could endanger Ms. Froman's physical and professional health. More importantly, however, these emotions can be a danger to the health of our society. To me, Ms. Froman still appears to be seeking revenge for her terror of long ago. She almost seems ready to administer capital punishment, even when this might later turn out to have been her response to an attempted misdemeanour.

What can we do with and about our enduring anger: we as individuals and we as a society? What can we do when that anger is our own? What can we do when it is someone else's? There are no easy answers to such questions, which may well be part of the reason that terrorism appears to be back on the increase. Today, more and more people appear to have more and more reasons to plan for revenge. And their anger also increases their likelihood of being recruited to perform acts of terrorism.

Effective controls over the world production of and trade in arms and ammunition could help reduce the potential for latent angers to cause widespread injury. In my enduring naiveté I always used to think that some benign superpower police, or maybe the UN, could rather easily stop ninety percent of all arms production and ninety-eight percent of the trade in arms. It seems, however, that the multiple arms industries, their lobbyists, governments themselves, and military groups around the world, all stand in the way of marshalling the resources necessary to achieve an effective control of dangerous arms. (I would exclude hunting rifles and shotguns from the category of "dangerous," and perhaps certain small arms as well, despite their potential for misuse.) We are left, then, with a renewed concern over the increasing risk that one or a very few angry people can get control of a weapon of mass destruction, be it nuclear, chemical, or biological. Once in possession, they will certainly want to trigger it. And so, again, what indeed are we to do?

Sunday December 24, 2006
Caledon (formerly Terra Cotta) Ontario

I now find myself at a point similar to one encountered by the Turkish writer Orhan Pamuk in his recent Stockholm address on the occasion of receiving the Nobel Prize in Literature. During his address, Pamuk appeared to find himself wishing to change the mood of his words and the direction that his thoughts seemed to be taking. So he "interrupted" his narrative to say: "The question we writers are asked most often, the favourite question, is: *Why do you write?*" Pamuk then offered a string of more than twenty potential answers to this question. And scattered among those many answers were the following three:

> *I write because I am afraid of being forgotten.*
> *I write because I am angry at everyone.*
> *Perhaps I write because I hope to understand why I am so very,*
> *very angry at everyone.*[*]

When I began writing this extended musing on anger, and on a certain cluster of senior emotions, emotions that hopefully might fall short

---

[*]   Translated from Turkish by Maureen Freely. Published in *The New Yorker*, Dec. 25, 2006.

of Erikson's description of the sour fruit of an unfulfilled life (Despair and Disgust), I had in mind what felt like a useful conclusion to share, as well as a scenic narrative route that nicely circled back to that conclusion. But during the time it took me to reach the above point in my writing, I lost this route home, and with it went my intended conclusion. Twice since that time I have glimpsed a different conclusion about Eriksonian Integrity, about bouts of late-life anger, and about the potential role of retirement in triggering or understanding, or dissolving the need for each. Both those glimpses occurred in the middle of the night. But predictably, neither of them came back into focus the following morning.

It is interesting, however, that since I began writing on this theme, and while waiting to rediscover the intended route home to my conclusion, I have finally discovered myself feeling somewhat more compassion for, and quite a bit more acceptance of, Ms. Froman. Even the article in praise of her career no longer offends me in the way it did at first. I began writing on this topic in part because I was so distressed by what I originally saw as a tacit celebration of anger and revenge in a world that seems to be in increasing danger from each. I felt the Stanford article lacked integrity in that sense, even as the journalist who wrote it seemed to be scrupulously matter-of-fact and neutral in his reporting.

The importance of many things happily drops away as we age, but I think Erikson has captured very well the essence of something that may gain in importance the older we get. And that something *is* integrity. Perhaps in retirement we revisit something that is first cousin to an early adolescent rage against perceived hypocrisy and the inauthentic in this world. Particularly when such states are imagined in others. Not that I think that rage is ever helpful. And not that I think anyone deserves rage.

But what about hypocrisy or a perceived lack of authenticity in oneself? Is it any easier to show integrity as a senior than it had been as an adult, or as an adolescent? As a senior it may in fact be harder to miss seeing the signs that we all fall short of the degree of integrity that we would prefer to possess.

Both the young adolescent and the mature retiree may share certain feelings of vulnerability in connection with a perceived lack of wished-for efficacy in life. From time to time, both may experience their lives as life-with-loss: the loss associated with restricted mobility, with restricted knowledge, limited memory, limited income, or depersonalized, involuntary dependency. With the adolescent we wish to give him or her hope, in the form of reassurance that this perceived state of loss is only temporary. For the retiree some might hope that he or she will find the key to turning perceived loss into acceptance, or perhaps into unimportance, or perhaps even into perceived opportunity. Retirement offers the opportunity to frame life afresh, to see our childhood, adolescence, and career years from outside, in a new way, a way that facilitates the work of sifting the past for what really has mattered and for what really offers us integrity in the present.

In his Nobel address, Pamuk emphasized another ingredient that may be required for achieving a sense of integrity: the laying to rest of any residual sense of powerlessness, any sense of marginality (which is, perhaps, another form of inauthenticity), but most of all, any sense of exclusion from the centre of things, from the social umbilicus that seems to bring "life" to a life. (Retirees know these feelings first-hand.) If anger comes from fear, and if our greatest fears are fears of exclusion, loneliness, and being unloved (or worst of all: becoming unlovable), does this mean that the answer to anger is receiving acceptance, approval, love, or esteem from others?

Apparently not. Or not fundamentally. For it is not others who ultimately trigger our fears. Rather, it is *we* who trigger them, having formed over the years what appear to be the habits of fearing whenever we are in particular situations. When our desires for attaining ever-receding mirages are disappointed, they appear to call out this habit of fear.

To combat fear of this sort we have to find an acceptance of reality, and particularly, an acceptance of ourselves. We must nurture a love of ourselves that has about it no selfishness, no pride, and no egotism; an acceptance that is framed neither by modesty nor immodesty; an acceptance that does not depend on comparing ourselves favorably with others. On the contrary, any such acceptance must facilitate the acceptance of others, just as they are. Yet this can be imagined to require accepting the "unacceptable" actions of others, actions that may be hurtful, cruel or selfish.

Happily, however, acceptance of others does not in fact require condoning all their actions, any more than accepting ourselves requires accepting our own regrettable (but no longer reversible) actions. It appears that though we need not condone another's harmful acts, we must not condemn them, lest we risk producing something that is toxic to integrity. Condemnation is one compound of anger. And anger erodes integrity, peace, and love of life.

How are we to create that acceptance of ourselves so necessary to accepting others, without at the same time "accepting," and giving up on changing, what is certainly a cruel and greedy world? I hate to say it, but to me it looks like we have to evolve a special form of *faith* to achieve such acceptance. In particular, I find it helpful to have *faith in the power of the unseen Good,* including that good we can accomplish through acts of patience, kindness, and compassion, the "good" of which flowers mostly while out of sight. Among all that we will never know there are important things that would bring us happiness and self-acceptance if only we were able to learn of them. (Not to deny the unknown things that it might dismay us to know.) Recognizing this, it seems not unduly hard to forge a faith in the unseen Good, and from that faith to build the foundations of a personal integrity.

～

Yes, I recognize the preachy streak in what I have said above. I recognize that it does not actually tell us how to create the integrity that we may agree we need for ourselves. I admit that I write those (and these) particular words more for myself than for anyone else. You see, I do not believe that "rational thinking" is sufficient to remodel emotion and to prevent evil and to win integrity. And yet I have seen the partial successes of so-called cognitive-behavioral therapy interrupting emotions like anger, and controlling some instances of impending evil. I have (and I'm sure you have, too) frequently talked myself out of actions that I would certainly have later regretted, even as I have knowingly ignored the little voice of conscience counselling me to inhibit certain other actions that I knew I might soon regret.

Why, then, did I do wrong on those occasions when I suspected it was wrong? Often I did so because I judged that there would be more regret for *not* having done such deeds than there would be for having done them. Because it felt to me that somehow there was some greater integrity in taking those actions than in not taking them. Nor have I generally changed my mind, later, about my previous moral calculus. What I do regret is having placed myself in certain situations where a choice later needed to be made between what seemed "right" and what seemed "best but wrong."

Still, we often have no way of knowing that we are headed for such situations, and that, to me, makes it easier to forgive. Yes, I am sure that Ms. Froman did not suspect what she was headed for when she joined the National Rifle Association in the United States. And for now I will be content with that.

39 | *Debatable Journalism*

*L*ast night, on TVOntario's current-affairs program *The Agenda*, five journalists were invited to debate whether or not global warming is debatable. This is just the sort of debate that grates on me these days, giving me yet another reason to worry about the debatable health of my retiring psyche while it is busy navigating its Eriksonian eighth stage.

It didn't help that some of what was said during last night's program seemed reasonable and interesting, albeit well off topic. The host, Steve Paikin, and his guest of honour, a doubting columnist from the *Wall Street Journal*, appeared to feel that environmentalists have generally been crying wolf about this global warming business and are using any means they can to out-shout and silence a reasoned opposition. All the participants seemed to agree that a "debate" should enable a sharing of relevant evidence and a critique of rhetorical logic. Yet last night's "debate" seemed more like a journalistic collage, one that was constructed from opinions layered on opinions that had been pasted on a background of suspicious motivations attributed to any "experts" with whom the various speakers disagreed.

While some of the Canadian panelists clearly did not share the sceptical view of the doubting columnist in New York, during the entire discussion no distinction was sought or kept between *opinion* and *evidence*, nor between the *possibility* of worrisome global warming, and the *likelihood* of potentially disturbing effects that might accrue therefrom. It was as if the opinions of certain people about the nature of environmental changes were the same as evidence for or against treating those hypothesized changes as real or as illusory. And attributed motives for holding worrisome beliefs were treated as sufficient reasons for ignoring any evidence about whether those beliefs might turn out to be sound or unsound.

It was thus rather ironic, I thought, that one interesting topic arising during this rather confused hour of discussion concerned the question of the media's proper role in current environmental reporting. Sadly missing from this discussion, and clearly needed by at least this audience of one, were the following:

- A clear distinction kept between *evidence* for and against hypothesized environmental threats, versus the resulting *opinions* or *conclusions* that might be suggested by any such evidence . . . and
- Clear distinctions among:

    (i) *actual data outcomes* and worrisome situations already well documented . . . versus

    (ii) *probable* (inferred) data outcomes and situations deriving from well-understood processes, be these processes physical, chemical, biological, social, or economic . . . versus

    (iii) hypothesized and imaginable *potential* outcomes based on plausible generalizations from what is currently assumed about climatology, agriculture, oceanography, capitalism, etc., particularly after making allowance for the sheer complexity of the imperfectly known systems under consideration . . . as well as

+ A clear recognition that each person must make his own determination of what is an *unacceptable level of risk*. Risk is always individually subjective, even when it must be collectively addressed . . . and

+ A clear recognition that a *risk* level, while never certain, can be worth reducing not only when it appears to be high, but even when it appears to be modest if the consequent risk event would be a catastrophic one . . . and finally

+ A clear distinction kept between *evidence* about the social and monetary *costs* of lowering identified risks (such as those that might come from global warming) versus *opinions* or *theory* or *preferences* about what such costs may or may not turn out to be.

One major problem with debating the existence and potential threats of global warming, even when the debaters are experts and even when they do try to observe the distinctions listed above, is the killing simplification that must occur to make the debate fit the limited timespan or page space available to the audience. The complexity of the topic is such that there are no simple counterexamples with which to refute what may be an erroneous inference or false hypothesis.

Thus, for example, a valid documentation of a few glaciers that have been growing larger over the past ten years would not invalidate the documentation of those major glaciers that are disappearing at an ever-increasing rate after many tens of thousands of years of existence. (And, vice versa.) There is no simple picture to paint, and no black-and-white conclusion to be expected, in matters of such complexity.

Yes, I'm suggesting here that some topics, some questions, may be too large to fit into any single TV debate, or into any few documentaries, or into any few journals or books, there to be nicely settled for any reasonable audience. Furthermore, an implication by the media that we *can* settle (or have already completely settled) such issues seems to me, at its extreme, to constitute an unethical disservice to a concerned public.

Having said that, however, I feel myself giving unintended aid and comfort to all those who stand to profit by insisting that the risks of (and associated with) global warming are somehow still very much debatable risks, and that consequently the economic status quo should not yet be jeopardized by any attempts to limit global warming in any way that might noticeably change our comfortable way of commercial and social life.

This latter argument seemed to me to be the one advocated by the *Wall Street Journal* columnist who joined in last night's discussion. He seemed to suggest that the economy, and economic theory, must be given (and must be allowed to play) their middling trump cards until the evidence for the impact of global warming becomes ever more incontrovertible and finally overtrumps the doubt of doubters such as himself. (Of course by that time it may well be too late for either side in this debate to enjoy any hollow "win.")

"Let us agree to disagree," I hear the weary debaters say. All right. But let us first try harder to articulate precisely the real sources of our disagreement. Perhaps we disagree in our estimates of how much harm will come to the economy should it be asked to accommodate to a marked reduction in the allowable production of greenhouse gases. (I believe the harm can be far less than some suppose.) If so, then let us admit this disagreement and examine the arguments and evidence for each side.

Perhaps we disagree in our estimates of how much harm will come to human life if we continue to go slow in reducing greenhouse gas emissions. (I believe the resulting harm to society, and to the economy, can be rather greater than is currently expected.) If so, then let us admit and examine the evidence for these different beliefs. Perhaps later we will again be able to focus on our differences, after more data have come to hand, permitting us to debate what will then have become more truly and productively debatable.

Meanwhile, however, though we may still disagree, let us not lose any further time before undertaking major trials of ways to markedly reduce emissions of greenhouse gases. Then, when or if it proves increasingly necessary to accelerate and expand the scope of that reduction process, we would at least know better how it might be effectively achieved. Communal "integrity" demands that we do no less, before it is too late. And "communal integrity" is something that retirees (for a time) may be well suited to help nurture.

40 | *Unamusing Deadlines*

SUNDAY NOVEMBER 10, 2007
CALEDON, ONTARIO

*W*hat is it about deadlines, even after one is retired? A recent deadline for completing an index, one that I managed to meet narrowly, but only after twice failing to receive promised materials on time, led to considerable irritability on my part, irritability that I soon regretted when it appeared to threaten a valued friendship. In retirement, of course, there seem to be far fewer deadlines to face, yet even now the ones I do accept feel no less important to me than they earlier did. What is it about missing deadlines that makes them so troubling at times, so stressful?

Could the "death" in deadlines be part of what is so troubling about the topic, the experience? There are still some things I would like to finish before I die. (Likely always will be.) And while my health appears excellent, and while all but one of my six primary forebears lived nearly two decades longer than my own recent seventieth birthday (the passing of which probably triggered some of this), I worry about "failing" to complete some planned retirement projects before encountering that proverbial river of no return

Somehow I had found it easy to imagine, on first electing unemployment, that I soon would no longer face deadlines. (How unobservant can one be?) Deadlines of one sort or another are all around us, freely available for the taking and self-imposed as always. And while retirement certainly does bring fewer deadlines, there is something that often feels rather more final about each deadline that it does bring. I still think of Orhan Pamuk's surprising question about his writing—"Why am I so angry?"—and I am beginning to wonder if the answer may have something to do with a felt shortage of time: the increasingly likely possibility that time will run out before the things that need understanding are understood and the things that need mending are mended, before the words that need discovering are discovered and the ideas that want their birthing are born. Anger, then, may be transmuted frustration, notwithstanding the fact that Psychology has long since abandoned that ancient hypothesis. Or perhaps anger is the expression of an intolerance of frustration. Could deadlines be seen, perhaps, as the ultimate frustrations?

Ah, the joys of retirement: all the time in the world (it once seemed) to solve the puzzles of existence and to enjoy doing so. But this retirement time seems to fill with detours, distractions, and with the time-consuming business of buying new time. We are learning these days that consumers need to start noticing how much energy others are using up to produce and deliver the transformed energy (e.g., gasoline, or electricity) that we consumers wish to use up. Similarly, it seems to me that the retiree must sooner or later examine the rather interesting question of how much time it takes to produce the new time that he or she wishes to make use of.

Producing that new "quality" time can use up a considerable amount of "ordinary" time when we enter the realm of the medical-industrial complex, or when we begin rebuilding a life that some surprising act of god has just shattered. We are tempted to say: "If only I could use the time I have now more fully. If only I could use it more effectively." But I'd rather be able to say: "If only I could use the time I have now to reach a point where I could freely give all the rest of it away and happily allow my temporal reservoir to empty, now that the era for such emptiness may be soon approaching."

Happily, for some lucky reason I have yet to feel the pressure of any deadline for completing this exploration of retirement, this book that I hope may one day slip into general circulation. In retirement, writer's block has also become much less of a problem than it used to be when I had deadlines to meet. I find I am in no hurry to write these chapters. (You will note how long the time between some of my reports can be.) If the words don't come today, then I'll shrug and see if they might come tomorrow. And so long as I "try" to write something on that morrow, words of some sort will come. In fact, I am continually amazed by the words that fall onto these pages. Sometimes I can sit down to write without any sense of where to begin or even where I want to go. There is only a vague sense of some theme calling to me. And yet more often than not surprising words emerge onto the page, or replace words already on the page, forming a story, the very story that I will recognize (only after the fact) as always having been *the* story that wanted telling at this point. And yet this is often a story that I had no inkling was the particular one I had been intended to hear.

I have reason to believe that many writers (by no means all) will know this experience for themselves. After rereading something one has previously written, one sometimes finds oneself saying, "Who wrote that?" And we have to admit: "I didn't write that" (happy though we may be to take credit for having done so). In fact, however, when we look closely, we can see that it truly has been one of our *muses* that deserves any credit, not our "self." There simply is no way to bully or to control a muse, residing as it does deep within the unconscious. When our muse chooses to be silent, we must allow it to rest. When it chooses to speak, we had best listen. We need to learn to ask our ego to get out of the way, to allow us to wait patiently for that right moment when our muse will again take us by the elbow and walk a little with us.

Of course deadlines can make any such patience very hard to achieve. The ego has its inconvenient pride, and a missed deadline becomes a tripwire that may send it sprawling. We must learn not to take credit for those gifts we receive from the muses. (It now seems rather likely that none of our gifts come from any other source.) And then, if our ego could be helped to give up both the giving and taking of either credit or blame, we might easily step over any tripwire that a deadline offers. In fact we might do far more: move more directly to a place of acceptance of others and of ourselves. And that in turn may permit us to understand rather better why it is that our anger had so troubled us for a time, a time that may be coming closer to its end.

41 | *Bottom Feeders*

*F*ifty years ago last month, in a delightful wreck of a room just northwest of Stanford University's outer quadrangle, I cemented a friendship with Ray Funkhouser while we began work together on the third issue of what would become volume 59 of *The Stanford Chaparral*. The *Chappie* was (and still is) Stanford's college humour magazine. In November 1957 I was its managing editor and Ray was one of our gifted associate editors.[*] The nine issues of volume 59 garnered for the *Chappie* the only award that we cared about back then: It was voted by the editors of all U.S. college humour magazines to have been the best of the breed over that academic year. (Those, too, were heady days.)

After leaving Stanford I lost contact with Ray, but a few years ago he and his wife made contact again and came to visit in Kaslo, since

---

[*]   Our editor that year was Jim Gleason. I became editor of volume 60 (in my senior year), and Ray became editor of volume 61 the year after I graduated.

which time Ray and I have had considerable e-mail contact. Prior to his retirement, Ray was a research professor and a consultant, special-izing in media communications, business organization, and manage-ment studies. My impression is that Ray and I share a strong priority for seeing democratic societies survive while at the same time we have very different views about some of what may be necessary to ensure that survival.

For instance, Ray appears to place considerable faith in capitalist economics but very little faith in any major risks to society that may be presented by (a) the current face of capitalism, or (b) by the environ-mental threats associated with carbon dioxide emissions and climate change, or (c) by the major political decisions taken to date by the Bush administration in the United States. Ray is professionally knowledge-able about propaganda, and he recognizes masses of it in Al Gore's *An Inconvenient Truth*, for instance, and in the reportage of the liberal press, but he finds much less of it in the best "balanced" reportage of the business press. With Ray's expert help I have recently boned up on "propaganda," and re-read his book chapters on the topic.* As a result I am recognizing even more "propaganda" in both the business press and in the liberal press than I did before. In both cases the volumes of propaganda appear roughly equal to me.

"Propaganda," of course, need not always equate either to "error" or to "evil." Adversarial debating societies, those that some of us live and work in, have sometimes admitted to their own propagandistic biases. And an informed public has long been imagined to constitute a fair jury in the trials of ideology versus ideology. One could argue that achieving a "balance" in news reportage is as much the responsibility of mem-bers of the public jury as it is of those journalist-witnesses who believe they have relevant evidence deserving consideration and credence by

---

*   See G. Ray Funkhouser, *The Power of Persuasion.*

that public. I agree with Ray when he bemoans the inhibiting effects of political correctness on informed debate these days. But I cannot follow him when he implies that political correctness has almost completely impeded the ability of climate-change deniers to marshal strong evidence supporting their view of things climatic. My guess is that Ray would not be willing to follow me when I assert that climate-change deniers (for instance) and Chicago-school economists seem incapable of recognizing that there is already a reasonable likelihood that their views might in the end be proved to be dangerously incomplete and socially quite harmful.

Last month, after my reading on such matters, Ray had occasion to respond to a question I had sent to him, saying: "But Barney, you're going to have to upgrade your selection of authors; you're dealing with real bottom feeders these days." These words discomfited me precisely because I am prepared to imagine that Ray may (in part) be right in this regard. However, I generally do feel I am in good company in my choice of authors, and I suspect that Ray would be much less willing than I am to contemplate that certain of my "bottom feeders" may be some of those we all need to heed after giving them a serious hearing.

Ray understands that currently I read (more or less thoroughly and with varying degrees of scepticism) authors who write in the following regular publications: *The New Yorker* magazine, *The Guardian Weekly* newspaper, and *Harper's* magazine. I don't think I've mentioned to Ray that I also subscribe to *The Sun* magazine and sometimes I peek through Lorraine's copies of *Mother Jones* magazine as well. On television I seek somewhat regular news via the BBC, the American PBS network and its current affairs programs, as well as similar Canadian programs originating on the CBC and TVOntario. A lot of what I hear while listening to the marvelous *Ideas* broadcasts on CBC Radio adds to what I learn from those authors whose books I choose to read or index. There is some recognizable propaganda in the writings of most of these media informants, these bottom feeders, but they do give me evidence that I find useful in evaluating what I hear from those carnivores living up near the top of Ray's journalistic food chain, carnivores that for the moment I prefer to call the bottom-line feeders.

Recently, while reading the words of a liberal bottom feeder writing in the latest issue of *The New Yorker*, I chanced on the following sentence:

> To live, the poet Yehuda Amichai writes, is to build a ship and a harbor at the same time: "And to finish the harbor / long after the ship has gone down."

These happened to be the final words in a review by James Wood of a new translation of Tolstoy's *War and Peace*.* In *War and Peace* the implied "Harbor" that was built would be Pierre and Natasha's hearth, i.e., the "peace" of their home life at the end of Tolstoy's book. The implied "ship" would be the War of 1812 and the journeys, adventures, and losses it offered and exacted before it sank into history.

How might we construe the harbour that you and I spend a lifetime building? And how might we construe our personal ship and its metaphorical sinking? Could the day of our retirement have been the day that our ship went down? Or mightn't retirement be instead, if it is timed well, the day that we *launch* the ship we have spent so long in building?

The metaphors of the harbour and the ship accommodate a variety of possible interpretations, which is partly why this fragment of Amichai's poem can be so haunting. I imagine the harbour that bottom-line feeders are dredging would feature their nest egg, the golden riches piling up in each king's counting house. But like the rest of us,

---

* Appearing in the November 26, 2007, issue of the magazine.

bottom-line feeders probably also seek calm and familial security, love
and admiration, i.e., Pierre and Natasha's hearth.

It appears to me that most uber-capitalists are able to achieve financial calm only by a convenient blindness in the face of so much want in
the world, so much inequality that could be reduced if only we put more
effort into building harbours with room for other people. Bottom-line
feeders do not usually see the share of resources, goods, and services
deserved by others as being any part of that share they have abrogated
for themselves. Maybe they are lucky in their blindness. But maybe we
are not.

Now I certainly do have some problems with *The New Yorker*, particularly with their business practices and their advertising. For instance,
subscriptions to a number of magazines that publish to both the U.S.
and Canada generally cost in Canada about $15 (or about thirty per-
cent) more than the cost to American subscribers. Not so, however, at
The New Yorker. Lately I have been receiving repeated offers, addressed
to me in Canada, for a one-year renewal of my subscription for U.S.
$40. But when I try to accept this offer I am told that as a Canadian I
must pay U.S. $90, and when I object to this I am referred to the small-
est of fine print at the very bottom of the offer noting that Canadian
subscriptions are $90. In short, the bottom-line feeders at *The New
Yorker's* business office will ask Canadians for their American $40 plus
125 percent of additional dollars to cover $15 of postage and Canadian
tax, plus an exceedingly generous further profit for themselves. There
is a distressing arrogance in this bait-and-switch "offer," an arrogance
to match that found in many of *The New Yorker's* advertisements and
some of the people portrayed in those advertisements.

Yet the editorial content in this magazine can be wonderful. The
authors are usually first rate, even the bottom feeders. The artwork,
too, is first rate. The humour that is to be found in *New Yorker* cartoons is justly famous, albeit generally idiosyncratic. I learned long ago,

while serving as editor of the *Chaparral*, that few cartoons will appeal to more than thirty percent of any audience, yet if only five percent of an audience finds a cartoon very funny, it is generally worth printing that cartoon for those readers. This week's *New Yorker* has a Mankoff cartoon, for instance, that I cannot imagine more than a small percentage of readers would find particularly funny, yet it is a cartoon that I greatly enjoyed, as much for its pseudo-truthful brutality as for its rich humour.* It shows a psychotherapist talking to a patient who appears exceedingly glum. The therapist is looking earnestly at this patient and is saying: "Look, making you happy is out of the question, but I *can* give you a compelling narrative for your misery."

Now some forms of psychotherapy have long been faulted for supposedly "compelling" patients to accept an "unprovable theory" (i.e., a story) that purports to explain why they have become unhappy and symptomatic. Some believe that the nature of such a story, if it is convincing, will permit the sufferer to put aside his or her sorrow and symptoms. Some others believe that happiness cannot be produced by any talking therapy, but only by changing one's behaviour. I am not a believer in therapists or therapies that require faith or compel belief. (There are a few, but not many, such therapies.) I *am* a believer in changed behaviour for relieving symptomatic pain or sorrow, and generally I would say that self-understanding is required for producing the necessary change in behaviour and the relief that follows it. However, there is often happiness to be had simply from better self-understanding, even if not always and not necessarily. Talking therapy, if skillfully done, is a wonderful facilitator of a certain amount of self-understanding. As is, of course, skillful reading and skillful listening.

One of the joys of reading *The New Yorker* is how helpful it can sometimes be for informing readers (well, this reader, I should say) about cer-

---

* Appearing on page 92 of the December 10, 2007, issue.

tain topics that retirement seems to promote in importance. An article in the same issue as the Mankoff cartoon, by another of my admired bottom feeders, has given me new reason to examine carefully those fears that bottom-line feeders appear to have about apparent threats to economic growth from actions to be taken in the name of reducing risk associated with global climate change. In particular, the fears I am referring to include expectations of huge and unacceptable costs associated with proposed social and economic changes, and/or negligible perceived benefits to be gained from any such proposed changes.

The article that I found so thought-provoking was by Dr. Atul Gawande.[*] In it he gives an account of the dramatic benefits and the modest costs that accrued recently from the introduction of required checklists to be employed by hospital personnel during routine (but somewhat complex) medical procedures. Typically there has been a growing, if understandable, resistance to the introduction of "more paperwork" in medicine. But the simple introduction of checklist usage by doctors and nurses performing routine medical procedures (similar to an airplane pilot checking off every item in the complex order of things to be done to prepare for a safe takeoff) now has repeatedly been demonstrated to reduce dramatically the number of unwanted side effects and complications following those medical procedures. This article traces the history of the recent introduction of checklist usage in a few hospitals, and it documents the fears about the apparent great costs and small benefits of this change that continue to delay the implementation of such procedures in more hospitals. Tried on an experimental basis, the introduction of these checklists has shown such fears to be phantoms, just as were the fears in years past of the perceived high costs and small benefits to be expected from requiring seat-belt usage in cars, or from introducing laws restricting smoking in public.

---

[*]   *The Checklist* (Annals of Medicine), *The New Yorker*, December 10, 2007, pp. 86–95.

My point is not that fears of change are always misguided. Often they are appropriate. My point is that fears about even *experimenting*, on a small scale, with changes that sound frightening to some, fears that prevent even the gathering of data about the *true costs* of introducing proposed changes and the *true benefits* to be had from introducing those changes, impede and delay the helpful solutions to many major problems we all face, from those with a global scope to those that are strictly personal. My point is that we should be *facilitating* small-scale experiments that can test the truth of our fears.* And when the experimental data do show our fears to be needless, the costs low, and the benefits large, then we need to broadcast those data, that evidence, to those who have the power to make the larger-scale changes that are needed using these proven techniques.

Among the authors (bottom feeders) whose writings suggest such morals to me are some who are preachy and propagandistic in ways that my friend Ray Funkhouser seems to find unworthy, uninformed, and sometimes even dangerous. Some of those that Ray calls bottom feeders do lack humility and a willingness to question their hard-won convictions. They simply wish to overpower their readers with "spin" and propaganda, for personal gain or glory. Before he retired, Ray had also carried out research on differing human motivations for (and differing cultural perceptions of) "personal power," as such power may be exercised over others.** Ray's work suggested that one of the common markers of those who enjoy accumulating power often turns out to be their enjoyment of fooling others, of tricking them, of besting them. Perhaps some of those *New Yorker* circulation marketers may be delighted by

---

* I would suggest, too, that facilitating such experiments in the arena of personal behaviour change is a primary goal of many good psychotherapies.

** See again, G. Ray Funkhouser, *The Power of Persuasion.*

their bait-and-switch trick on Canadians, the one I mentioned earlier, and by the "gotcha" nature of their successes each time their ploy works. Bottom-line feeders, too, can be corrupted by the powers they enjoy, by the winning game of financial hardball they may love to play.

Yet even bottom-line feeders can sometimes be quite gentle and humorous. Recently I was told another wonderful joke that on the surface appears to be a subtle putdown of professor-types (i.e., of me), a joke that certain bottom-line feeders in particular seem to delight in telling.* It goes like this:

> A small group of philosophy professors is gathered in the faculty club early one evening when suddenly an angel appears in their midst. The angel turns to one of the men and tells him that his lifetime of service to others, his many anonymous good works, and his profound religious learning have all pleased his God, who wishes to bestow on him a great favour.
>
> "You may have any one of these three gifts," says the angel. "You may have five million dollars, or universal love and admiration, or deep and ultimate wisdom. Which is it to be?"
>
> Being a professor, the man chooses ultimate wisdom.   "So be it!" says the angel and there is a flash of brilliant light, a popping sound, and in a puff of smoke the angel disappears.
>
> As the smoke clears, the man's eyes widen and fill with tears. He looks miserable.
>
> "Did you receive ultimate wisdom?" asks one of his colleagues.
>
> "Oh yes," he answers.
>
> "Then why do you look so miserable?"

---

* I say "another" joke here, thinking back to the wonderful Menken quip quoted earlier in chapter 14 ("Peacekeeping"): "Academic disagreements are so bitter, because the stakes are so low."

The man slowly shakes his head, then looks up and says, "I should have chosen the money."

So many of us are ready to see ultimate "wisdom" in choosing the money. But this is the tragedy of the commons all over again. Bottom-line feeders assure us that a rising tide raises all ships, that wealth is continually renewable, and that there is so much wealth that its distribution is *not* a zero-sum activity.* Yet the truth is, fundamentally, that monetary wealth and the non-renewable resources consumed to create it are each zero-sum. One can invent a world in which the distribution of wealth and resources would not be a zero-sum activity, but that world would be special in ways that human nature currently seems to forbid in our world. There would need to be effective caps on human population in that happier world and effective cultural limitations on the degree of allowable individual differences in privilege and consumption.

Part of the humour I find in the joke about the philosophy professor is the special irony of knowing that I, too, have sometimes wished that I had chosen the money. Yet I do have quite enough to be content. Even better, I am learning how to corral more of my unwise wishes, and how to live content with less and less. It seems that, sooner or later, old age requires this of each of us.

---

*   A zero-sum activity is one in which a finite number of discrete resources are available to be allocated to a given number of recipients. Thus any one unit allocated to one recipient means one less unit is available to be given to some other. "The tragedy of the commons" refers to a situation in which any one person who takes from the common store of resources one unit more than their fair share of the units will create only a tiny, essentially undetectable, difference to the store of resources that remain for others and for future use. Thus many people may be tempted to cheat just a little by taking slightly more from the store than can be sustained if others were to do the same thing. But the tragedy is that because so many are tempted and are not prevented from slight pilfering, the resource fails and everyone then suffers.

42 | *Arabesque*

From time to time I still add to the contents of my Brown Paper Bag. About a year ago it was three compact discs, comprising all three episodes of the CBC *Ideas* series *Arabian Nights* (produced and narrated by Barbara Nichol). These broadcasts, based on *The Book of the Thousand and One Nights*, offer listeners some wondrous perspectives, including some surprising insights associated with topics as varied as true listening; the rewards of patience; amazement-as-an-aesthetic; fate; life-as-an-arabesque; human anger; and trusting.

A few of these insights came to me with particular force last October while I was again travelling eastbound along U.S. Highway 2, through Montana, North Dakota, Minnesota, and Wisconsin. As America's landscape flowed past, and as these three broadcasts rolled out their stories in repeated hearings, I became aware of some previously unappreciated overtones to the familiar metaphor of every Life as being lived, but also as being narrated, i.e., told as a *story*. Our lives are a story we continually tell to ourselves. As are the stories we may narrate to ourselves about anyone else we may be coming to know ever-so-partially, ever-so-personally, and so very uniquely. Journeys, too, can become stories. And vice versa. A story is, in one sense, a journey through mental space-time. Memoirs in particular are stories, mapping past journeys. And often that mapping can resemble an arabesque.[*]

As I am using that word here, an arabesque refers to an endless (sometimes eventually circular) Arabic design that is repetitive in nature, frequently turning back on itself, one that may border and frame symbols having religious implications that lie beyond verbal specification. *The Book of the Thousand and One Nights* is a work that circles around and around certain themes, one that uses stories to suggest relevant morals while never overtly moralizing. These stories and themes are nested one inside another, echoing one another and expanding one another. On the surface they seem to be just a series of bedtime stories, often bawdy, but it is sometimes possible to see in them a grand design and a grand commentary on human nature and on storytelling itself.

This week I am again looking at these retirement memoirs, these chapters of mine, as storytelling. Not in any pejorative sense, but rather in a sense implying that the proper work of retirement may include a kind of proper storytelling, storytelling that is told both for and to the storyteller, as well as being told for those unknown listeners, the ones who may stumble on the telling while they themselves happen to be on a journey.

Today, then, one unappreciated aspect of "retirement" seems to me to be its arabesque quality, one that spirals around, and frames, a life that may become more focused by the weaving of that frame.

---

[*] The theme of the arabesque in the CBC *Ideas* programs about *The Book of the Thousand and One Nights* was developed from an interview with Sandra Naddaff, and it derived in part from her book, *Arabesque: Narrative Structure and the Aesthetics of Repetition in the 1001 Nights.*

Retirement also seems to present new variations on the themes embroidered during earlier years, themes that it is easy to imagine had been tied off and left behind many years before. But of course nothing is ever finished, except possibly when our own storytelling ceases. And even then, our storytelling echoes in the retellings and further embroidery of others. Like an arabesque, life turns back on itself on a regular basis, even while every cycle of repetition may move us closer to the closing of a circle.

I hear a voice at this point saying, "Wait! Are these stories you are telling yourself really *true* or are they 'only stories'?" That question is a difficult one to answer because it implies that there are some stories that are true and other stories that are not true. But following my encounters with *Arabian Nights* I am even less sure that *stories* of either sort exist. Stories are simply what they are. They are foods that nourish our wish to hear and to see and to discover, our wish to have our horizons expanded, our wish to be surprised. Are chocolates *true*? Are some glasses of milk, or malt, *false*? Ahh, but then, do they nourish?

So a better question might be: "What is *proper* storytelling?" And the answer to that question, certainly for the retiree, may be that proper storytelling is storytelling that nourishes the hunger to gain a greater perspective. Also perhaps, for the lucky ones, storytelling may nourish a hunger to share with others some expanded perspective that we ourselves have newly enjoyed. (Of course, one can never be sure that what has nourished us will prove digestible to someone else.)

By this definition, proper storytelling can be either fiction or non-fiction. Both types of literature can, and often do, expand our perspectives and deepen our understanding. In particular, the hunger to achieve an expanded perspective appears to be a driving force behind all forms of *history*. There is a wonderful pun residing in that word, with clear echoes in the French language. Depending on the context, *histoire* can be translated as a story (a tale), an account of, or a history. The various and sometimes contradictory histories we have today, histories of world religions, histories of science, of economics, of the forms of government, of warfare, of our families, etc., all these perspectives can expand our horizons and our partial understandings of those complex and fortuitous events that have nudged our local lives to the places they occupy today. At one and the same time these histories can show us how different today's world might easily have been, and how unpredictable tomorrow's world may soon become.

Stories of where we have come from (and sometimes why) simultaneously satiate and amplify our curiosity, our hunger for another story. But people differ. The psychological dispositions that we call curiosity, a love of learning, a love of reading, and the love of listening to stories have each wandered along their own particular pathways as we grew up, sometimes leaving us drifting apart from each other while at other times bringing us unexpectedly to the same point of psychological longitude and latitude. Each of us seems to weave an arabesque as we track and backtrack, as we hunger and satiate, as we summer in a land of novels and winter in a land of memoirs.

Early in *The Book of the Thousand and One Nights*, Scheherazade, the mistress of storytelling, offers herself as the next wife to a once-betrayed king who since that betrayal has had each of his new wives killed at dawn so that he might never again be cuckolded. Each night, however, Scheherazade tells the king parts of a never-ending story, and she always stops her latest chapter exactly at dawn, in mid-story, leaving her narrative hanging in midair. Her sister, who shares the time listening to these stories, then says aloud (in ritual fashion) something like: "What an amazing and lovely story."

And Scheherazade responds, "But this is nothing compared to what happens next. This coming night I shall tell you something even more wonderful."

And the king, Scheherazade's husband, silently vows to spare Scheherazade's life for a further day, that he may hear more.

Thus each storytelling begins and ends with this little arabesque that frames the story of the stories of the stories. An arabesque that, for all its predictability, is as delicious in its irony as in its promise.

According to tradition, this queen of storytelling bears her king three sons over the course of one thousand and one nights of lovemaking and storytelling. Actually, we do not know how the original frame story about the storyteller Scheherazade ends, because the original written accounts of the oral tradition have all been lost. The imagined endings that have been offered to us, in the existing written accounts about the queen, generally agree that after a thousand and one nights Scheherazade directly asks her husband, *for the sake of his three sons*, to permanently spare their mother's life. In the account that rings truest to me, he answers, "My dear Scheherazade, I did that long ago."

Let us not disguise the moral here: The antidote to enduring anger and mistrust is Love. Love that is thinly disguised as exceptional storytelling fools no one for very long.

43 | The Wand Chooses the Wizard

TUESDAY MAY 20, 2008
KASLO, B.C.

*J*ust over two weeks ago Page and I completed our annual four-day drive westbound, from Ontario back to
Kootenay Lake and Kaslo. Tomorrow Lorraine flies out
to join us.

Kaslo has just concluded its 116th annual May Days celebrations,
and yesterday, Victoria Day Monday, was the day of our grand parade
and the children's Maypole dance. As a special treat, prior to watching
this year's parade, I decided to take Page with me into town for an inau-
gural walk on the brand new Kaslo River Trail. This trail is a remarkably
engineered affair, one that has been two years in the making, almost all
of it created with volunteer labour and donated materials. It offers visitors and residents alike a leisurely forty-five-minute circuit that closely
follows the Kaslo River upstream along the river's north bank, then
across a handsome covered footbridge and back downstream along the
south bank of the river. For most of its length the path wends through

natural forests and rocky cuts, out of sight of any houses or roads. The river remains close by, always audible and generally visible.

Plans call for a second footbridge to complete the circuit, but for now the eastern end of the river trail connects to the highway bridge into town, so after crossing that bridge one currently walks three short blocks, past lovingly tended gardens, to return to the parking area at the start of the trail. This year those May Days gardens are particularly lush from the plentiful spring rains and warm sunshine that we have recently enjoyed, so this last portion of our river walk proved to be the icing on the cake.

Page always knows there is something up when she sees me reach for my walking stick, and yesterday she was as keen as ever to race out the door to find her own short stick, and to prance proudly with it in her mouth as we made our way out to the car. Upon opening the car door, I noticed that I had neglected the day before to bring indoors my copy of J. K. Rowling's *Harry Potter and the Deathly Hallows*, a copy that still lay on the seat after having been returned to me by a friend who had wanted to borrow it. As I lay my walking stick beside the book, it suddenly struck me that Page and I were carrying "wands" for our planned wander along Kaslo's new path, the path that would pass close by a copse of woods known to be the habitat of a resident bear. My walking stick, so comfortable in my hand (and possibly Page's gruff bluff) would be our only protection should we encounter that bear. True, any other people on the path would also provide a margin of safety. (I was once told by an expert that no bear has ever attacked a group of five or more people, which can sometimes be reassuring even if not quite believable.) It happened, however, that Page and I encountered no bears and very few other people on yesterday's magical forest walk. And thus, no extra magic was required from the wand that I carried. Both Page and I hope to repeat this amble soon, and next time with Lorraine.

On the topic of wands, during the course of the past nine years Lorraine and I have read aloud together each one of the Harry Potter books. And bit by bit I have also read each of them aloud to Lorraine's mother, Audrey. The rich humour in Rowling's books, their impressive psychological insights and depth, their remarkable craft and intricacies, and of course their storytelling wonders, all justify their fame, in my view. (All seven books can now be found among those other treasures I keep in my brown paper bag, with its magically expanding space for holding everything I have asked of it.)

Recently, I have become particularly taken with Rowling's observation that "it is the wand that chooses the wizard." I think this observation is as true in my muggle world as it is in the wizarding world of Mr. Olivander's wand shop. In that wand shop neither the elder shopkeeper nor a young wizard-in-waiting can presume to suppose that they know correctly which wand will prove to be right for the wizard. And yes, years ago, while I was poking around in certain British muggle shops, in the market to buy "a proper English walking stick," I now recall that I found it necessary to wave each stick around a bit to see what sparks might ensue, and to walk around the room with it for a time, and to snap it in-to and out-from an armpit, all the while noting if this might be the wand that wanted to choose me. Yes, a walking stick *is* a kind of wand, possessing its own kind of potential magic. And, I dare say, so are a conductor's baton, a lecturer's pointer, an oriental's chopstick, an artist's brush or pencil, even each drumstick in the hands of a gifted percussionist.

My favourite walking stick was given to me by my father, who had inherited it from his father, who had made it with his own hands. That stick came from a young madrone tree (what in British Columbia we would call an arbutus tree), one selected from many such saplings growing on my grandfather's weekend "ranch" at the top of California's Napa Valley, north of Calistoga.

This sapling would have been one of a cluster of shoots, all of them perhaps chin-high, each of them growing up out of a small knurl of roots the tops of which would have been slightly visible, humped up at ground level. The young madrone would have been pulled up by the roots, the roots then cut off, and the rounded knurl lightly sanded into a smooth grip-end. Finally, the straight slim trunk would have been cut to proper length and capped. Madrones have a deep magenta bark (a smooth skin), and this gave my grandfather's walking stick a very distinctive appearance. Even better, it fit my hand and frame like no other walking stick I have ever used. Needless to say, it was my favourite walking stick from the moment it was presented to me, and I kept it handy at all times. Soon after I moved to Toronto, however, this treasure was stolen from my locked car. It was the *only* thing stolen from the car. As you can probably tell, I've never quite gotten over that loss.

Walking sticks can indeed have magic about them. And if ever I needed proof of this (and I never really did), then certain events at Kananaskis confirmed this for me in no uncertain terms.

Lorraine and I were spending a day at the Lodge in Kananaskis, which was the site of the alpine ski competitions during the 1988 Calgary winter Olympics and the site of a contentious G8 summit meeting of world leaders in 2002. We took a walk on a major trail uphill from the lodge, where we came on what appeared to be a yearling female moose foraging alone on aspen leaves beside the trail. We stopped until the moose had ambled well off to the side and then we walked on. But on our return to the lodge the young moose was back again, foraging not far from the trail. We walked slowly by and the moose did not stop feeding while we did so. Consequently we felt quite safe.

Once we were well past the moose, however, and furtively glancing back at it, we noticed that it had stopped feeding and was eyeing us. We continued walking slowly away, but glancing back more frequently we saw that the moose had started walking quickly in our direction.

Suddenly it began running directly at us, head low (without antlers) in a full-blown charge. There was no way we could outrun the animal so I whirled around to face it, raised my walking stick like a sword and began my own slow charge directly at the oncoming moose. The startled animal immediately did a cartoon-like stop at full skid, turned tail, and dashed away uphill.

I looked at Lorraine in disbelief, she at me, and we decided then and there that my walking stick was much more than it appeared to be. (This was also the day I learned that, apparently, my patronus is a bald moose. If true, I have no idea why that should be.)

The magic of the Kaslo day that had begun with the new river walk continued later in the morning with Kaslo's May Days Parade. Yes, the parade did go around twice this year, but it has become longer than ever now, and so yesterday it was routed around two deep blocks. This newer route brought it right past the Village Hall. The hall's crescent-shaped staircase leading up to the main entrance on the second floor became a splendid set of bleachers for watching the parade in comfort. I was able to secure a place at the top of the stairs, facing the oncoming parade with my challenging new digital camera (my other wand) at the ready. Presently I could hear the Kootenay Kiltie Pipe Band from nearby Nelson marching down Front Street. The drummer's beats grew louder, and the grand growl of the droning pipes rose slowly over the crowd noise. And then Kaslo's two Mounties marched into view at the distant corner of the street dressed in their scarlet uniforms. They executed a smart right turn toward us, followed by the first row of the band of pipers who performed their own smart turn as the music swelled.

Good old Kaslo: The Mounties marched past us, immediately turned right again and headed back up B Avenue beside the Village

Hall as had always been intended. The impressive pipe band, ceremonially dressed in tartan for the occasion, followed their lead. And then (sad to say) came three automobiles bearing the May Days Queen and her Princesses. (The float of Kaslo's *Moyie* steamer, the one that rightfully would normally bear them, has apparently left us for good.) And then . . . And then . . . nothing. A gap. A huge gap. I could hear visitors on the steps below me asking, "Is that all then? Shall we go?"

At long last the reason for the gap became clear. Around the corner on Front Street came the amazing sight of some very tall stilt walkers, each dressed in flowing costumes of vibrant colours, their slow pace dictated by their awkward steps. Yet the effect was not at all of awkwardness; it was of magical creatures, with extended wing-like arms of billowing fabric, floating slowly past us like giant, benign fairies.

Far beneath them were a few Kaslovians carrying homemade signs that urged everyone to help stop the privatization of nearby watercourses that tumble down forested Crown land. Recently, certain proposed power-generation projects have upset a large portion of the local citizenry. These are projects that appear likely to degrade unique local stream habitats and existing wilderness, i.e., projects that will "sell" our water for private exploitation and will noticeably erode our commons. In short, this colourful protest celebrated Kaslo's green *bona fides*. Very Kaslo, all of it. And for me, very reassuring to see.

There was much more to the parade. As always. But I left my seat soon after the end of the first coming in order to try to reach the Maypole park before the Pipe Band arrived there. I was able to get quite a satisfactory photograph of the band as they neared the park, and my new camera seemed to react well to each of the various spells that I asked it to perform.

As on so many previous occasions, I had planned to watch the children's Maypole dance next. But this year I was unexpectedly invited to sit off to the side and to share lunch and then a beer with good friends.

I ended up sitting for a long time at the edge of the ballpark outfield, my walking stick across my lap and my camera around my neck. To the west, dramatic snow-covered peaks were visible, providing their own appropriate backdrop to the lush green of our park and to its carpet of yellow dandelions, just beyond which could be seen Kaslo's many chestnut trees with their open candles towering over the flower gardens and fruit trees in bloom below. This was magic indeed. It was for moments like these that I had retired.

From where we were sitting I could faintly hear the music for the Maypole dance wafting over the heads of the crowd gathered around the pole. Also, I could see the top few feet of the pole itself as it was being laced and unlaced with alternating yellow and blue ribbons. I assume there were the usual missteps, as predictably there will always be. Nevertheless, the dance ended with the pole artfully surrounded in colour.

Cumulus clouds began spilling toward us over the mountains in the west. There was no threat of rain in them. Still, I was reminded again of that final magic trick in this same park in 1992, just before a downpour scattered the crowd. The wizard who was entertaining us that year waved his wand to refill a water jug repeatedly, endlessly, with water. For a number of years now, ever since that day, the glaciers feeding our lake have each been melting away. This year the spectre of those privately dammed, formerly wild rivers that feed into our lake has made Kaslo aware that *our* water supply is *not* endlessly renewable. Many citizens have been waving pencils and pens over local petitions, hoping to produce a shield charm against the loss of key local streams and the water they bring us. Those wands might not be up to the job, but somewhere, hopefully, there are other wands that will choose the wizards who *can* perform the required political magic.

It's true: Once upon a time I had thought that the title of Kaslo's favourite film, *Magic in the Water*, was a bit daft. But today I'm thinking that it was simply prescient.

Epilogue

*H*appily, the journey that has led to the publication of this book has also provided me with unexpected help from some timely new muses.

Some time ago I was advised by an expert that this book probably contained too much memoir (i.e., to sell), too much rant (i.e., to inform properly), and insufficient insights into the retiree's dilemma (i.e., yet to be of much service). Listening carefully to this person, I could see the temporary truth for her (and even for me) in such a point of view.

More recently, however, a second expert has reminded me that I must not forget that I have been writing primarily for readers (experts) with different requirements, including amateur experts (among whom I count myself), on the puzzles of senior psychology, on reading writers' lives, and on dissecting out the large yet subtle differences between the worlds in which we actually live and the worlds in which it is repeatedly suggested that we do live. Insofar as we are all "beginners" awakening each day to a changing world, in this sense, too, we are all "retirees" and we have been for a very long time.

The writing of *On Retirements* was finished almost two years ago as I sit typing these closing words early in 2010. Of course there continues to be much more that might be written about the psychology of retirements and about the new experiences and new perspectives we sometimes encounter near the end of a life. For myself, I have not stopped writing on these topics, nor do I currently expect to stop anytime soon.

Writing has its rewards and its potential importance for almost everyone. Reading, or hearing written words read aloud, completes those virtues. We read because doing so can sometimes be so life-enhancing. We write because the time has come for us to do so, for ourselves particularly, but sometimes, too, for an unknown future audience. Perhaps then it is time for others to write on the topic of retirements, even if just for themselves. Some of such writing certainly should be shared with readers, however. And perhaps (for a time, anyway) some selected parts of such writing might properly be shared with me.

Should you wish to write to me, and while I am still able to read limited amounts of what others may wish to offer to me, the means for your doing so can be found on the web at jbgilmore.ca.

And so, if you are a muse (and of course you are), I salute you. If you are a writer, I wish you the courage to persevere. If you are a reader, and in particular a reader-retiree, one who sometimes may be disturbed by the puzzles of a changing life, one who sometimes may be irritable, sometimes playful, and sometimes awed, then I wish you good reading in the future. And if you happen to be one of that small majority of skillful readers who might be each of these and more, then I am especially grateful for your invitation to have spent this reading time together.

Thank you, dear reader, for your reading of this book.

Acknowledgments

The number of people who have inspired, facilitated, shared, and framed these reflections on retirements far exceeds the rather small number who you will find named below and in the index of this book. These unnamed others range, for instance, from "my retirement barber" in Nelson (that would be Gene) to the staff inside the Kaslo post office (including Norma) to the many people in Toronto's publishing world who continue to offer me indexes (particularly Deirdre) and to the anonymous staff who provide the nourishing music and ideas on the radios of Nelson and Toronto. Let's all of us acknowledge the communities we cannot name who support our readings, our writings, and our retirement life itself.

Throughout my retirement years to date there have been some key people who have helped to make this book possible, in ten ways or twenty. My brother, Scott, and my stepmother, Helga, have been key in ways they probably still underestimate. My wife, Lorraine, hopefully recognizes the forty or fifty ways she has helped. Still, no muse I've yet experienced could help me to write those ways for her, or for you.

There are other key people, too, and my former wife, Elizabeth, who made possible the timing of my first retirement, well deserves the thanks I offer to her here.

Others who have helped to make this book possible include Holley Rubinsky, who was among the earliest of my new Kaslo friends, who encouraged my writing while sharing her own, and whose home and support was placed at my disposal during times of need. The same was true of Jessie Herreshoff. And of Pat Forsyth. And of Paul Erickson.

Early on, Perry Bauer and Verne Sparkes and Barrie Richardson introduced me to the Kootenay alpine. Dave Edmeads and Chris Temple consented to build my homes. Denis Saffran brought me to curling and Marion Saffran brought me to my senses (strategic and gustatory). I began reading and concert-hosting with Jack McDowell and David Herreshoff and Mary Weiler, and dozens of others. Today, Jill Fryling generously continues to nourish both Lorraine and me, and to symbolize all that is right about our Kootenay retirements. Kaslo and Ainsworth and Woodbury Village truly became home because of such people.

I have also received many forms of encouragement from warm Woodbury neighbours, retirees all, particularly Allan and Marianne Hobden, and Vicky and Barrie Richardson, but also, for instance, from Paul Wilton (who created the wonderful forest walk I take each day) and the nautical ladies who launch. Marianne, more than any other person, helped me to see these "chapters" as a book.

It isn't just people that need to be acknowledged; it is institutions, too. The Langham Cultural Centre in Kaslo, for instance, and the society of volunteers who maintain the water system in Woodbury Village, and the Kaslo and Nelson hospitals (crippled though these have become in some respects), the Kaslo Historical Society, and the staff at the *Moyie* museum and the Silver Spoon Café: All of these have taught me much about retirement and the environments that facilitate it.

In Ontario, too, there are many to acknowledge, people who made (and continue making) retirement a rich and warm experience, including: the Barrel-Stavers (our cross-country ski group), my fellow curlers, and the members of Caledon's Coalition of Concerned Citizens. A few names must stand for all here. Judy and Doug Biggar made retiring an adventure and a joy. Marnie Kramarich and Don Bastian made publishing my common cold book an adventure and a joy. And now Don has made publishing this book equally appropriate fodder for some future retirement reflections.

Lynd and Georgiana Forguson, my dear friends for many years, saw me off from Toronto (and Collingwood) when I retired, and later reconnected with me when they moved west to North Vancouver. Lynd, a philosopher whose interests were very close to my own, helped me to put many things in perspective over the years. His death still feels recent, and his presence still feels palpable. That is helpful, too.

In Ontario there is one further person to single out, to acknowledge, and to remember. Audrey Symmes, my amazing, perceptive, warm, sociable mother-in-law, died a few days before I sat down to write these last three pages. Together, she and I often read aloud, and watched major curling events, and attended concerts. She read a recent draft of this book and encouraged me, both directly and via Lorraine, in ways that mattered very much to me and to the creation of this book. She was a "retired" farmer and teacher, artist and gardener, yet she never retired. What a lesson she taught me. Life is short, but it is very long, too. For that insight, and so much else, I thank Audrey.

Index, Including a Selective Concordance

LaVergne, TN USA
10 March 2011
219487LV00004B/6/P